EUREKA, AGAIN!
K-2 SCIENCE ACTIVITIES AND STORIES

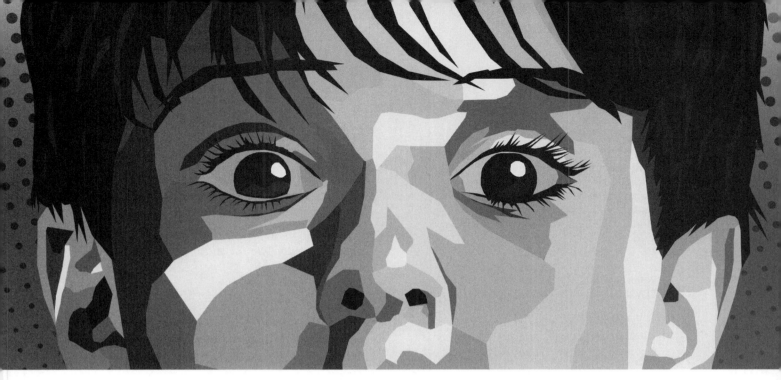

EUREKA, AGAIN! K-2 SCIENCE ACTIVITIES AND STORIES

DONNA FARLAND-SMITH

JULIE THOMAS

National Science Teachers Association

Arlington, Virginia

National Science Teachers Association

Claire Reinburg, Director
Rachel Ledbetter, Managing Editor
Deborah Siegel, Associate Editor
Andrea Silen, Associate Editor
Donna Yudkin, Book Acquisitions Manager

ART AND DESIGN
Will Thomas Jr., Director
Joe Butera, Senior Graphic Designer, cover and
    interior design

PRINTING AND PRODUCTION
Catherine Lorrain, Director

NATIONAL SCIENCE TEACHERS ASSOCIATION
David L. Evans, Executive Director

1840 Wilson Blvd., Arlington, VA 22201
www.nsta.org/store
For customer service inquiries, please call 800-277-5300.

Cataloging-in-Publication Data
Names: Farland-Smith, Donna, author. | Thomas, Julie, 1947- author.
Title: Eureka, again! : K-2 science activities and stories / by Donna Farland-Smith and Julie Thomas.
Description: Arlington, VA : National Science Teachers Association, [2018] | Includes index.
Identifiers: LCCN 2018019041 (print) | LCCN 2018022737 (ebook) | ISBN 9781681403175 (e-book) |
    ISBN 9781681403168 (print)
Subjects: LCSH: Science--Study and teaching (Elementary)--Activity programs--United States. |
    Next Generation Science Standards (Education)
Classification: LCC LB1585.3 (ebook) | LCC LB1585.3 .F36 2018 (print) | DDC 372.35/044--dc23
LC record available at *https://lccn.loc.gov/2018019041*

CONTENTS

CONTENTS

CONTENTS

CONTENTS

GUIDELINES FOR SELECTING BIOGRAPHY-THEMED TRADE BOOKS IN YOUR CLASS   **295**

FOREWORD

Julie Thomas

Jane Goodall showed considerable interest in science and nature as a young girl. She is known for watching a chicken until she understood how the egg came out (Winter 2011) and tucking a handful of earthworms under her pillow (Goodall 1999). As Jane remembers, her mother did not scold her for bringing the soil and worms to bed. Instead, her mother took time to explain that the worms needed to be returned to the outdoors or they would die. Still today, Jane insists her mother's support greatly influenced her early thinking and lifelong passion for scientific understanding. What's important here is that Jane's mother didn't shy from teaching a young child about the relationships between organisms and their environment. The worms, of course, needed the moisture and nutrients found in soil—and some plants needed the benefit of the worms' tunneling and some animals looked to the worms as food.

Certainly, developing complex understandings of the interdependence of living things also seems a lofty goal for K–2 children. However, giving some thought to purposeful ways we can begin to deepen students' knowledge and awareness of science and engineering lays a foundation for later learning. The purpose of this foreword is to provide some insight into what research says about children's developing capacity to learn science and what teachers can do to broaden K–2 students' interests in science, engineering, and medical (SEM) careers.

Early Science Learning

Have you ever watched a toddler's playful high-chair game—the one where the child repeatedly pushes a spoon over the edge of the tray and then leans over to watch the spoon hit the floor? These repeated actions (and observable feedback loops) help young children gather information about the mechanics of physical objects and help us know they develop general reasoning and problem-solving skills (i.e., underpinnings of the scientific processes) from a very young age. In fact, research tells us children are not as cognitively limited as we once thought. Rather, they bring a wealth of capabilities to the learning process (Duschl, Schweingruber, and Shouse 2007). Young children have a natural interest in science, and their reasoning abilities suggest they can benefit well from relatively complex lessons. Our challenge as teachers is to build on children's prior knowledge as we help them further understand and apply scientific knowledge.

One thing to keep in mind is that not all children experience the same early science learning opportunities. There is likely great variability across your students' prior experiences when it comes to visiting science museums, reading science books, engaging in experiments, or interacting with scientists. Teachers can help equalize opportunities for all K–2 students by exposing them to a variety of resources to help broaden their knowledge and understanding of the work of scientists and engineers and inspire SEM careers.

How Do Children Form Career Aspirations?

Curricula and assessments that are based on the *Next Generation Science Standards* (NGSS Lead States 2013) are intended to improve students' understanding of science and boost interest in science careers. Importantly, though most career awareness programs begin with middle or high school, career choices actually begin as early as kindergarten (Wahl and Blackhurst 2000) and are primarily influenced by socioeconomic status (Auger, Blackhurst, and Wahl 2005). One way to make sense of this is to think about how children first become aware of the work world via the people and places their parents know. For example, my research among elementary students with low socioeconomic status in rural Oklahoma helped explain why so many fifth graders aspired to medical careers (Hulings, Thomas, and Orona 2013). Conversations with the children helped me learn they regularly accompanied their pets and grandparents to visit the doctor—and usually went right along with them into the examination rooms. These students could tell us a lot about the tools and procedures these doctors used. One unique student, Brittney, aspired to a career in cosmetology—and she had learned what she knew by spending time in her aunt's beauty shop:

> I think [cosmetologists] need to know about science … what types of chemicals [they're] using and how to use them in the right way so they don't affect the person. So there won't be any problems. You need to know how much you need to put in their hair … and whether or not it's too much or too little. (Hulings, Thomas, and Orona 2013)

Some research reveals how children view scientists and engineers—and the kinds of experiences that influence children's drawings of scientists and engineers. Draw-a-scientist studies conclude that most students organize stereotypical views of scientists as white males and occasionally monsters who primarily work indoors (Barman 1997); even students of color are likely to draw white scientists (Finson 2002). Similarly, draw-an-engineer studies find elementary students have a limited conception of the work of engineers (i.e., they mistakenly expect engineers to be mechanics, laborers, and technicians). Chambers (1983) determined children's images of scientists usually begin to appear in when they are in second or third grade and are fully formed by the time children are in fourth or fifth grade. Clearly, the long view of elementary science education is to recognize that scientists and engineers include a broad representation of diverse males and females and encourage and inspire young children to consider SEM careers. So, given that children's home and community experiences limit children's career awareness, how can teachers expand students' career awareness via school experiences?

What Can Teachers Do?

Efforts to broaden children's knowledge and understanding of the work of scientists and engineers will help expand SEM career awareness and aspirations for all—regardless of race, gender, or socioeconomic status. These efforts can include connecting science lessons to science and engineering careers, inviting scientists and engineers to visit your classroom and talk about their work, engaging and involving parents as SEM education allies, and introducing biographies and the personal traits of scientists and engineers.

Connect science lessons to science and engineering careers. Think about linking science lessons to real-world career applications (e.g., when and why scientists or engineers measure things). This purposeful addition will illuminate children's observations of scientists and engineers' work and help motivate and inspire students' thinking about SEM careers. Figure 1 shows the importance of augmenting science lessons with conversations about how hands-on classroom activities link to the real world of SEM workers. Of course, opportunities to link lessons to the real world will grow as you become more aware of the work of scientists and engineers—but you can begin in your own community. You might choose to take photographs of these community workers yourself or simply share community news with your students. Consider sharing a photo and asking your students to think about the picture (e.g., how the conservation biologist is observing migrating monarch butterflies). You might be surprised to find real-world connections embedded in science lessons you are already using or in a little-used-section of your science textbook.

Invite scientists and engineers into your classroom. Local career role models can both share the excitement of their work and familiarize your students with the ways scientists and engineers in your area are working to make the world a better place. Certainly, nothing can approximate the personal opportunity to meet an SEM professional. Think about looking to medical groups, engineering societies or firms, universities, or city and state agencies (e.g., transportation and city planning, utilities, recycling, or waste management departments)—even students' parents and families—to recruit enthusiastic SEM professionals. Endeavor to reflect diversity in the workforce (e.g., females, varied ethnic and racial backgrounds) with these classroom guests and to represent a variety of fields and disciplines.

You might also think about the possibility of bringing in virtual classroom guests. There is an ever-increasing number of internet sites designed to demystify the work of scientists and engineers and otherwise encourage SEM career aspirations. My absolute favorite among these is PBS's The

Figure 1

Science Lesson Misconceptions

Some children's drawings of scientists show us how science lessons can confuse students' thinking about the work of scientists. Scientists do not actually use an eyedropper to count how many water drops fit on a penny (a common lesson to teach about water properties) but scientists do follow similar practices to observe phenomena. For example, scientists may not build model volcanoes to watch them erupt but they might build model volcanoes to understand or explain how and when they erupt. Classroom conversations can help deter these misconceptions.

Secret Life of Scientists and Engineers website (*www.pbs.org/wgbh/nova/secretlife*), which is appropriate for people of all ages. Two distinct features of this website are suitable for use with early elementary students: video clips of scientists and engineers telling about their "secret lives" and explaining how their unique passion relates to their work (*www.pbs.org/wgbh/nova/blogs/secretlife/teachers/#video*) and teaching tips that offer ideas about how to incorporate the scientists' stories into your teaching (*www.pbs.org/wgbh/nova/blogs/secretlife/teachers/#teachers*).

At the very least, these scientists and engineers will help you and your students break down stereotypes about who can aspire to an SEM career. The video clips bring young SEM researchers to life and introduce them via a surprising secret life that fuels their work, and vice versa. Some of the inspiring researchers featured on the website include the following:

- Bisi Ezerioha (*www.pbs.org/wgbh/nova/blogs/secretlife/engineering/bisi-ezerioha*) is a high-performance engineer and drag racer. As an engineer, he creates fire-breathing automotive beasts for the track and the street. As a drag racer, he sets speed records but "drives like a grandma" when off the race track.

- Cheri Blauwet (*www.pbs.org/wgbh/nova/blogs/secretlife/blogposts/cheri-blauwet*) is a medical doctor and an accomplished athlete. As a doctor, she specializes in sports medicine and, as a champion wheelchair racer, she earned a gold medal in the Athens games.

- Kathy Reichs (*www.pbs.org/wgbh/nova/blogs/secretlife/anthropology/kathy-reichs*) is a forensic anthropologist and a TV hero. As a scientist, she studies remains to solve real-life crime mysteries and, in the TV world, she was a producer and writer for the series "Bones," which is based on her novels.

Include parents. One way to expand your students' science learning opportunities is to also teach parents and guardians. Are you thinking this idea is "out there" or beyond the call of duty? Well, parent education programming helps parents appreciate what you are teaching and why it makes a difference. Research suggests that parents who "get the message" support the teacher and encourage school learning opportunities (Weiss et al. 2009).

Your parent education efforts could be as simple as regular science feature stories in a school newsletter or on a classroom website. The "work" here might be as simple as posting pictures and stories about the science goings-on in your classroom or alerting parents to science learning opportunities in the community (e.g., programs at a nearby museum or community library). Another easy way to educate parents is to invite them to help (e.g., manage materials) when you plan an engineering design activity with your students. Consider creating some at-home science learning opportunities such as literature-linked science activities from *More Picture-Perfect Science Lessons* (Ansberry and Morgan 2007) to encourage children to explore bubble fluid recipes and bubble wand shapes with their families.

You might also consider organizing parent learning through creative workshops, social gatherings, or content-focused event nights. Family night events—informal, interactive activities—can be a great way to engage family members as engineering teams to imagine, plan, create, and improve together. Smetana et al. (2012) encourage us to think broadly about family—not only parents and grandparents but also siblings, caregivers, and neighbors, too. As these educators learned, multigenerational family units particularly enjoy working together at these events.

When it comes to organizing family learning events, a guidebook titled *Family Engineering* (Jackson et al. 2011) is particularly useful for both novice and experienced planners. This guide, modeled after the popular book *Family Math* (Stenmark, Thompson, and Cossey 1986), provides excellent details about how and why to organize a family engineer event—from how to put together the planning committee, to choosing the location, to developing volunteer roles, agenda guides, and sample room layouts. *Family Engineering* includes two types of event formats (opener activities and engineering challenges); lists of simple, inexpensive materials (e.g., plastic cups, brads, and craft sticks); and step-by-step directions. *Opener activities* are self-directed tabletop activities families can engage in at their own pace and *engineering challenges* are more in-depth activities that introduce a variety of engineering fields and engage families in the processes of engineering. One especially nice feature is the organization of the two-sided tabletop activity directions. One side provides a leading question and activity guide while the other side provides an explanation or *engineering connection*. Having organized several family engineering events using this guidebook, we can attest to how easily diverse audiences are drawn in to these activities and engage in thinking and problem-solving challenges as family units.

Introduce biographies and the personal traits of scientists. *Eureka, Again!* presents a series of science lessons linked to biographical books about the accomplishments and early interests and inclinations of famous scientists and engineers. Here, a focus on specific character traits helps us understand how the human dimension of such traits both encourages and supports SEM career choices. One book, *Me … Jane* (McDonnell 2011), introduces Jane Goodall as a young girl whose favorite toy was a stuffed chimpanzee. Jane's career as primatologist began with backyard observations of birds and squirrels. She set her mind to observing animals in Africa when she was 10 years old. As a scientist, Jane showed her observant nature in the discovery of chimpanzees' ability to make and use tools. Another of the books, *Shark Lady* (Keating 2017), tells the story of Eugenie Clark, a young shark lover whose zoology career began with reading about sharks in the library and studying fish in school. As a scientist, Eugenie demonstrated her *fearless* nature when she dove into the open ocean and proved herself "smart enough to be a scientist and brave enough to explore the oceans" (p. 21).

These biographies can help your students realize they possess some of these same character traits and can become scientists and engineers themselves. After all, famous scientists and engineers were once young children who began with a particular disposition or character trait, found a passion, and became famous adults. It just makes sense that explicit focus on character traits (while reading a story and doing a science activity to learn more about a scientist or engineer) will help students understand more about potential SEM career choices. Such explicit connections may be a necessary component to the National Science Foundation's (2008) mission to broaden SEM participation among diverse populations by providing "for the discovery and nurturing of talent wherever it may be found" (p. iii).

References

Ansberry, K., and E. Morgan. 2007. *More picture-perfect science lessons: Using children's books to guide inquiry, K–4.* Arlington, VA: NSTA Press.

Auger, R. W., A. E. Blackhurst, and K. H. Wahl. 2005. The development of elementary-aged children's career aspirations and expectations. *Professional School Counseling* 8 (4): 322–330.

Barman, C. R. 1997. Students' views of scientists and science: Results from a national study. *Science and Children* 35 (1): 18–24.

Chambers, D. W. 1983. Stereotypic images of the scientist: The draw-a-scientist test. *Science Education* 67 (2): 255–265.

Duschl, R. A., H. A. Schweingruber, and A. W. Shouse, eds. 2007. *Taking science to school: Learning and teaching science in grades K–8.* Washington, DC: National Academies Press.

Finson, K. D. 2002. Drawing a scientist: What we do and do not know after fifty years of drawings. *School Science and Mathematics* 102 (7): 335–345.

Goodall, J. 1999. *Reason for hope: A spiritual journey.* New York: Warner Books.

Hulings, M., J. Thomas, and C. Orona. 2013. Influences on 5th grade students' images of scientists and career aspirations. Paper presented at the annual conference of the Association for Science Teacher Educators, Charleston, SC.

Jackson, M., D. Heil, J. Chadde, and N. Hutzler. 2011. *Family engineering.* Portland, OR: Foundation for Family Science and Engineering.

Keating, J. 2017. *Shark lady: The true story of how Eugenie Clark became the ocean's most fearless scientist.* Naperville, IL: Sourcebooks Jabberwocky.

McDonnell, P. 2011. *Me … Jane.* New York: Little, Brown and Company.

National Science Foundation (NSF). 2008. *Broadening participation at the National Science Foundation: A framework for action.* Washington, DC: NSF.

NGSS Lead States. 2013. *Next Generation Science Standards: For states, by states.* Washington, DC: National Academies Press. *www.nextgenscience.org/next-generation-science-standards.*

Smetana, L. K., J. C. Schumaker, W. S. Goldfien, and C. Nelson. 2012. Family style engineering. *Science and Children* 50 (4): 67–71.

Stenmark, J. K., V. Thompson, and R. Cossey. 1986. *Family math.* Berkeley, CA: Lawrence Hall of Science.

Wahl, K. H., and A. Blackhurst. 2000. Factors affecting the occupational and educational aspirations of children and adolescents. *Professional School Counseling* 3 (5): 367–374.

Weiss, H. B., S. M. Bouffard, B. L. Bridglall, and E. W. Gordon. 2009. *Reframing family involvement in education: Supporting families to support educational equity.* Equity Matters: Research Review, Brief No. 5, The Campaign for Educational Equity, Teachers College, Columbia University, New York.

Winter, J. 2011. *The watcher: Jane Goodall's life with the chimps.* New York: Schwartz & Wade.

Dedication

This book is dedicated to my budding young scientists, Leo and Luke.
—Donna Farland-Smith

This book is dedicated to my most supportive husband, who has helped me brainstorm, craft, and edit these ideas and lessons from the very beginning.
—Julie Thomas

Acknowledgments

We would like to thank NSTA Press for the opportunity to publish this work. Special thanks to Rachel Ledbetter, whose unflappable nature is like a rudder on a ship.

Special thanks to the teachers (Erin Barrett, Melissa Miller, Michelle Prince, and Melanie Worley) at Ridgewood Elementary in the Hilliard City School District for their willingness to participate in the development of many of these lessons. It has been an honor to teach the students at Ridgewood Elementary about science and scientists! I will never forget the fun we had.

Special thanks to Tiffany Kuck, who worked with me to develop a few lessons in this book. Thank you for allowing me into your classroom and collaborating with me. I always say, "first grade is the hardest grade to teach," and you make it look easy! Thank you for being both my boys' first grade teacher. We will never forget you!

About the Authors

Donna Farland-Smith has over a decade of experience in the classroom and previously taught science in all grades K–12. She currently serves as an associate professor of science education in The School of Teaching and Learning at The Ohio State University-Mansfield. Her areas of expertise include teacher education, students' perceptions of science and scientists, and encouraging girls to explore science and engineering fields. Along with several book chapters and many articles about science education, Farland-Smith has written and published four books that inspire children to understand and appreciate scientists and their work: *Jungle Jane* (Authentic Perceptions Press, 2002), *It Takes Two: The Story of the Watson and Crick Team* (Authentic Perceptions Press, 2002), and *The Simple Truth About Scientists* (Authentic Perceptions Press, 2002). Farland-Smith received a BA in elementary education, a BA in natural science, an MA in science education, and an EdD in mathematics and science education from the University of Massachusetts-Lowell. In 2017, she published the book *Many Hands, One Vision: 20 Principles That Built a Children's Museum and Revitalized a Downtown Community* (CreateSpace), which tells about her experience founding The Little Buckeye Children's Museum in Mansfield, Ohio. She is the mom of two young scientists.

 **Julie Thomas** is an experienced elementary classroom teacher and elementary gifted-program coordinator. Now a research professor of science education in the College of Education and Human Sciences at the University of Nebraska-Lincoln, Thomas focuses her efforts on elementary science for teachers *and* their students. She has led both state-funded and federally funded projects and has published research about children's science learning and teacher professional development. Thomas's accomplishments include collaborative efforts such as No Duck Left Behind, a partnership with waterfowl biologists to promote wetland education efforts and Engineering Is Everywhere (E2), a partnership with a materials engineer to develop a time-efficient model for STEM career education. Throughout her teaching career, Thomas has been active in professional associations such as the School Science and Mathematics Association, for which she is a past executive director; the National Science Teachers Association, for which she has authored articles in the journal *Science and Children* and has served on the Awards Committee and Nominations Committee; and the Council for Elementary Children International, for which she is a past president.

1

Introduction

WHAT WE DID IN THIS BOOK AND WHY

We are so grateful you are reading this book right now! It is intended to make what you do in your classroom both easy for you and meaningful for your early childhood students. As former teachers, we have a deep and long-standing passion for teaching science and an unwavering respect for your efforts to meet new demands associated with the teaching profession. Today's classrooms are multifaceted; we know what you do is challenging and you have many choices for the resources you select in your classroom. We also realize you choose to spend a great deal of your personal time and money to maximize learning options for your young students. So we have designed these lessons to enable you to borrow trade books from your school library and manage these hands-on activities on a modest budget.

The Book's Title

The book title is inspired by a familiar, centuries-old saying: "Eureka, I've found it!" This saying comes from a legend about Archimedes, one of the very first scientists (and the founder of modern-day physics). As the story goes, Heiro, the king of Syracuse at that time, was skeptical about the goldsmith who had made his new crown, so he began looking for someone who could prove that the crown was made of gold and not silver.

Thus, King Heiro summoned Archimedes, the greatest mathematical thinker of the time. Archimedes mulled over the problem night and day—and, as luck would have it, the answer came to him as he was stepping into his bath. He was so excited about solving the problem that he forgot he wasn't wearing clothes and, wearing nothing but his birthday suit, ran up and down the street yelling, "Eureka! Eureka! I have found it! I have found it!"

You might be wondering, "How did the bathtub help Archimedes answer his question?" Well, as Archimedes stepped into the bathtub, he noticed that his body caused the water to rise and some of it to flow over the sides of the tub. He connected this experience to the problem with the king's crown. Archimedes expected that the specific weights of gold and silver would be different, which would allow him to easily discern how much water a gold crown should displace and thus show whether King Heiro's crown was made from pure gold.

The children's book *Mr. Archimedes' Bath* (Allen 1980) tells a whimsical version of this story, with some detail about how Archimedes might have measured the displaced bathtub water. You are likely to find this book in your school library. We caution you to read this story yourself before sharing it with your students because some teachers have expressed concern about the "naked man" illustrations (which are cartoon-like views of Archimedes's backside). But we have found that children do understand the author's intended humor.

We were inspired to use the word *eureka* because we expect that many people are familiar with that old expression and the storied connection it has to the character and work of a scientist. There are many wonderful stories about scientists and their work, and we incorporate 27 of them in the activities of this book. These biographical stories will expand students' knowledge and understanding of who scientists are, what scientists do, and why science is important—and will inspire children to see themselves as budding scientists. In addition, these activities will help children recognize their own character traits and encourage them to think about their potential as future scientists.

The Backstory

Our experiences as educators have led us to understand the importance of children's understandings of scientists' work as a human endeavor. Several other researchers have examined how children view scientists and determined that students hold stereotypical views of scientists as white males and occasionally monsters who primarily work indoors (Barman 1997; Finson 2003; Finson, Beaver, and Cramond 1995; Losh, Wilke, and Pop 2008). We, too, have conducted a number of studies using the Draw-a-Scientist Test (DAST) or some variation of this drawing measure and have developed new prompts and scoring rubrics for the DAST (Farland-Smith 2012).

Donna Farland's research (2003, 2006) examined the influence that reading historical, nonfiction trade books has on children's images of scientists. The finding was that in Full Option Science System (FOSS) unit instruction, when teachers read biographies to their students, the students more fully recognized the science processes they were applying in their lessons. The study (2003, 2006) involved students ($n = 156$) in 13 classrooms, each with one teacher. Six classrooms (with one teacher each; $n = 72$ students) were randomly assigned to supplement their third-grade FOSS instruction by reading one scientist biography each week for six weeks (FOSS + Biography [FB] group). Seven classrooms/teachers ($n = 84$ students) followed the usual FOSS lesson procedures (FOSS-Only [FO] group).

To evaluate the difference between the FO and FB classes, we reviewed scientist drawings completed by all students before the unit of instruction and another set of drawings from a readministered test after the unit instruction. We found that compared with the FO students, the FB students demonstrated a broader perception of who does science, where science is done, and what activities scientists do.

The Chapters and Lessons

This book includes 27 lessons linking nonfiction historical trade books and science content that uniquely enable you to model scientific thinking by linking stories of scientists with your elementary (grades K–2) science lessons. This bold new idea is that biographies of scientists can allow you to highlight the human dimension of scientists and engineers while you encourage science learning. We think these stories will help to broaden students' perceptions of scientists and engineers as real people and will add explicit and implicit opportunities for your students to consider science and engineering careers.

Think of this book as a way to invite scientists and engineers into your classroom without the hassle of finding and scheduling guest speakers. Each chapter of this book presents three lessons based on a children's literature biography of a scientist. Each lesson is organized according to the

Next Generation Science Standards (*NGSS;* NGSS Lead States 2013) alignment, the character trait or disposition of the scientist, personal story, and the learning-cycle format described in the following sections.

Next Generation Science Standards Alignment

Each book chapter is aligned with the science and engineering practices outlined in the *NGSS* (NGSS Lead States 2013) for grades K–2. The *NGSS* alignment provides the most universal organizational structure; however, we expect teachers to approach these lessons from the standpoint of a variety of state standards and expectations. Within the *NGSS* alignment, we have focused on the *NGSS* language but have linked the activities to grades K–2 as a group rather than to the specific grade-band end points in *A Framework for K–12 Science Education: Practices, Crosscutting Concepts, and Core Ideas* (*Framework;* NRC 2012).

The real innovation of the *NGSS* is its integrated, three-dimensional performance expectations (NRC 2012): disciplinary core ideas (DCIs), science and engineering practices (SEPs), and crosscutting concepts (CCs; ideas and practices that cut across the science disciplines). To help you and your students recognize science as a human endeavor, we encourage applying a fourth dimension of performance expectations: the nature of science.

Thus, the lessons in *Eureka, Again!* are structured to include four elements—the three dimensions of high-quality science (DCIs, SEPs, and CCs) and their connections with the nature of science as outlined by the *Framework* (NRC 2012). First, each chapter is organized according to one of the eight SEPs. Three scientist and engineer biographies will help students recognize these practices, and the lessons will guide students' active experiences with them. Next, each scientist

biography and associated lesson support the CCs and the performance expectations in the DCIs. Teachers' decisions about how to implement each lesson may vary, and these *NGSS* references will help to guide lesson selection and implementation. Appendix C (p. 303) lists the *NGSS* alignment by chapter and by scientist.

Character Traits

Each featured scientist and engineer is introduced with a character trait, which is given as a descriptive adjective. These character traits capture the unique human qualities of the scientists and introduce the human assets of scientists' dispositions. Every individual has such character traits, and the focus here is on helping our students understand that scientists and engineers are people and express a personal, human trait that enables them to become successful.

Character traits will be a familiar focus for your students from their previous learning involving review of fictional literature and development of insight into the specific events in a story (for example, "Why was Goldilocks asleep in the mother bear's bed when the bears returned home?"). Character traits include a person's behaviors, thoughts, and beliefs related to universal principles, moralities, and integrity and his or her commitment to live by those principles. Positive character traits can have personal and societal benefits and encourage other people to believe in you—and have been integral to the successful endeavors of the historic men and women of science and engineering depicted in the biographies in this book.

Scientists' character traits also reflect their dispositions toward science. Binns, Koehler, and Bloom (2015) became interested in the universal nature of the character traits and dispositions of scientists because these guide our perception of scientists and their work. Through their study of popular films about scientists, they identified nine such dispositions: passionate, excited, pragmatic, collaborative, intuitive, inquisitive, creative, risk taking, and persistent. In this book, we expanded on the work of Binns, Koehler, and Bloom (2015) to identify the dispositions or character traits of the 24 scientists and engineers introduced in this book. The explicit teaching of a human character trait or disposition, along with learning the stories of scientists and engineers, will help to humanize children's conceptions of scientists and engineers and the nature of their work. As suggested earlier in this chapter, this improved awareness of the nature of scientists' and engineers' work may be integral to inspiring the next generation of science, technology, engineering, and mathematics (STEM) workers.

Personal Story

At the beginning of each chapter is a personal story by one of the authors. We have included detailed science teaching stories because they provide context and make these practices relevant. We hope these will provide valuable insights into teaching this exciting grade range.

Lesson Format

Each science lesson has been formatted in one of two learning-cycle formats because this is similar to what is being asked in the *NGSS*. We began with the predict–explain–observe (P–E–O) strategy as described by Page Keeley (2014). The P–E–O strategy has three parts. The first step is *predict*—this is where students' prior knowledge is elicited when they are asked to provide opportunities to voice their predictions. The second step is for children to *explain* their understandings. The third step is to *observe* a situation related to the science activity.

However, in our book, we reordered the Keeley model into the predict–observe–explain (P–O–E) sequence for K–2 students because this provides developmentally appropriate learning sequences

for early childhood learners. Therefore, you may see some of the activities outlined in the chapters using the P–O–E sequence.

In other lessons, you will see the learning-cycle format as described in Trundle, Mollohan, and McCormick (2013): a model for hands-on, inductive science teaching with early learners that is based on three phases: play, explore, and discuss. Here, the learning cycle is important, as each part represents an important process in learning and is an ongoing process. Although Trundle, Mollohan, and McCormick intended it to be for preschool students, we have included it here for four reasons: (1) It is developmentally appropriate for early childhood scientists, (2) it works with the lesson structure in most elementary classrooms, (3) it supports the types of lessons in this book, and (4) it fits within modern time constraints in elementary classrooms (which last an average of 30 to 45 minutes). Also, if teachers begin implementing three phases of the learning cycle at the younger grades, they will be most likely to incorporate additional phases in other learning cycles in the upper elementary grades. The purpose of each stage is as follows:

- **Play:** To awaken student interest or prior knowledge, lead students into the topic of the lesson, and connect with students' prior experiences. In this phase, students notice, question, and wonder—all natural occurrences for young learners (and essential components of quality science instruction). This phase is developmentally appropriate because we meet students where they are and with what they are interested in and what questions they have. Play is an integral part of intentional learning because it allows students to notice and wonder on their own about whatever physical properties they might be "playing" with.

- **Explore:** To provide a shared experience to guide students' investigations of concrete materials and to provide a record of their work. At the early childhood level, students make and record through drawings, which have several advantages for science learning. These records are the process through which children focus on written language skills to help document their experiences. For young children who are still developing their fine motor and gross motor skills, alternatives such as visual clues or verbal prompts may be used instead of a written observation.

- **Discuss:** To express experiences from the Explore phase and refine and deepen understanding of the science concept(s) by focusing on collected data. A simple data chart or graphic organizer can be used with the youngest of students to pictorially represent an experience. Depending on the age of the students (and ability level) and the data to be collected, there are three possibilities for data collection: (1) independent data collection, (2) partner data collection, and (3) small-group data collection. This phase is also an opportunity for teachers to identify the focus of the science lesson and introduce scientific vocabulary after the students have had an experience. The naming of science concepts *after* the experience helps children use common language to verbalize what they experience. In this way, young children are encouraged to think about what they have observed or explored and how it is related to what they already knew.

The *How* and *Why* of the Lesson

In addition to a description of each lesson and the *NGSS* standards addressed, we have included a *how* and *why* section for most lessons. The *how* section focuses on exactly how the lesson is taught and provides detailed directives for the teacher. The *why* focuses on why this particular activity meets the three components of the *NGSS* (DCI, CC, and SEP).

Evaluation

Assessing young children's science progress can be challenging at times. It is important to realize that with young children, no single assessment method or model will work for evaluating every child because of his or her own individual strengths (Trundle, Mollohan, and McCormick 2013). Although it is important to gather a variety of assessments from young learners as they progress, throughout this book you will find rubrics at the end of each lesson based on three forms of student work:

1. **Drawings:** Are the drawings moving from imagination to evidence-based realities?

2. **Participation in Class:** Are the students able to link their reasoning back to the evidence observed in class?

3. **Questions:** Are students able to ask new questions from the Explore phase? Are these new questions based on evidence?

Lessons will be evaluated for both the content and the character trait.

How to Use This Book

In each chapter, you will find three different literature-based lessons that follow the *NGSS* and introduce complementary skill building and inquiry investigations to highlight the science processes and the human nature of scientists' endeavors. You may decide to teach one lesson from each chapter or all three—it's up to you.

The appendices might guide your choices. For example, Appendix C (p. 303) might inspire you to teach one of these science lessons because your students learned about one of these scientists or engineers in another class. Or you may decide you want to teach a lesson on patience, and it fits in with your science curriculum. Or you may need to find creative ways to meet the standards and you are looking for a lesson (say, on friction) that would be appropriate.

It is our goal for the lessons in this book to be the kind you cannot wait to teach the following year with a new group of students. In addition to teaching science content and addressing the *NGSS* standards, *Eureka, Again! K–2 Science Activities and Stories* is unique in that it brings to life the personal traits of well-known scientists and engineers as they are portrayed in biographical trade books.

Safety Considerations for Hands-On Activities

Hands-on, process-based, and inquiry-based classroom and laboratory activities can make the teaching and learning of science and STEM today both effective and exciting. The challenge to securing this success needs to be met by addressing potential safety issues as appropriate relative to engineering controls (e.g., ventilation, eye-wash station), administrative procedures and safety operating procedures, and the use of appropriate personal protective equipment (e.g., indirectly vented chemical splash goggles or safety glasses meeting the ANSI/ISEA Z87.1 D3 standard, chemical-resistant and nonlatex aprons and gloves). Teachers can make it safer for students and themselves by adopting, implementing, and enforcing legal safety standards and better professional safety practices in the science classroom and laboratory. Before undertaking any science or STEM activity or investigation, a

hazard analysis, risk assessment, and review of safety actions should be done to ensure a safer teaching and learning experience. Also remember that personal protective equipment should be worn during the setup, hands-on, and takedown segments of the activity.

Always provide safety training and demonstrate the proper use of hand tools, laboratory equipment, personal protective equipment, and so forth before having students undertake any hands-on activities. Also provide follow-up safety reminders before each activity.

Throughout this book, safety precautions are provided for classroom and laboratory activities and should be adopted and enforced to provide a safer teaching and learning experience. Teachers should also review and follow local policies and protocols used within their school districts and schools (e.g., chemical hygiene plan, Board of Education safety policies).

Additional applicable standard operating procedures can be found in the National Science Teachers Association's "Safety in the Science Classroom, Laboratory, or Field Sites" position paper (*www.nsta.org/docs/SafetyInTheScienceClassroomLabAndField.pdf*). Students should be required to review the document or one similar to it under the direction of the teacher. Both the student and the parent or guardian should then sign the document, acknowledging procedures that must be followed for a safer working and learning experience in the laboratory.

The Council of State Science Supervisors (CSSS) provides information about classroom science safety, including a safety checklist for science classrooms. See the CSSS website (*www.csss-science.org/safety.shtml*) to access this information and for links to other science safety–related resources.

Disclaimer: The safety precautions of each activity are based in part on use of the recommended materials and instructions, legal safety standards, and better professional practices. Selection of alternative materials or procedures for these activities may jeopardize the level of safety and therefore is at the user's own risk.

References

Allen, P. 1980. *Mr. Archimedes' bath.* New York: HarperCollins.

Barman, C. R. 1997. Students' views of scientists and science: Results from a national study. *Science and Children* 35 (1): 18–24.

Binns, I. C., C. M. Koehler, and M. A. Bloom. 2015. Dispositions of scientists in mainstream film: The extraordinary person called a scientist. In *Application of visual data in K–16 classrooms,* ed. K. Finson and J. Pederson, 153–166. Charlotte, NC: Information Age Publishing.

Farland, D. 2003. The effect of historical non-fiction trade books on students' perceptions of scientists. PhD diss., University of Massachusetts–Lowell.

Farland, D. 2006. Trade books and the human endeavor of science. *Science and Children* 44 (3): 35–37.

Farland-Smith, D. 2012. Development and field test of the modified Draw-a-Scientist Test and the Draw-a-Scientist Rubric. *School Science and Mathematics* 112 (2): 109–116.

Finson, K. D. 2003. Applicability of the DAST-C to the images of scientists drawn by students of different racial groups. *Journal of Elementary Science Education* 15 (1): 15–26.

Finson, K. D., J. B. Beaver, and B. L. Cramond. 1995. Development and field test of a checklist for the Draw-a-Scientist Test. *School Science and Mathematics* 95 (4): 195–205.

Keeley, P. 2014. *What are they thinking? Promoting elementary learning through formative assessment.* Arlington, VA: NSTA Press.

Losh, S. C., R. Wilke, and M. Pop. 2008. Some methodological issues with "Draw a Scientist Tests" among young children. *International Journal of Science Education* 30 (6): 773–792.

National Research Council (NRC). 2012. *A framework for K–12 science education: Practices, crosscutting concepts, and core ideas.* Washington, DC: National Academies Press.

NGSS Lead States. 2013. *Next Generation Science Standards: For states, by states.* Washington, DC: National Academies Press. *www.nextgenscience.org/next-generation-science-standards.*

Trundle, K. C., K. N. Mollohan, and M. McCormick. 2013. Plants, alike and different. *Science and Children* 50 (6): 52–57.

2

Asking Questions and Defining Problems

The practice of asking questions and defining problems is integral to both science and engineering. This chapter will focus on three scientists—Jane Goodall, Albert Einstein, and Kathy Sullivan—who all asked questions to define problems in their science and engineering work. Through the processes of asking questions and redefining problems, scientists and engineers were able to study chimpanzees (Goodall), be an incredible thinker and inquirer (Einstein), and be the first woman to walk in space (Sullivan). It is easy to see why the words *observant, imaginative,* and *explorer* might be used to describe these character traits or dispositions for these three scientists.

The *Next Generation Science Standards* (*NGSS*; NGSS Lead States 2013) explain that science mostly begins with asking questions, whereas engineering mostly begins with defining problems to solve. Although reverse instances may occur, asking questions provides a frame for thinking about the similarities and differences between these two disciplines in the classroom. In our experience, although children are naturally curious, schooling tends to disconnect them from their natural inclination to ask questions of all kinds. We have learned to model explicit and implicit questioning to help students hold onto their curiosities in the school setting. In addition

to asking particular questions about their understanding of content, we focus on asking questions to promote students' thinking about what scientists do for work, such as the following: What do you know about the work of scientists and engineers? What activities have you heard or seen scientists or engineers doing? How did you know they were scientists or engineers?

At the K–2 level, the focus on asking questions is based on observations to find more information about the natural or designed world. It is important at this level that early childhood students ask questions that can be answered by investigations. Science then becomes about answering questions and defining simple problems. For the youngest of students, a simple problem that can be solved through the development of a new or improved object or tool *is* science.

Questions help generate children's interest in science and mathematics if they are allowed to investigate and satiate their curiosity. Although the culture of classrooms has changed over time, questioning is one of the things that will never go out of style. In this chapter, you will find three very different lessons to connect students' questions about scientists and their biographies.

As the *NGSS* suggest, the goal of science is to construct explanations of the world in which we live. Scientists, then, ask and answer questions to improve our understanding of the natural world, whereas engineers figure out how things work and make new things to improve the quality of our lives. Whether students are engaged in science investigations or engineering designs, it is critical that they plan a course of steps and measure outcomes that will answer their questions. In time, children will naturally come to carefully plan their investigations as they experience experimental error and see how it affects their work.

There is great value in highlighting the investigation process by telling students that they are answering a question. It's important for teachers to recognize that children need practice asking questions and that their questions improve with practice. *How?* and *Why do you think?* are good places to start with young children. Questions help identify what needs to be investigated, and both teachers and students play a critical role in asking productive questions (Schwartz, Passmore, and Reiser 2017).

We frequently remind students that the best science and engineering investigations both answer the initial exploratory questions and allow us to revise these questions to generate a new question. An activity like the Alka-Seltzer activity described in the following section will provide lots of opportunities for students to ask questions.

Donna's Personal Story

For the Alka-Seltzer activity, all you need is one resealable plastic bag (quart size), three sodium bicarbonate tablets such as the commercial brand Alka-Seltzer, a half cup of water in a clear plastic cup, and a hand lens (per group or team of students). *(Teacher Note: I remove the tablets from the packaging so the students do not know what they are unless they have had experience with them before or have seen the box in the classroom).* Simply ask students to observe the tablets with a hand lens. Ask them to make statements about the tablets

using their senses. I begin by asking students to tell me what the senses are and review all five (smell, touch, taste, sight, and sound). I caution them that we never eat anything in science class, so we are really working with four senses today. After a few minutes, I gather their observations and record them on the board for the whole class. Most students say things like "It's white," "It has numbers or letters on it," or "It feels like chalk." These are all good observations. If students have not smelled the tablet, I ask them to do so. Most children make sounds when they smell the tablet because it smells of vinegar. I prompt the students to tell me what this "smells like" because the best observations are observations where children make an analogy (e.g., "soft as a bunny"). These analogies provide the most descriptive observations and set children down the path of scientific reasoning. I keep asking questions during this process of observation until someone responds that the tablet smells like when they color eggs in the spring.

Then I ask the students to make a prediction with their partner or their group. What do they think will happen when they place the tablet into the cup with water in it? I am careful to make sure that every group has a prediction before we actually do this experiment as a group, and that is because I want my students to gain experience in making a prediction. I count to three, and as a class we place the tablets into the water. By now the class is filled with sounds of science— eeks and shrills of excitement that I could bottle up forever! Children are either surprised by the reaction or excited because what they thought would happen actually happened. Some children will automatically place their hand over the cup or place their ear near it. If you see that happen, direct other students to do the same. If you do not see that happen, model it yourself and children will follow.

Ask the students what they observed. Almost always, one student will say that the tablet is melting. If a child says this, challenge his or her misconception by asking where the heat comes from to "melt" the tablet. Usually, the child will change his or her first answer and come up with a better explanation. Use the classroom conversation to elicit a response before telling the students that the science word for what they have just observed is *dissolve* or *dissolving*. Alert the children to the plastic bags on their desks. Ask children what they think will happen when they place the water in the bag along with the two remaining tablets and then seal it up. First I model how I want the children to place the water from their cup into the plastic bag. Then I ask students to work with their partners, with one holding the cup of water and one holding the resealable plastic bag. As a class, we seal three quarters of the plastic bag tight, leaving only enough to slip the two tablets in the water. This is critical because you want the reaction to happen as quickly as possible. I do a countdown to help with classroom management and to ensure that all students place the tablets in the bag at approximately the same time. When they do, once again you will hear shrills of excitement and joy! They will observe the plastic bag filling with air from the chemical reaction inside the bag. Encourage students to feel the outside of the plastic bag for a temperature change.

Although there are many benefits to this lesson (e.g., opportunity for observations, a visual chemical reaction), I use it for questioning. At the culmination of the lesson, I instruct all the groups or teams to come up with a new question using the materials we used to investigate. I model saying "I wonder what would happen if … ." Students often vary the amount of tablets, or they change the size of the plastic bag—for example, "I wonder what would happen if we changed the size of the plastic bag to a snack size and added more tablets." I let them have free rein with *I wonder what would happen if …* statements because I want them to see that science is about asking questions.

A simple experiment like this one with a few household materials can help your students understand the importance of asking questions. Although this activity might also teach about solids, liquids, and gases, my intent is to focus on the process that scientists follow when they ask and answer questions.

What's Important to Remember About the Practice of Asking Questions

- Children need practice asking questions, and their questions improve with practice.

- *How?* and *Why?* are good places to start with young children.

- Questions help identify what needs to be investigated.

- Both teachers and students play a critical role in asking productive questions.

See Schwartz, Passmore, and Reiser (2017) for more information.

SCIENTISTS AND ENGINEERS ARE

OBSERVANT

Learning About **Jane Goodall**

Observant (adj.): good at noticing things

Lesson: Ghost Shrimp
Description

In this lesson, students observe ghost shrimp and discover patterns of what plants and animals (including humans) need to survive.

Objectives

Students will consider how the observant character trait helped Jane Goodall make careful observations and will engage in observations of ghost shrimp while identifying patterns of living things.

- In the Predict portion, students will predict whether animals need air in a formative assessment probe.

- Students will hear the story *Me … Jane* by Patrick McDonnell and discuss how it relates to the word *observant*.

- In the Observe section, students will observe ghost shrimp and create a list of wonderings about the ghost shrimp. They can either complete the worksheet at the end of this chapter or make a drawing (using both words and pictures) in their science journals if they are keeping a journal.

- In the Explain portion, students will revisit their questions about ghost shrimp and plan some possible investigations to answer their questions.

Learning Outcomes

Students will (1) discuss what being observant means and why being observant is an important trait for scientists and engineers and (2) use observations to describe patterns of what plants and animals (including humans) need to survive.

Connections to the *NGSS*

The following sections make one set of connections between the instruction outlined in this lesson and the *NGSS*. Other valid connections are likely; however, not all possibilities are listed.

Performance Expectation	Connections to Activity
K-LS1-1: Use observations to describe patterns of what plants and animals (including humans) need to survive.	• Observe ghost shrimp and describe what they need to survive; compare this to the needs of humans and plants.
Science and Engineering Practice	**Connections to Activity**
Asking Questions and Defining Problems	• Students pose questions about their observations based on the shrimps' external physical characteristics such as color, size, and body covering.
Disciplinary Core Idea	**Connections to Activity**
LS1.C: Organization for Matter and Energy Flow in Organisms All animals need food in order to live and grow. They obtain their food from plants or from other animals. Plants need water and light to live and grow.	• Observe and discover how ghost shrimp use food to survive and grow.
Crosscutting Concept	**Connections to Activity**
Structure and Function	• The shape and stability of the structures of ghost shrimp are designed specifically to relate to their functions.

Jane
Goodall

Overview

In this lesson, students observe ghost shrimp in the classroom to mimic the way Jane Goodall observed chimpanzees in the wild. Students learn how one person who had a passion for animals made a significant, long-lasting improvement in how we view animal communications. Jane Goodall shared her observations about chimpanzees with others and improved the way people understand how these animals live and communicate. By reading the featured book, students will learn that people from all backgrounds choose careers as scientists. The scientist trait of *observant* refers to how Jane Goodall's patient chimpanzee watching led to carefully planned investigations. In the hands-on portion of the lesson, students experience what it is like to observe live, wild animals for a period of time.

Materials

You will need one copy of the featured book *Me … Jane* by Patrick McDonnell (2011) and a few (two to three) ghost shrimp. *(Teacher Note: Ghost shrimp will cost about $1.00 per handful at your local pet store. The ghost shrimp can be stored in tap water with added conditioner [purchased at the pet shop], or you can simply use the water they come home in from the pet store. If you have a fish tank with oxygenated air, they will last longer in that than if you simply place them in a jar for observations without oxygenation [see Figure 2.1]. Make sure you plan accordingly for your lesson; if you do not have oxygenated water, they will only last a couple days. They eat off the bottom of the tank or jar, so feed them fish food that travels to the bottom of the water [not flakes that remain at the top of the water]. Ghost shrimp are basically maintenance free—except that they do not do well in extreme temperatures, mostly cold.)* You will need one container or jar for the class. *(Teacher Note: In this lesson, we used a small fish tank I found in my basement.)* You will need the worksheets that are included for the Predict, Explain, and Observe portions of the lesson (pp. 21–25).

Figure 2.1

Ghost Shrimp in the Tank

Safety Notes

(1) Make sure activities are not near electrical receptacles—this can be a shock hazard if water comes into contact with a live receptacle. (2) Immediately wipe up spilled water—it creates a slip-and-fall hazard.

Setting the Context
Predict

Use the formative assessment probe (p. 25) to elicit children's ideas about the needs of living things. This probe—Do They Need Air?—comes from *Uncovering Student Ideas in Primary Science, Volume 1* by Page Keeley (2013) and is designed to find out if students recognize that all animals need air to live, including animals that live under water. Show this probe to your students and gather their thoughts about living animals. The best answer comes from Mei: "I think all pond animals need air to live." All animals need air. When they take in air, they capture oxygen, which goes to their cells. Cells use oxygen to help release energy from molecules that come from the food the animal has eaten. All animals get their energy from food and therefore need oxygen for energy-releasing chemical reactions to take place in their cells. Land animals get their oxygen by breathing in air (some animals, such as amphibians, can absorb air through their skin). Aquatic animals must get their oxygen from the air that is dissolved in water. They use structures such as gills to extract dissolved oxygen from the water (Keeley 2013, p. 32).

Guided Reading

Students will be learning about animal behavior, animal body parts, and the life work of a scientist who was especially observant by reading *Me … Jane.* Introduce the book: *Can you find the person on the front cover? What does it look like is happening on the front cover?* Read the story aloud. Encourage students to notice and think about the challenges Jane Goodall may have faced as a woman alone in the jungle and observing chimpanzees.

1. **Pages 1–15:** How did Jane act like a scientist from a very young age? *Jane hid in a henhouse because she was curious where eggs came from, she named a tree, and so on.*

2. **Page 5:** The author states: "She read about animals in books like Dr. Dolittle and Tarzan of the Apes." What did Jane dream about after reading these books? *Jane dreamt about a life of living with and helping animals. When Jane Goodall was 10 years old, she decided that when she grew up she would go to Africa, live with animals, and write about them. Almost everyone told her this goal was impossible, except her mother.*

3. What did Jane end up doing at the end of the story? *Jane was studying chimpanzees out in the wild. Jane finally earned enough money to get to Africa in 1957. There she met famed anthropologist Louis Leakey and began studying chimpanzees in Tanzania. One of Jane's most important observations was her discovery that chimpanzees are able to make and use tools. Until this time, scientists had thought that they were not able to use their hands in this way.*

Observe

(Teacher Note: Ghost shrimp, also known as glass shrimp, are inexpensive and efficient aquarium cleaners. What makes them interesting is that they have transparent, segmented bodies with 10 sets of legs. The first four sets have tiny claws that aid the shrimp in feeding. Ghost shrimp are relatively small invertebrates, reaching a maximum size of only 2 in. They survive best in a freshwater aquarium of at least 10 gal. with plenty of hiding places and can live with small, peaceful fish that will not pose a threat to the shrimp.)

Ask students if they have ever watched wild animals. Where and why did they watch animals (or would they watch animals)? Tell the class they are going to be watching ghost shrimp for a few days. They are aquatic animals. Ask students how these animals might take in oxygen (from the probe). Some students may say that they would expect to see gills on the ghost shrimp because of what they just learned in the probe. Allow enough time for children to watch and generate questions about the ghost shrimp while completing the journal entry on page 22. If you have time, ask them to select one of their questions and write down how they might go about investigating it using the journal entry on page 23. *(Teacher Note: Their answer does not have to be accurate. The point is to try to get children to ask questions and define problems. Therefore, this lesson will be evaluated on their ability to observe and ask questions [see rubric in Table 2.1, p. 20].)* Collect their questions in a visible place in your classroom where students can reference them as they observe the ghost shrimp over the next few days. Invite students to observe in groups of four to five. Place the tank or jar of ghost shrimp in the middle of each group for observation.

THE *HOW* OF THE OBSERVE

Direct students to record their observations in the form of words (if developmentally appropriate, in sentences) and drawings (with labels; see Figures 2.2 and 2.3). Review the difference between observation and inference and/or between fact and opinion. You want students to write and draw what they actually see, and this can require fairly focused observations. Hand lenses might be helpful in encouraging children to view details of the ghost shrimp. In our experience, students will rise to the occasion and provide thoughtful, detailed observations if they know you will be reviewing them or reading them aloud. Ask, "What did you find out? What have you learned about ghost shrimp and/or their body parts that you did not know before?" Encourage students to write or illustrate their observations and reasoning in their

Figure 2.2

A Child's Sketch of a Ghost Shrimp With Labels

Figure 2.3

Student's Journal Entry of a Ghost Shrimp Habitat

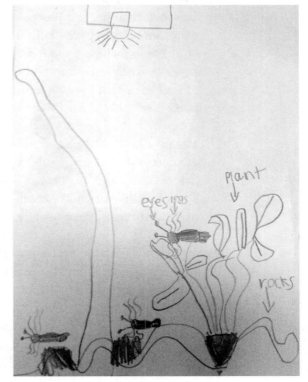

science notebooks or on a piece of paper. (Look for an accurate illustration of the observation; although artist skills are not necessarily important here, it is important that children pay attention to detail.) Visit each group as the students work, asking them questions about what they see and what they have drawn. Challenge them to be accurate.

THE *WHY* OF THE OBSERVE

As teachers, we often accept children's first attempts at drawings in elementary school without hesitation. This is the perfect opportunity to introduce the concept of diagrams versus illustrations. Introduce the difference or ask students what makes a picture an illustration. An illustration includes text and arrows or lines for identification purposes. If this opportunity is taken now, when children are young, they will not be surprised when they encounter diagrams on standardized assessments. Another strategy you could try is to show students an illustration and a diagram and ask them to compare the two. This may seem like a trivial detail, but it helps them start to think about the connection between science and art.

Explain

Encourage students to summarize their observations and questions prompted by this investigation. Introduce discussion about the anatomy of the ghost shrimp—for example, can they easily find the eyes, head, and antennae? If so, encourage students to include these terms when they label their illustrations. Ask students if they observed any other body parts—maybe the legs? The abdomen? The importance here is that they begin to recognize body parts such as legs, eyes, and antennae. *(Teacher Note: Ghost shrimp are among the more interesting types of aquatic creatures you could keep as a pet. They are interesting because they are translucent and children can see through them. They are not fish. They are crustaceans, and they can most often be found dwelling at the bottom of a fish tank feeding on waste or debris of any kind. A ghost shrimp's natural habitat is in the brackish water of wetlands.)*

Ask students to make connections between what plants, animals, and humans need to survive by completing the worksheet on page 24. Begin by projecting the three-circle Venn diagram on the board and asking students what things plants and animals (including humans) need to survive. Discuss this question as a class and help students find similarities and differences between plants and animals (e.g., both need food and water, plants cannot move themselves but animals can). Prompt students by asking them the three questions on the worksheet: How do they get food? How do they grow? Do they need water? These questions can be answered as a class or on individual worksheets at the teacher's discretion.

Once this discussion is complete, ask students, "How does this science activity help you think about Jane Goodall's observant nature? What considerations do you think Jane Goodall had to make when planning and carrying out her investigations?"

Evaluate

Summative evaluation of this lesson will include assessment of students' understanding of (1) the observant character trait and (2) the ability to generate questions during their observations of the ghost shrimp and their ability to use observations to describe patterns of what plants and animals (including humans) need to survive.

CHARACTER TRAIT

Encourage students to answer the following questions: What made Jane Goodall such an observant scientist? *(Teacher Note: For example, she was patient and she watched the chimpanzees every day, all day. She kept notes about it all.)* Why is being observant an important character trait of scientists? *(Teacher Note: Careful observations allow scientists to collect accurate data. In Jane Goodall's case, her carefully skilled observations helped her to earn the trust of the chimpanzees she studied—and thus gather even more data.)* Ask students to think about a time when they were observant.

CONTENT

Students will have a diagram of ghost shrimp in their science journals (or on their worksheets). Students' questions and observations may be evaluated by a rubric like the one shown in Table 2.1 (p. 20). To conclude this lesson, revisit students' questions about ghost shrimp and plan some investigations to answer their questions.

Table 2.1

Rubric for Assessing Ghost Shrimp Activity

Content or Skill	Not Yet	Beginning	Developing	Secure
Participation or Observation	Student did not provide written observations.	Student is not able to link his or her reasoning back to the evidence observed in class.	Student is able to link his or her reasoning back to the evidence observed in class.	Student is able to link his or her reasoning back to the evidence observed in class and correctly identify several parts of the ghost shrimp.
Drawing	Student did not provide a drawing or an illustration.	Drawing is still at the imagination level.	Drawing is moving from imagination to evidence-based realities.	Drawing is moving from imagination to evidence-based realities and words are included with arrows or lines.
Questions	Student did not generate any questions.	Student is not able to ask new questions from the Explore phase or new questions based on evidence.	Student is able to ask new questions from the Explore phase or new questions based on evidence.	Student is able to ask new questions from the Explore phase or new questions based on evidence. Student has an idea of how to begin to answer these questions.

GHOST SHRIMP JOURNAL

NAME: _____

LIST OF WONDERINGS

I wonder _____

I wonder _____

I wonder _____

I wonder _____

Name: _____

Draw what you see with pictures and use words and arrows to describe what you observe.

Pick one of your wonderings to investigate. How would you investigate?

WONDERING:

STEP 1 _____

STEP 2 _____

STEP 3 _____

STEP 4 _____

Name: _____

Fill in the common traits of animals, plants, and humans.

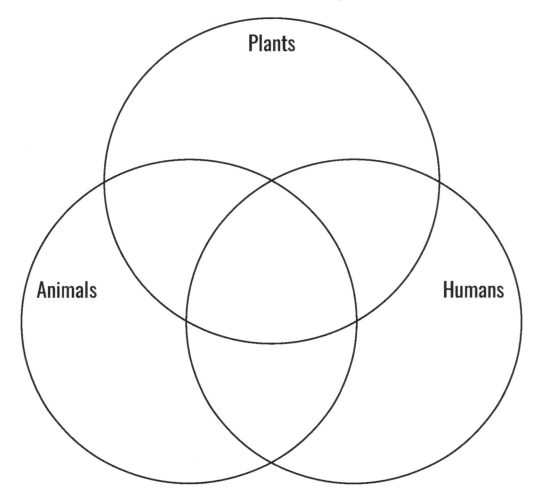

Question	Plants	Animals	Humans
How do they get food?			
How do they grow?			
Do they need water?			

Do They Need Air?

What are you thinking?

SCIENTISTS AND ENGINEERS ARE
IMAGINATIVE

Learning About **Albert Einstein**

Imaginative (adj.): having or showing an ability to think of new and interesting ideas

Lesson: A Beam of Light
Description

In this lesson, students investigate what happens when light strikes several different objects.

Objectives

Students will consider how being imaginative helped Albert Einstein investigate light.

- In the Predict portion of the lesson, students will complete their predictions about how light will interact with the materials provided.

- Students will hear the story *On a Beam of Light: A Story of Albert Einstein* by Jennifer Berne and discuss how it relates to *imaginative* as a character trait.

- In the Observe portion of the lesson, students will discuss which objects are transparent, translucent, and opaque based on their investigation with a flashlight and materials.

- In the Explain section, students will discuss why light passes through some objects and not others.

Learning Outcomes

Students will discuss (1) what being imaginative means and why being imaginative is an important trait for scientists and engineers and (2) plan and conduct an investigation to determine the effect of placing objects made with different materials in the path of a beam of light.

Connections to the *NGSS*

The following sections make one set of connections between the instruction outlined in this lesson and the *NGSS*. Other valid connections are likely; however, not all possibilities are listed.

Performance Expectation	Connections to Activity
1-PS4-3: Plan and conduct investigations to determine the effect of placing objects made with different materials in the path of a beam of light.	• Students will plan the best way to answer their questions and then develop the steps necessary to find the answers to their questions.
Science and Engineering Practice	**Connections to Activity**
Asking Questions and Defining Problems	• Children will ask *Can light travel through _____?*
Disciplinary Core Idea	**Connections to Activity**
PS4.B: Electromagnetic Radiation Objects can be seen if light is available to illuminate them or if they give off their own light.	• Students will learn that some materials allow light to pass through them, whereas others allow only some light through and still others block all light and create a dark shadow on any surface beyond them, where the light cannot reach. • Students will learn that mirrors can be used to redirect a light beam. (*Note:* Assessment does not include speed of light.)
Crosscutting Concept	**Connections to Activity**
Cause and Effect	• Students will plan and carry out an investigation to learn that events have causes that generate observable patterns.

Albert Einstein

Overview

In this lesson, students learn how light travels. The book *On a Beam of Light: A Story of Albert Einstein* discusses Albert Einstein's observation of a "beam of light," and in this experiment students actually test how light travels. In the story, Albert Einstein is portrayed as a young boy endlessly distracted by his curiosities and then as a man who would embody genius and shine a profound light on our understanding of the universe. By reading the featured book, students will learn that men and women from all backgrounds choose careers as scientists. The character trait of *imaginative* refers to Albert Einstein uncovering the mysteries of the universe—he was forced to use his imagination simply because no one had dared to before. Students share ideas about scientists as engineers and discuss how mathematical and computational thinking is used to solve problems.

Materials

Students will need a copy of the featured book *On a Beam of Light: A Story of Albert Einstein* by Jennifer Berne (2016). For this group activity, you will need the following items per group: one flashlight, a glass jar (any size), a plastic cup (clear—any size), a sheet of white paper, a piece of cardboard (at least 4 in. × 4 in.), aluminum foil (at least 4 in. × 4 in.), wax paper (at least 4 in. × 4 in.), tissue paper (at least 4 in. × 4 in.), a cup of water (in a clear cup), a mirror, a piece of cloth (at least 4 in. × 4 in.), and a paper plate. Encourage students to try out the experiment with any other items they are curious about.

Safety Notes

(1) Use caution when handling glass jars. These can shatter and cut skin. (2) Use caution when handling mirrors made of glass. These can also shatter and cut skin. (3) Immediately wipe up spilled water—it creates a slip-and-fall hazard. (4) Never drink any liquids used in a class activity.

Setting the Context
Predict

The Predict portion of this segment is on the Einstein worksheet included with this lesson (p. 34). Children predict whether they think light will pass through the items listed (pictured for young learners). *(Teacher Note: In this portion of the lesson, remind students that a prediction is what they believe will happen. Scientists learn the most when they make predictions and when what they thought was going to happen does not happen. Therefore, children should make their best guess and then see what happens.)*[1]

Guided Reading

Students will be learning about the work of Albert Einstein and the contributions he made to science as a result of his work. Introduce the book by holding up the cover and asking, *What do you think this story is about?* Read the story aloud. The following questions may be used to guide children's attention to detail as you read. (Page numbers reference unnumbered book pages, beginning with the title page as page 1.)

1. **Pages 1–12:** From the time he was very young, Albert was very quiet, and then he began asking a lot of questions. How did Albert Einstein come to experience the scientific mysteries of the world? *Albert loved reading about light, sound, magnetism, and gravity. He also loved reading about numbers—to him, they were like a secret language for figuring things out. Through reading, he kept wondering and learning.*

---

1   This lesson has been adapted with permission from "Just Passing Through," by AIMS Education Foundation, 2010, *Energy Explorations: Sound, Light, and Heat,* Fresno, CA: AIMS Education Foundation. Copyright 2010 by AIMS Education Foundation.

2. **Pages 21–22:** What kinds of questions did Albert ask? *He asked questions such as "How could one thing dissolve in water but not another?"* Why were those kinds of questions important? *These kinds of questions can be answered by conducting an experiment and had not necessarily been asked before.*

3. **Pages 27–28:** Albert Einstein is probably one of the most famous scientists. Many children know his name and can picture his crazy hair. He is often regarded as a genius. How did people come to regard Albert Einstein as a genius? *Albert wrote down his ideas and sent them into a science magazine. When they were published, he found out how interested other people were in his ideas. This is when Albert began to be called a genius—a title most people still associate with him today.*

4. **Pages 45–46:** On the last page of the story, the book says, "Albert thought and figured until the very last minute of the very last day of his life. How did Albert's imagination help him form questions?" *Albert did not limit himself in terms of the types of questions he asked or the amount of questions. One of Einstein's most remarkable talents was his ability to visualize experiments in his mind. It has been determined that most of Einstein's ideas first came to him as images, and later he turned them into words and equations.*

Making Sense
Observe

Gather the materials in a central location. Designate one student in each group as a "material" person. That person can be allowed out of his or her seat to get and return materials as needed for the group. Give each group a flashlight. Instruct students that they will be developing a plan to test how light behaves with different objects and that they will be looking for patterns in how light shines through objects.

THE *HOW* OF THE OBSERVE

Allow students to have about 10 minutes of exploration with a variety of objects and the flashlight, then gather them back together as a group and address their observations thus far. Ask them to figure out how they can find out what objects allow light to pass through and which objects block light. Ask each group how they would like to proceed answering this question; once everyone's procedures are formed, let students begin investigating. Students should notice at least two obvious reactions: Light either passes through the object or it does not. The third reaction—partial light passing through the object—may be difficult for students to observe. Ask students to show you what they are observing. Can they show one example of light passing through and one example of light being blocked?

Figure 2.4 ————————————————

An Example of a Transparent Reaction of Light

Figure 2.5 ————————————————

An Example of an Opaque Reaction of Light

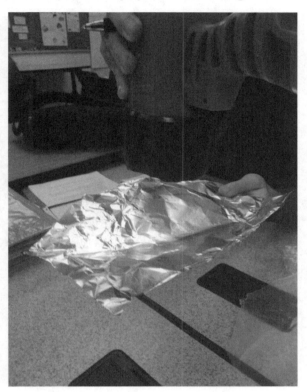

THE *WHY* OF THE OBSERVE

Students should have come to three very different conclusions based on their observations: (1) the object lets light pass through easily, (2) the object does not let light pass through easily, and (3) the object casts a shadow. Ask each group to show you an example of one of these reactions. Some objects allow light to pass through easily—these are plastic objects. Some objects block light completely—these are metal objects. Other objects will cast a very dark shadow. Pass out the Einstein worksheet (p. 34), and ask each group to make their predictions by filling out the left side of the worksheet first. Go around the room and check that each group has completed all its predictions, and then give students permission to progress with the activity as a group and record their data on the Does Light Go Through It? worksheet (pp. 35–36). Students should use the tools and materials to develop, design, and observe a cup that allows light to pass through it.

Figure 2.6

An Example of a Translucent Reaction of Light

Explain

In this portion of the lesson, you will be introducing the science words for each of the observations students have witnessed. Begin by asking students if they know the science words associated with the different ways the light reacted or behaved. It is very important that students have concrete experience with the materials before you provide the science term they are learning. Try grouping observations into three categories: (1) one lets light pass through, (2) one blocks light, and (3) one lets partial light through. Review each of these by having students demonstrate with objects. Then help them scaffold their science experience with the correct science word. The object that lets light pass through easily and does not cast a shadow is called *transparent* (Figure 2.4, p. 31). Ask students if they have ever heard this word before and ask them to record it on their worksheets. When the light is totally blocked and the object casts a very dark shadow, it is called *opaque* (Figure 2.5, p. 31). Ask students if they have ever heard this word before and ask them to record it on their worksheets. When the object allows some light to pass through and casts a dim shadow, it is *translucent* (Figure 2.6). Ask students if they have ever heard this word before and ask them to record it on their worksheets.

Evaluate

Summative evaluation of this lesson will include assessment of students' understanding of (1) the character trait of *imaginative* and (2) how to plan an investigation using a flashlight to discover which materials will let light pass through easily, which materials will let some light pass through, and which materials will block the light entirely.

CHARACTER TRAIT

Encourage students to answer the following questions:

1. If Albert Einstein had not explored unknown mysteries of the universe, how might our knowledge of what lives there today be different? *Of course someone might have eventually thought to explore the universe and discover the laws to do so. But Albert Einstein was imaginative and envisioned this before anyone else we know of did. He used his imagination to think outside the box. (Teacher Note: The point here is to review Einstein's efforts to create new understandings using mathematical and computational thinking.)*

2. Why is imagination an important character trait for scientists and engineers in the development of new ideas? Ask students to recall a time when they were imaginative.

CONTENT

Evaluate students' responses on their worksheets. Look for steps to investigate light on their worksheets and in their observations. Use a rubric like the one shown in Table 2.2 to assess students' worksheets.

Table 2.2

Rubric for Assessing Beam of Light Activity

Content or Skill	Not Yet	Beginning	Developing	Secure
Observation	Student did not record any observations about light passing through objects.	Student recorded observations about light passing through objects, but these were missing many details and had no clarity.	Student recorded some observations about light passing through objects with either details or clarity but not both.	Student recorded observations about light passing through objects with detail and clarity.
Planning and Carrying Out Investigations	Student did not provide evidence of how he or she went about answering the question.	Student provided some evidence of how he or she went about answering the question, but the steps were still unclear.	Student did not provide evidence of how he or she went about answering the question, but the basic steps were present.	Student provided clear and concise evidence of how he or she went about answering the question.

Name: _____

EINSTEIN WORKSHEET

QUESTION: Does light pass through these objects?

How can I find out? First, I will _____ .

Second, I will _____ .

Third, I will _____ .

Object	Prediction: Light Will Pass Through	Observation: Circle One	Observations
Paper plate	Yes or No	Yes Some No	
Aluminum foil	Yes or No	Yes Some No	
Tissue paper	Yes or No	Yes Some No	
Cup of Water	Yes or No	Yes Some No	
Piece of Cloth	Yes or No	Yes Some No	
Mirror	Yes or No	Yes Some No	
Fork	Yes or No	Yes Some No	
Add an item from your classroom	Yes or No	Yes Some No	

Name: _____

DOES LIGHT GO THROUGH IT?

Use the materials to explore light. Observe the three distinct differences in the amount of light that is able to pass through. Draw what you see in the empty boxes below. Label all materials used. Be sure to fill in the information for each section.

Translucent

This is translucent because _____

I was/was not (circle one) able to measure the light passing through it.

The light was _____ inches long.

Transparent

This is transparent because _____

I was/was not (circle one) able to measure the light passing through it.

The light was _____ inches long.

Opaque

This is opaque because _____.

I was/was not (circle one) able to measure the light passing through it.

The light was _____ inches long.

Conclusions:

The _____ (translucent, transparent, or opaque) let the most amount of light pass through.

The _____ (translucent, transparent, or opaque) let the least amount of light pass through.

SCIENTISTS AND ENGINEERS ARE
EXPLORERS

Learning About **Kathy Sullivan**

Explorer (n.): one who travels in search of geographical or scientific information

Lesson: Fun in the Sun
Description

In this lesson, students make observations to determine the effect of sunlight on Earth's surface.

Objectives

Students will consider how the character trait of being an explorer helped Kathy Sullivan make observations in outer space.

- In the Predict portion of the lesson, students will observe the Sun's position during the day.

- Students will hear the story *To the Stars: The First American Woman to Walk in Space* by Carmella Van Vleet and Kathy Sullivan and discuss how it relates to being an explorer.

- In the Observe portion of the lesson, students will compare observations of sand, soil, rocks, and water to determine the effect of sunlight on Earth's surface.

- In the Explain portion of the lesson, students will draw conclusions as to the effect of sunlight on Earth's surface.

Learning Outcomes

Students will (1) discuss what being an explorer means and why being an explorer is an important trait for scientists and engineers and (2) make observations to determine the effect of sunlight on Earth's surface.

Connections to the *NGSS*

The following sections make one set of connections between the instruction outlined in this lesson and the *NGSS*. Other valid connections are likely; however, not all possibilities are listed.

Performance Expectation	Connections to Activity
K-PS3-1. Make observations to determine the effect of sunlight on Earth's surface.	• Students will observe sand, soil, and water and compare their temperatures.

Science and Engineering Practice	Connections to Activity
Asking Questions and Defining Problems	• Students will ask the question *Which one is warmer? Which one is cooler? Why?*

Disciplinary Core Idea	Connections to Activity
PS3.B. Conservation of Energy and Energy Transfer Sunlight warms Earth's surface.	• Students will observe how sunlight warms the Earth's surface through observing sand, soil, rocks and water and comparing temperature.

Crosscutting Concept	Connections to Activity
Cause and Effect	• Students will learn that the Sun heats different objects at different rates.

Overview

In this lesson, students learn how one scientist worked through many challenges to achieve her dream of being the first woman to walk in space. Students will study the effect of sunlight on Earth's surface. This is meant to be an introduction to a "big idea" lesson. By reading the featured book, students will learn that men and women from all backgrounds choose careers as scientists. The character trait of being an explorer refers to Kathy Sullivan's bravery in preparing to venture into space during a time when no woman had ever done so before.

Materials

You will need a copy of the featured book *To the Stars: The First American Woman to Walk in Space* by Carmella Van Vleet and Kathy Sullivan (2016). Teacher will need: Three disposable polystyrene foam trays (if you cannot get polystyrene foam, then use plastic trays or three containers of the same size and make); aluminum foil (should not be used on trays because it can heat up, which would cause flawed data); sand, soil, and water (enough to fill the trays); a classroom thermometer

Kathy Sullivan

or a computer; a single "Go!Motion" temperature probe ($29); and Logger Lite software (free download available).

Individual students will need the Predict the Warmth worksheet (pp. 43–44). We recommended grouping students into teams for the Explore portion of the lesson. Teams for the Explore portion of the lesson will need the following materials: three disposable polystyrene foam trays (if you cannot get polystyrene foam, then use plastic or, at the very least, three of the same size and make of containers; otherwise, experimental error may affect the experiment); aluminum foil (trays should not be used because they can heat up, and this would cause flawed data); sand, soil, and water (enough to fill the trays); a classroom thermometer or a computer; a single "Go!Motion" temperature probe ($29); and Logger Lite software (free download available).

Safety Notes

(1) Remind all students that personal protective equipment should be worn during the setup, hands-on, and takedown segments of the activity. (2) Immediately wipe up spilled water—it creates a slip-and-fall hazard. (3) Never look directly at the Sun—this can cause irreparable damage to the eye. (4) Wash hands with soap and water upon completing this activity.

Setting the Context
Predict

The Predict portion of this segment is included in the worksheet with this lesson (pp. 43–44). Children predict which item they think will be the warmest and which item they think will be the coolest from the items listed (pictured for young learners). *(Teacher Note: In this portion of the lesson, we would remind students that a prediction is what they think will happen. Scientists learn the most when they make predictions and when what they thought was going to happen does not happen. Therefore, children should make their best guess and then see what happens. Note that larger versions of the graphs on p. 44 are available at www.nsta.org/EurekaAgain.)*

Guided Reading

Introduce the book by holding up the cover and asking, *What images on the book cover show us what we will learn about Kathy Sullivan?* Read the story aloud. The following questions may be used to guide children's attention to detail as you read. (Page numbers reference unnumbered book pages, beginning with the title page as page 1.)

1. **Pages 1–2:** From a young age, Kathy loved adventure. What was Kathy like as a young girl? *She was full of wonder and loved to study and explore.*

2. **Pages 9–10:** Kathy had many passions that were considered "boy's things." As a young girl, Kathy thought she might become a spy or a diplomat. How did her friends respond when she told them the kinds of jobs she was interested in? *They told her that those kinds of jobs were not for girls. They told her that girls are supposed to be teachers, nurses, or mothers.*

3. **Pages 17–18:** What did Kathy learn to do when she was a teenager that would help her in later years? *She learned how to pilot a plane, and later she learned about another kind of instrument panel from a spaceship. Kathy's first mission in space, called STS-41-G, was aboard the* Challenger, *and this was historic for two reasons. The space shuttle crew included two women (Kathy and Sally Ride), and Kathy was the first American woman to walk in space on this mission. Kathy would fly on two more missions aboard the* Discovery *and the* Atlantis.

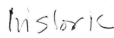

4. How does Kathy's story help you reach for the stars? *Kathy had the courage to set big goals for herself and go against ideas people had about girls and what they can and cannot do. Kathy flew in three space missions and logged over 500 hours in space. In 2004, she was inducted into the United States Astronaut Hall of Fame. She fulfilled her childhood dream and traveled all over the world to visit exotic and mysterious places—even the South Pole.*

Making Sense
Observe

This lesson requires some preplanning on the part of the teacher. First, find a good spot for your students to go out and observe the Sun several times. You will want to select a spot that gets the most sunlight during the longest part of the day.[1]

THE *HOW* OF THE OBSERVE

To begin, ask students if they have ever noticed where the Sun is when they enter the school building. If they have not noticed, give them some time—a day or so—to make these observations. Invite students to share their observations about the Sun. Tell students that they are going to test their predictions of which of the three

Figure 2.7
How to Set Up This Experiment

items in the lesson—sand, soil, and water—absorb the most heat from the Sun (see Figure 2.7). They are looking for the cause and effect between the Sun's rays (heat) and the temperature of the materials. Earth is composed of these materials (sand, soil, and water), and they heat Earth at different rates. (*Teacher Note: Most students can verbalize that the Sun is in different places during the day. They are familiar with the Sun being hot and having a high temperature. You can ask your students if they have ever gotten a sunburn. This is because the Sun's energy on its way to Earth gets converted into heat energy. Students may also be familiar with solar energy or energy from the Sun. Light energy from the Sun is received in wavelengths, and differing wavelengths mean different temperatures.*)

THE *WHY* OF THE OBSERVE

This is the perfect opportunity to use Kathy Sullivan's experience in space to address how she studied Earth. Earth is made up of land (continents) and water (oceans, lakes, and rivers). In this activity, students will explore how infrared energy from the Sun is converted into heat energy at different rates by three different materials: sand, soil, and water.

---

1 This lesson has been adapted with permission from "Sunsational Changes," by AIMS Education Foundation, 2011, *Earth Book: Hydrosphere, Geosphere, Atmosphere, and Their Interactions*, Fresno, CA: AIMS Education Foundation. Copyright 2011 by AIMS Education Foundation.

Explain

Land will heat up and cool down faster than water, so students should notice the sand and soil heating up faster than the water. They should also notice the sand and soil cooling down faster than the water.

Evaluate

Summative evaluation of this lesson will include assessment of students' understanding of (1) the character trait of being an explorer and (2) the effect of the Sun on Earth's surface: sand, soil, and water. Did students circle a prediction on their worksheet? Did they write or draw a conclusion? These pieces of evidence can be reviewed for assessment purposes.

CHARACTER TRAIT

1. In this story, Kathy Sullivan was an explorer because she ventured to travel where no woman had traveled before. Why is being exploratory an important character trait for scientists and engineers? *This is important because some discoveries by scientists may be beyond the understanding of the general population. It takes people who are brave to go beyond what we know to explore the unknown.*

2. When might other types of scientists need to be explorers? Ask students to work in pairs and tell each other about a time when they were explorers.

CONTENT

Evaluate students based on the graphs in the worksheet included with this lesson. Did students answer the overarching question of which materials heat up the fastest from the Sun? Were students able to make a prediction on the coolest and hottest materials? In assessing their worksheets, remember that it is not important whether students made correct predictions; instead, focus on whether they were able to make a prediction and what they learned from their prediction if it was incorrect.

References

AIMS Education Foundation. 2010. Just passing through. In *Energy explorations: Sound, light, and heat.* Fresno, CA: AIMS Education Foundation.

AIMS Education Foundation. 2011. Sunsational changes. In *Earth book: Hydrosphere, geosphere, atmosphere, and their interactions.* Fresno, CA: AIMS Education Foundation.

Berne, J. 2013. *On a beam of light: A story of Albert Einstein.* San Francisco: Chronicle Books.

Keeley, P. 2013. *Uncovering student ideas in primary science, Volume 1: 25 new formative assessment probes for grades K–2.* Arlington, VA: NSTA Press.

McDonnell, P. 2011. *Me … Jane.* New York: Little, Brown Books for Young Readers.

NGSS Lead States. 2013. *Next Generation Science Standards: For states, by states.* Washington, DC: National Academies Press. *www.nextgenscience.org/next-generation-science-standards.*

Schwartz, C. V., C. Passmore, and B. J. Reiser. 2017. *Helping students make sense of the world using next generation science and engineering practices.* Arlington, VA: NSTA Press.

Van Vleet, C., and K. Sullivan. 2016. *To the stars! The first American woman to walk in space.* Watertown, MA: Charlesbridge.

Name: _____

PREDICT THE WARMTH

Circle with a red crayon which one you think will be the hottest after one hour in the sun.

Sand   Soil   Water

Material	Start Temp (sun)	End Temp (sun)
Sand		
Soil		
Water		

Circle with a blue crayon which one you think will be the coolest after one hour in the shade.

Sand   Soil   Water

Material	Start Temp (shade)	End Temp (shade)
Sand		
Soil		
Water		

Record your observations below on these graphs.

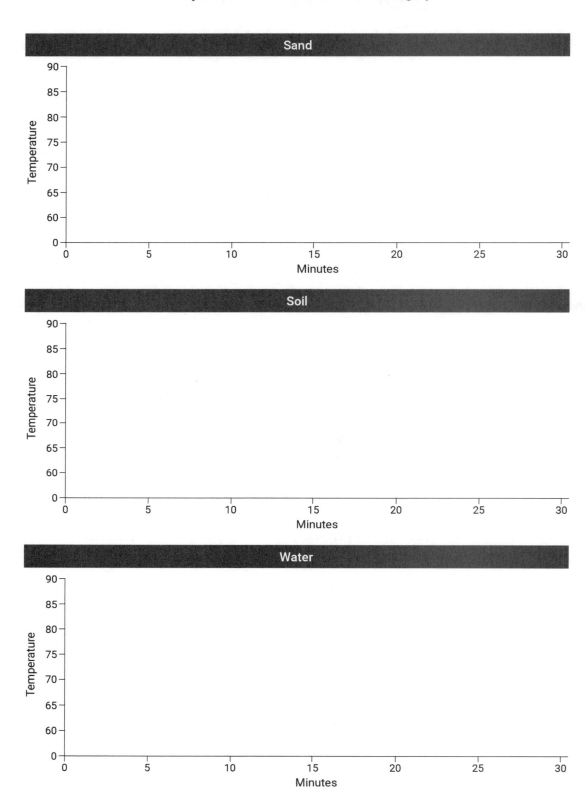

3

Developing and Using Models

The practice of developing and using models is very important in both science and engineering. The chapter will focus on Alfred Ely Beach, the citizens of the island of Samsø, and Maria Merian, who all ended up developing and using models in their work. An underground transit (Beach), energy sustainability (the citizens of Samsø), and the discovery that metamorphosis is a natural process (Merian) all advanced society. It is easy to see how the character traits of being a *thinker,* being *united,* and being *artistic* describe these scientists' and engineers' dispositions toward science.

The *Next Generation Science Standards* (*NGSS;* NGSS Lead States 2013) suggest that science models include diagrams, physical replicas, mathematical representations, analogies, and computer simulations. Engineering models, however, help to explain a system or help you understand where and under what conditions flaws might develop and how to test possible solutions to a problem. Models can also be used to visualize and refine a design, to communicate a design's features to others, or to illustrate a new prototype's design performance. Models can often be the source of misconceptions—especially if students don't also have a direct experience with the "real thing."

Although models do not correspond exactly to the real world, they do provide a visual representation that explains a phenomenon or how something works. Children need opportunities to experience models so that they can understand the limitations of models. In the K–2 classroom, children can benefit from building and revising simple models and from using a variety of models to represent events and design solutions. These experiences will also help children recognize the limitations of models.

Donna's Personal Story

One of the best examples I can think of to relate the practice of building models involves electricity. It was many years ago before the current *NGSS* were developed; however, it is a great visualization to me, as a teacher, how models help children to think through solutions. We were learning about conductors and insulators, and we had the typical kinds of materials (e.g., batteries, bulbs, wires). Through a series of classroom activities, children placed the wire to the batteries and lightbulb to make their lightbulb light up. When I asked the students how they thought electricity was used in their homes, they were silent. Developmentally, they were not at an age to be able to understand such an abstraction. So the next day I began bringing in cardboard boxes. The children asked what I was doing cutting these boxes and reconnecting them to each other. I constructed a "dollhouse" for our class as a model and asked the students to place lightbulbs in appropriate places and then "connect" what they needed to connect to get the lightbulbs to work. Our class worked diligently on that model, and the students went way beyond any time I had set aside for my electricity unit, but in the end, that model helped those students understand what a three-way switch was when going up and down stairs and why it's important simply because their doll would have to run back up the stairs to turn the light off. Because of the age of my students, I created one concrete model for the class. The students were able to experience the ins and outs of its effectiveness and visualize conductors and insulators in a whole new way. Soon, dolls and props filled "our house," and children were playing electrician during many, many indoor recesses!

What's Important to Remember About the Practice of Developing and Using Models

- Models help identify questions and predict answers.

- Models can be revised to answer or explain, predict, and solve.

- Models use mathematics to formulate some models and mathematical reasoning to evaluate models.

- Argumentation is involved in both developing and evaluating models.

- Models hold and organize relevant information and become the focus of communicating ideas.

See Schwartz, Passmore, and Reiser (2017) for more information.

SCIENTISTS AND ENGINEERS ARE
THINKERS

Learning About **Alfred Ely Beach**

Thinker (n.): one who has an idea or opinion

Lesson: Tunnel Travel
Description

In this lesson, students will build a model for underground transportation.

Objectives

Students will consider how the character trait of *thinker* helped Alfred Ely Beach create the subway.

- In the Play portion of the lesson, students will play with toy cars and cylinders.

- Students will hear the story *The Secret Subway* by Shana Corey and discuss how it relates to the word *thinker*.

- In the Explore portion, students will work in teams to build a model for underground transportation.

- In the Discuss portion, students will discuss how their model works and the benefits of their model.

Learning Outcomes

Students will (1) discuss what being a thinker means and why being a thinker is an important trait for scientists and engineers and (2) develop and use a model for underground transportation.

Connections to the *NGSS*

The following sections make one set of connections between the instruction outlined in this lesson and the *NGSS*. Other valid connections are likely; however, not all possibilities are listed.

Performance Expectation	Connections to Activity
K-2-ETS1-1: Ask questions, make observations, and gather information about a situation people want to change to define a simple problem that can be solved through the development of a new or improved object or tool.	• Students will be asked to think about underground travel and design a model using toy cars for underground travel.
Science and Engineering Practice	**Connections to Activity**
Developing and Using Models	• Students will develop a simple model based on evidence to represent a proposed object or tool.
Disciplinary Core Idea	**Connections to Activity**
ETS1.B: Developing Possible Solutions Designs can be conveyed through sketches, drawings, or physical models. These representations are useful in communicating ideas for a problem's solutions to other people.	• Students will create a physical model of a way to transport people and/or vehicles underground other than (or not limited to) a subway.
Crosscutting Concept	**Connections to Activity**
Structure and Function	• Students will learn that parts and pieces of models are shaped for their purposes. For example, a funnel might be used to move sand from one area to another. There is a relationship between structure and function; for instance, a paper towel tube might be used to simulate a tunnel because their structures are similar.

Overview

In this lesson, students learn how the subway was developed and create a new invention of their own. Alfred Ely Beach created his invention to address the problem of trash in the street to meet societal needs. By reading the featured book, students will learn that men and women from all backgrounds choose careers as scientists. The character attribute of thinker refers to Alfred Ely Beach's creative attempts to use pneumatic power—the power to move things with air pressure—to solve New York City's traffic crisis.

Alfred Ely Beach

Materials

You will need the following materials for this lesson: a copy of the featured book *The Secret Subway* by Shana Corey (2016); empty paper towel and toilet paper rolls; a variety of scraps and cylinders for play; empty cans like the ones used for the commercial brand Pringles (with the bottom removed); empty oatmeal containers (with the bottom removed); cardboard boxes of varying sizes; duct tape and masking tape; scissors; and safety glasses or goggles.

Safety Notes

(1) Remind all students that personal protective equipment should be worn during the setup, hands-on, and takedown segments of the activity. (2) Watch for sharp

plastic or metal edges on cans. These can cut skin. (3) Use caution when handling scissors, wires, and so on. They are sharp and can cut or puncture skin.

Setting the Context
Play

For this lesson, students should be using their imaginations and wondering skills to "play" with objects in a science center. Arrange a variety of cylinders and matchbox cars so that children can easily select them. The only direction children should be given is to play with the items with their classmates (in small groups). The play should be both unstructured and uninterrupted (see Figure 3.1).

Guided Reading

Students will be learning about Alfred Ely Beach, a scientist who was a thinker, by reading *The Secret Subway*. Students will connect Alfred Ely Beach to efforts with connecting pneumatic power (the power to move things using air pressure). Introduce the book by asking, *Can you find the person on the front cover? What seems to be happening on the front cover?* Read the story aloud. Encourage students to notice and think about the challenges Alfred Ely Beach faced as a man who needed permission to build a railway under the streets of New York City. The following questions may be used to guide children's attention to detail as you read. (Page numbers reference unnumbered book pages, beginning with the title page as page 1.)

Figure 3.1

A Student Working on the Play Portion of the Activity

1. **Pages 1–4:** At the beginning of the story, how did the streets look? Why does the author say "something had to be done"? *The book says that the streets were filled with so much garbage that stagecoaches and horses had a hard time passing through.*

2. **Pages 5–6:** Show an illustration where people were thinking about and dreaming up new ideas to solve their problem, yet all they did was talk about solutions, not create any. How was Alfred Ely Beach different from most people? *The book describes Alfred Ely Beach as a thinker who took action. His ability to take action is what set him apart from others. Whereas others just*

dreamed about ideas, he tried to visualize a way to make travel happen. His idea involved an underground transit powered by a fan called a pneumatic system.

3.   **Pages 11–18:** The name of the book is *The Secret Subway.* Why did Alfred Ely Beach have to keep the tunnel a secret while it was being built? What roadblocks did he encounter? *Obtaining permission to build a railway underneath New York City was such a complicated process with a variety of political implications that Alfred Ely Beach decided to go around the legal system. He disguised the project as a travel system for mail delivery and built it at night to accomplish building the model for underground transportation.*

4.   **Pages 21–28:** The public was invited to view and ride on the wind-powered (pneumatic) transit that Alfred Ely Beach had invented. Why did he not get permission to expand this successful invention? *Some people did not like Alfred Ely Beach's idea for a variety of reasons, such as the possibility that it was not safe and because it affected the shopkeepers above ground. (Teacher Note: There is a great deal of controversy about this period in history as to why Alfred Ely Beach was not allowed to continue building his underground train. Some historical documents point to Boss Tweed's influence on the project.)*

5.   **Pages 35–36:** Today we have a subway that is not powered by a fan but is the result of Alfred Ely Beach's efforts. What did workers find when building the modern-day subway? *They found remnants of Alfred Ely Beach's pneumatic transit system. (Teacher Note: Beach died in 1896. His tunnel was destroyed while the current system was being built, but the memory of his magical subway station still exists, buried deep beneath New York City's sidewalks.)*

Making Sense
Explore

Invite students to practice brainstorming and invent something that would make underground travel safer or more fun for people in vehicles. To begin, engage students in a conversation about how Alfred Ely Beach might have planned to build an underground travel system. Students will be creating an invention of their choice using household or recyclable materials provided in a mini-makerspace in the classroom.

THE *HOW* OF THE EXPLORE

Your classroom can include any safe materials you can gather. Some simple craft items have been suggested in the materials list, but you might also include electric components (e.g., magnets, wires, bells, or bulbs to extend students' knowledge of electric circuitry) and invite students to bring additional materials from home. This type of lesson, which uses recyclable scraps for children to create a model, can be very different from routine classroom lessons. For this lesson, teachers organize processes and materials that help structure students' freewheeling problem solving and guide students to a finished product that meets the lesson goals and objectives.

THE *WHY* OF THE EXPLORE

Models are tools for thinking, making predictions, and making sense of experiences (NRC 2012). In this lesson, students are being asked to create a model and think about underground travel in a unique way. If a child uses a subway system of any kind in his or her daily life, he or she may very well be familiar with the underground structures. If a child does not have concrete experience with a subway system, it may be a little more challenging for him or her to visualize and/or articulate what the structures could possibly look like underground. This is why this activity will vary based on your student population. It should not be interpreted as a simple *build a subway* task but rather as a task to *create an underground way for people or cars to travel*. As children begin to imagine and create, they will appreciate an opportunity to learn about the design cycle.

Children will gradually become familiar with the design cycle, which involves repeated steps of asking questions, inventing, testing, improving, and retesting. Ask students if they are aware of the design cycle. If they are not, they can work in groups to generate a pictorial representation of how an invention works. This can easily be done with sticky notes on a page in the students' science notebooks. Arrange students into groups and encourage them to answer this question, *What are the steps to creating something new?* Most children will benefit if you limit the number of steps to three or five. Pass out sticky notes so they arrange the design steps on the page. If students are struggling at this point, create a class list on the chalkboard of some of the words (generated as a class) to describe the invention process. *(Teacher Note: Prompt students to wonder whether scientists or engineers make an invention perfectly the very first time. How do they know when it is perfect? What evidence do they have? This will help guide students' realization about revision being a natural part of the process. There is no perfect model of the design process. Your students will likely produce varying answers as they begin to think about the design process. The most important point here is the value of testing and revising.)*

Figure 3.2

A "Subway" That Students Created Out of a Box, Paper, and Paper Towel Rolls

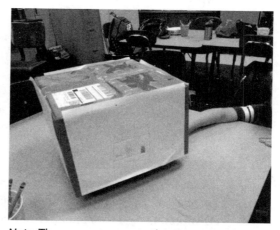

Note: The paper represents the cityscape. The paper towel rolls represent the transit underground.

Discuss

Now that students have an underground travel system (see Figures 3.2 and 3.3), ask them to work together to identify the steps in the design cycle used in creating their solution. Provide ample time for all groups to present their ideas, which should include their system of underground travel and the steps of the design process used. *(Teacher Note: This lesson encourages children to actually tinker with objects and ideas until they build something unique—just like scientists and engineers. These experiences allow students to improve their thinking skills and to connect in-school learning to real-world applications. In this lesson, you are giving them the idea for the finished outcome [underground system for transportation]; however, each group's design should be unique to accomplish this task.)*

Figure 3.3

The "Subway" Turned Upside Down

Evaluate

Summative evaluation of this lesson will include assessment of students' understanding of (1) the thinker character trait and (2) how to build a model for underground transit.

CHARACTER TRAIT

The ability to solve problems and invent new ideas is important for scientists and engineers. Therefore, the thinker character trait is central to this way of thinking.

1. How was Alfred Ely Beach a thinker? *Alfred Ely Beach was able to visualize, try out, and test several ideas, constantly thinking about the problem he was trying to solve.*

2. Describe a time when you were a thinker.

CONTENT

The idea here is that students create a way to solve the original problem in the book—a way for underground travel to happen. Some students' creations will look like what we know as subways; some will not. Students can use a checklist like the one shown in Table 3.1 (p. 54; larger version available at *www.nsta.org/EurekaAgain*) to evaluate their design process as a result of team effort. If you want to evaluate the activity, you may use a rubric like the one included after the self-evaluation checklist (Table 3.2, p. 54), where students can circle the smiley that matches their answer.

Table 3.1 ──

Method of Student Self-Assessment for Tunnel Travel Lesson

Question	Yes	No	Maybe/Unsure
Did We Follow the Design Process?	☺	☹	••
Does Our Invention Allow for Underground Travel?	☺	☹	••
Can It Be Improved?	☺	☹	••

Table 3.2 ──

Rubric for Assessing Students for Tunnel Travel Lesson

Content or Skill	Not Yet	Beginning	Developing	Secure
Participation	Students are not able to create a means for underground travel as a team.	Students are able to create a means for underground travel as a team but their design may not be functional or realistic.	Most students on the team are able to create a means for underground travel as a team and the design appears to be functional and realistic.	All students on the team are able to create a means for underground travel as a team and redesign it as necessary to improve their original design during the process.
Drawing	Student did not provide a drawing.	Student's drawing is still at the imagination level.	Student's drawing is moving from imagination to evidence-based realities and includes a mode for underground travel.	Student's drawing is moving from imagination to evidence-based realities and words are included with arrows or lines. The drawing includes multiple ways for cars to travel underground.
Design and Redesign Process	Student is not able to analyze data from tests of underground travel.	Student is not able to analyze data from tests of underground travel designed to solve the problem of underground travel to compare the strengths and weaknesses of how each car performs.	Student is able to analyze data from tests of three cars designed to solve the problem of underground travel and can compare the strengths and weaknesses of how each car performs.	Student is able to analyze data from tests of three or more cars designed to solve the problem of underground travel, and he or she can compare the strengths and weaknesses of how each car performs. The team is able to redesign its model based on this information.

SCIENTISTS AND ENGINEERS ARE
UNITED

Learning About **the People of the Island of Samsø**

United (adj.): involving people or groups
working together to achieve something

Lesson: Round and Round We Go!
Description

In this lesson, students learn how a group of citizens came
together to solve a problem by building a model for wind energy.

Objectives

Students will consider how being united helped the people of the island of Samsø solve
their problem. They will test which windmill design is the sturdiest and which will be
better at capturing the wind's energy.

- In the Play portion of the lesson, students will explore with wind tools.

- Students will hear the story *Energy Island: How One Community Harnessed the Wind
  and Changed the World* by Allan Drummond and discuss how it relates to the word
  united.

- In the Explore portion, students will create a simple model of a windmill.

- In the Discuss portion, students will discuss how the model of the windmill they
  created can be used for capturing energy.

Learning Outcomes

Students will (1) discuss what being united means and why being united is an important
trait for scientists and engineers and (2) develop and use a model of a windmill and test
different materials for sails.

Connections to the *NGSS*

The following sections make one set of connections between the instruction outlined in this lesson and the *NGSS*. Other valid connections are likely; however, not all possibilities are listed.

Performance Expectation	Connections to Activity
K-2-ETS1-3. Analyze data from tests of two objects designed to solve the same problem to compare the strengths and weaknesses of how each performs.	• Students will build mini windmills out of different materials and test and compare which one is best for capturing the wind's energy.
Science and Engineering Practice	**Connections to Activity**
Developing and Using Models	• Students will build mini windmills so they can use this model to simulate the motion of a real wind mill.
Disciplinary Core Idea	**Connections to Activity**
ETS1.C: Optimizing the Design Solution Because there is always more than one possible solution to a problem, it is useful to compare and test designs.	• Students will use the windmill material of their choice to try to improve their design.
Crosscutting Concept	**Connections to Activity**
Structure and Function	• Students will observe and test the shape and stability of the different windmill sails.

Overview

In this lesson, students learn how one community of ordinary people collaborated to harness energy for their island. When the ordinary citizens decided to do something extraordinary, they drastically reduced their carbon emissions and became almost completely energy independent. This inspiring true story proves that with a big idea and a lot of hard work, anyone can make a huge step toward energy conservation. By reading the featured book, students will learn that men and women from all backgrounds choose careers as scientists. The character trait of being united refers to the combined efforts of all the people on the island of Samsø; this is an example of how scientists and engineers use models to solve real-world problems.

The People of the Island of Samsø

Materials

You will need a copy of the featured book *Energy Island: How One Community Harnessed the Wind and Changed Their World* by Allan Drummond (2015). For the Play portion, you will need a blow-dryer (tape it with duct tape on the cool setting prior to bringing it into the classroom) and Ping-Pong balls. For the Explore portion, you will need the following materials: construction paper, card stock, bulletin board paper or newsprint, plastic straws, string, paper clips, tape, scissors, tacky stuff, wooden skewers (trim the pointed edges off before bringing these into the classroom), a hole punch, a blow-dryer (duct tape on the cool setting), and gallon-size resealable plastic bags. For ease of classroom management, place the following items into the plastic bags: precut squares made out of three different types of paper, a straw, 6 in. of string, a paper clip, one small piece of tacky stuff that will later be divided into four and skewered. Pass these out to teams of two students (see Figure 3.4). *(Teacher Note: Create 8 in. × 8 in. squares by holding two 8 in. × 12 in. pieces of paper: one vertically, one horizontally. Cut along the edge that is off the center, and once you remove the second piece of paper you will have an 8 in. × 8 in. square. Draw a line from one corner to another twice to make a large X on the square. Cut on the lines of the X until 3 in. from the center. Place a hole punch in the center to create a hole. Depending on the amount of experience your children have and their ages, you can modify this experiment in several ways. The ideal way to do this experiment is to let all groups create a windmill from all three types of paper [card stock, construction paper, and bulletin board paper]. The benefit of this method is that children can compare the structure and function of three different types of paper, and this way the type of paper becomes the variable. However, if you do not have enough time or if your students are not very skilled with the experimentation process, you can provide only one piece of paper to each group, and as a class the students can compare the data of the three different types of paper. Another way to teach this lesson would be to allow everyone in the class to use the card stock because it works best.)*

Figure 3.4

Sample Bag of Experimental Materials

Safety Notes

(1) Remind all students that personal protective equipment should be worn during the setup, hands-on, and takedown segments of the activity. (2) Watch for sharp edges on cans, skewers, clips, and so on. These can cut or puncture skin. (3) Use caution when handling scissors. They are sharp and can cut or puncture skin. (4) Only an adult should operate the electric blow-dryer. (5) Do not operate the blow-dryer near a water source—this can create an electrical shock hazard. (6) The blow-dryer is a potential heat source. This should be handled with caution, as it can burn skin.

Setting the Context
Play

Ask students if they have ever seen the wind. We don't see wind—we see the *effects* of wind. Ask students if they think wind is powerful. Ask students, *Have you ever seen a windmill before? What do you think windmills are used for?* If possible, allow students to "play" with wind by providing a couple of Ping-Pong balls and blow-dryers at the science center. Invite students to place the Ping-Pong ball over the blow-dryer and then turn the blow-dryer on. Ask, *What do you observe?* Encourage students to draw this picture in their science notebooks and record three to five observations. Discuss these observations with the entire class. *(Teacher Note: The ball will gravitate over the blow-dryer due to Bernoulli's principle. It is not important that the children know these details—it is only important for them to experience "playing" with the blow-dryer and Ping-Pong ball and wondering what happens and why [see Figure 3.5]. The book you will be reading to the students provides extensive background information for teachers in the green sections on every page, including information about renewable and nonrenewable energy and global warming.)*

Guided Reading

Students will be learning about the island of Samsø in Denmark. Find Denmark on a map and show the students how far away it is from where they live. Introduce the book by holding up the cover and asking, *What do you think this story is about?* Read the story aloud.

The following questions may be used to guide children's attention to detail as you read. (Page numbers reference unnumbered book pages, beginning with the title page as page 1.)

1. **Pages 1–12:** This story tells of the people of the island of Samsø, Denmark. What was special about "Energy Island"? *The Danish Ministry of Environment and Energy chose Samsø as the ideal place in Denmark to become independent*

Figure 3.5

Students in the Play Portion of the Lesson

from nonrenewable energy (sources of energy that cannot be replaced—they must be used up). A teacher named Søren Hermansen was selected to lead the energy independence project.

2. **Pages 12–16:** Soon, two renewable energy projects had begun: one small wind turbine and one big wind turbine. How did the idea of conserving wind energy come about on the island of Samsø? *As the story implies, wind is plentiful on the island. Søren Hermansen was growing weary of the idea because it was taking so long to convince people to give energy independence a chance. Then one day, an electrician offered to put up a secondhand wind turbine near his house, and a farmer agreed to invest his own money to build a large wind turbine there.*

3. **Pages 19–20:** The weather helped the people conclude that they could produce enough energy with their large turbine. How did they learn that they could make energy for themselves? *The power went out, and when they realized that the wind turbine produced enough electricity, everyone wanted one for themselves. This also motivated people to try different energy-saving ideas on their own, such as using electric cars, making their own tractor fuel from crops, and using solar panels. People became excited about and motivated to use renewable energy.*

4. The book says that we have renewable energy all around us. How can our community work together to make the best of it? *The book talks about how we waste energy in the winter to stay warm and in the summer to stay cool. The author recommends thinking about how we use energy every day. We can bike or walk to save gas. We can also use better gas and build vehicles that use less gas. (Teacher Note: Students can generate ideas about how they might be able to save energy in their community.)*

Doing the Activity
Explore

Invite teams of two students to explore windmills. *(Teacher Note: Windmills are machines that convert energy from the wind into useful work by rotating. Using wind power dates back to the first century in Greece. Windmills have been used to lift things up and down, especially water from the ground, to power machines that crush grain and process food and [in this story's case] to power motors to generate electricity. Windmills work because the wheel is able to rotate freely on an axis, harnessing the wind's energy to move it by using sails or shapes that can catch the wind.)*

THE *HOW* OF THE EXPLORE

Allow each group to select a square from the various types of materials you have provided (newspaper, card stock, printer paper). *(Teacher Note: Have an X already drawn on each of the squares from corner to corner.)* To create the sails of the windmill, bend each corner down to where the cut stops near the center of the paper and secure it with tacky stuff (see Figure 3.6; *do not cover up the premade hole*). Instruct students to insert a straw through the center of each windmill; this will help the windmill rotate. Tie or tape a piece of string onto the straw (*not the skewer*). *(Teacher Note: The string should be precut and handed out to groups with tape.)* Tie the other end of the string to a paper clip.

Instruct students to hold the ends of the wooden skewer and blow on the sails of the windmill model. Encourage students to observe what happens. Depending on your classroom, call students up one group at a time to "test" their windmill with a really big gust of wind using the blow-dryer (see Figure 3.7, p. 62). This is the fastest way for them to see the effects of wind. They should notice the string and paper clip rotating around the straw. Encourage them to build a second design—what would they change? What differences do they notice between the windmills with different materials? Encourage students to answer the question *Which windmill works best and why?* Follow this outline for the activity:

Figure 3.6

Making the Pinwheel Shape

Note: Fold down every other corner piece and secure shape with tacky stuff. Push firmly for best results.

1. Build the windmill.

2. Record the number of times it rotates in X amount of time. We suggest coloring one flap to ease counting.

3. Try to increase the rotations per minute (rpms) while exploring variables such as the design of the blades or base, the weight of the paper blades, the speed of the wind, or other variables the students think of (even better!). *(Teacher Note: Some types of paper will not hold up to more rotations; students should have the opportunity to redesign their blades as necessary.)*

4. Have students record their observations on the chart shown in Table 3.3, p. 62.

THE *WHY* OF THE EXPLORE
Asking students to create a windmill and observe the spinning process will get them thinking. By asking students to compare materials and use different materials for the wind sails, they can test their ideas quickly and easily.

Making Sense
Discuss

Explain to children how, as they blow on the windmill, their breath (or the air from the blow-dryer) then rotates the wheel, which will rotate the shaft. Because the axis is connected to the string and the paper clip, it will convert the energy from the breath, harnessed by the wheel, into useful work by twisting up the string and lifting the paper clip. This is how windmills produce energy. *(Teacher Note: Windmill blades, like aircraft propeller blades, turn when the wind blows and power an electric generator that supplies an electric current. Instead of using electricity to make wind, like a fan, windmills use wind to make electricity. The wind turns the blades, which spin a shaft, which connects to a generator and makes electricity.)* Card stock will likely produce the best sails because it is the stiffest material. Bulletin board or newsprint paper will have the weakest sails because the shape created when folding the corners of the paper into the center creates a sail, which will catch the breath (or blow-dryer) when it is blown on.

Figure 3.7

Students Testing Out Their Designs With a Blow-Dryer

Table 3.3

Data Collection Chart for Students

Design	Number of Rotations (Person 1 Blowing)	Number of Rotations (Person 2 Blowing)	Number of Rotations (Person 3 Blowing)
First Design or Construction Paper			
Second Design or Card Stock			

Note: A larger version of this table is available at *www.nsta.org/EurekaAgain.*

Evaluate

Summative evaluation of this lesson will include assessment of students' understanding of (1) the character trait of being united and (2) the design and function of their windmill.

CHARACTER TRAIT

Encourage students to answer the following questions:

1. The people on Samsø became united around the idea of energy conservation. What struggles do you think they faced before they became united? How about *after* they became united? *They would have struggled with communicating with others and spreading the word. After they became united, they would have struggled with ensuring that everyone's voice was heard and keeping everyone informed. (Teacher Note: Encourage students to think about a time they became united for a purpose, either at school or at home. It is also important to mention that energy independence did not happen overnight—it took years and many, many meetings. The story also mentions that the children were quick to generate ideas and the adults were slower to generate ideas about energy conservation.)*

2. Describe a time when you united with others to solve a problem.

CONTENT

Challenge students to compare the different materials their classmates used—maybe the students could make all three and compare them. Find a way to compare the different models that the groups in the class built. How are they alike or different? Prompt students to think about what improvements they could make in the redesign process. You can use a rubric like the one shown in Table 3.4.

Table 3.4

Rubric for Assessing Students' Windmill Designs

Content or Skill	Not Yet	Beginning	Developing	Secure
Design and Redesign Process	Student is not able to create a model of a windmill.	Student is not able to create a model of a windmill and/or test different materials for sails.	Student is able to create a model of a windmill and test at least one material for sails.	Student is able to create a model of a windmill and test more than one different material for sails. Student or team is able to redesign the model based on this information.

SCIENTISTS AND ENGINEERS ARE

ARTISTIC

Learning About **Maria Merian**

Artistic (adj.): having or showing the skill of an artist

Lesson: Interesting Insects
Description

In this lesson, students develop a simple model that mimics the function of an animal dispersing seeds or pollinating plants.

Objectives

Students will consider how being artistic helped Maria Merian.

- In the Predict portion of the lesson, students will use their prior knowledge about life cycles to complete a formative assessment.

- Students will hear the story *Summer Birds: The Butterflies of Maria Merian* by Margarita Engle and discuss how it relates to the word *artistic*.

- In the Observe portion, students will observe and interact with a model that mimics the function of an insect in pollinating plants.

- In the Explain portion, students will discuss interdependent relationships in ecosystems (plants and insects).

Learning Outcomes

Students will (1) discuss what being artistic means and why being artistic is an important trait for scientists and engineers and (2) observe and interact with a model to explain the relationship between plants and insects.

Connections to the *NGSS*

The following sections make one set of connections between the instruction outlined in this lesson and the *NGSS*. Other valid connections are likely; however, not all possibilities are listed.

Performance Expectation	Connections to Activity
2-LS2-2: Develop a simple model that mimics the function of an animal in dispersing seeds or pollinating plants.	• Students will develop a simple model that shows how insects disperse seeds and help pollinate plants.
Science and Engineering Practice	**Connections to Activity**
Developing and Using Models	• Students will develop a simple model that shows pollination.
Disciplinary Core Idea	**Connections to Activity**
LS2.A: Interdependent Relationships in Ecosystems Plants depend on animals for pollination or to move their seeds around.	• Students will use one-to-one correspondence with concrete materials to help gain an understanding of how pollination occurs.
Crosscutting Concept	**Connections to Activity**
Cause and Effect	• Students will observe the cause-and-effect relationship between flowers and plants.

Overview

In this lesson, students learn about one woman who, as a teenager, was responsible for disproving spontaneous generation and introducing people to the fact that insects go through a cycle called metamorphosis. This was during the mid-1600s when people were often afraid of the natural changes of butterflies, moths, and frogs and tended to label these living things as evil. Through careful observation, she discovered that metamorphosis is natural, not supernatural. Her studies were simple, yet far ahead of her time. By reading the featured book, students will learn that men and women from all backgrounds choose careers as scientists. The scientist character trait of *artistic* refers to Maria Merian's careful observations and beautiful paintings of butterflies, moths, and frogs during a time when her scientific ideas were not culturally accepted.

Maria Merian

Materials

You will need a copy of the featured book *Summer Birds: The Butterflies of Maria Merian* by Margarita Engle (2010). For the Predict portion of the lesson, you will need the Chrysalis probe by Page Keeley. For the Observe portion, you will need puffed cheese snacks such as the commercial brand Cheetos, black and orange pipe cleaners, and the paper flower pattern (p. 72).

Safety Notes

(1) Watch for sharp edges on the pipe cleaner wires. These can cut or puncture skin.
(2) Never eat food that is used in a class activity.

Setting the Context
Predict

Use the Chrysalis probe from Page Keeley's book *What Are They Thinking?* (p. 73). The point of using this probe is to get children thinking about insects before they read the book about Maria Merian. Just about every student in the class will have had some experience with butterflies or life cycles. Most children in kindergarten can tell you the stages of development (yet this is one thing we teach over and over again). This topic is quite common in preschool and kindergarten. Many preschools do these kinds of caterpillar activities with young children. The goal of this lesson is not to reteach the life cycle but to expand the children's knowledge about insects and how they interact with the environment in both good and bad ways. Have books available at the science center as well as materials for students to re-create a life cycle. Some popular books are those by Eric Carle such as *The Very Hungry Caterpillar* or books about frogs. Think about discussing life cycles before you read *Summer Birds: The Butterflies of Maria Merian*. Summarize information from the students' ideas or comments—for example, "I noticed all of your ideas about a caterpillar included a chrysalis; let's investigate further with this probe." Show the class the probe on an interactive white board or other projector. Discuss the probe with students to generate their prior knowledge ideas about insects and life cycles before reading the story.

Guided Reading

Students will be learning about Maria Merian, a teenage girl who studied insects. Introduce the book by holding up the cover and asking, *What do you think this story is about?* Read the story aloud. The following questions may be used to guide children's attention to detail as you read. (Page numbers reference unnumbered book pages, beginning with the title page as page 1.)

1. **Pages 1–8:** During a time when people believed that insects came from mud, a young girl challenged their ideas. This story tells of a teenage girl who dared to be different in the 1650s and began observing butterflies, moths, and frogs. What did Maria do to find out how insects and frogs change over time? *(Teacher Note: Students' responses will vary but should include how Maria observed the animals over time. The title of the book,* Summer Birds, *comes from the medieval name for the mysterious butterflies and moths that appeared suddenly during warm weather and then vanished again in the fall.)*

2. **Pages 10–18:** The book describes how Maria used observation to disprove what adults believed. What did Maria do with her observations? *Maria drew the "summer birds" at all stages and painted her pictures. (Teacher Note: Maria eventually became a famous scientist, an artist, and an explorer. Eventually, Maria's paintings were published in beautiful books that helped people understand the life cycles of flowers and insects.)*

Figure 3.8

Three-Step Process for Building the Flower Model

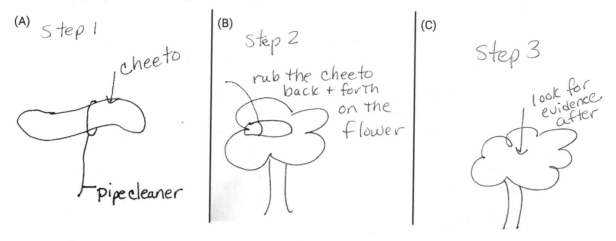

(A) Step 1
cheeto
pipe cleaner

(B) Step 2
rub the cheeto back + forth on the flower

(C) Step 3
look for evidence after

Doing the Activity
Observe

As a group, generate a list of ways insects help the environment and ways they hurt plants. If students do not have any ideas, you could visit Encyclopedia Britannica for Kids (*http://kids.britannica.com/comptons/article-285163/insect*) for some help.

One answer for how insects help plants is that they visit and pollinate them. Insects hurt or harm plants by eating them. Some children may have noticed large bite marks in the leaves of their garden in the summer. Some insects do eat plant leaves, and usually this is a problem for the plant. In this portion of the lesson, connect life cycles (the focus of the book) and pollination (the activity). Build on students' prior knowledge by allowing them to demonstrate what they know about life cycles first. Remember that the point of this lesson is to build on their existing

Figure 3.9

Children Building Their Models Using the Three-Step Process

knowledge about insect life cycles in an attempt to teach some new content about insects and the environment. To learn about how insects interact with the environment, the students will build a model.

THE *HOW* OF THE OBSERVE

Students will create a model to show how bees help the environment by pollinating flowers. Divide students into groups. Each group should get one puffed cheese snack and cut out three flower patterns on construction paper. Figures 3.8 and 3.9 show the three-step process. Instruct students to wrap one orange pipe cleaner around the puffed cheese snack so it can be held in their fingers as a handle. Wrap a black pipe cleaner around this to represent the bee's wings. Instruct students to put their "bee" (cheese snack figure) in their fingers and to "fly" their bee over to the flower (see Figure 3.10). Give the students several minutes to create a model using the "bee" and "flower" to simulate how bees pollinate flowers (see Figure 3.11).

THE *WHY* OF THE OBSERVE

An appropriate model would include students having their bees "land" on the flower. Instruct students to rub the end of the cheese snack onto the construction paper flower. Ask the students to look for evidence that the bee has visited the flower. They should discuss the orange dust left behind on the flower from the puffed cheese snack. Talk to

Figure 3.10 ————————————————

Student Rubbing the Puffed Cheese Snack "Bee" on the Paper Flower Model

Figure 3.11 ————————————————

Student Using the Bee and Flower Model to Explain Pollination

each group about their model and about what happened when their bees landed on the flower. Some questions you might ask as you approach each group include *Which model did you make and why?* and *What does the cheese snack dust represent?* (pollen). Encourage students to draw a picture of what the cheese snacks and the bee represent and to write a sentence about it.

Making Sense

Explain

Discuss with students their previous answers about how insects harm or help the environment. Ask students to come forward and share their ideas about pollination using their model. Can they make another model of any of their responses about how insects harm or help the environment? Work as a class to accomplish this if possible.

Evaluate

Summative evaluation of this lesson will include assessment of students' understanding of (1) the artistic character trait and (2) pollination as evidenced by their illustration and sentence.

CHARACTER TRAIT

Encourage students to answer the following question:

1. Why is being artistic an important disposition for scientists and engineers to have? *(Teacher Note: Answers will vary, but some kind of acknowledgment about enduring struggles to be a scientist should be the focus of the discussion. Focus here on how Maria Merian's artistic disposition helped her observe and communicate accurate science information to dispel assumptions and superstitions.)*

2. Describe a time when you were artistic.

CONTENT

Challenge students to think about the many ways insects help and hurt our environment. See the handout "How Insects and Other Arthropods Help and Harm Us" (*www.umes.edu/cms300uploadedFiles/HOW%20INSECTS%20HELP%20AND%20 HARM.pdf*) for more ideas on helpful and harmful insect behaviors. Evaluate students' drawings and sentences with the rubric shown in Table 3.5.

Table 3.5

Rubric for Assessing Interesting Insects Lesson

Content or Skill	Not Yet	Beginning	Developing	Secure
Participation or Observation	Student does not participate in the activity.	Student is not able to see the physical connection between insects (bee) and the flower (environment).	Student is able to see the physical connection between insects (bee) and the flower (environment).	Student is able to link his or her reasoning back to the evidence observed in class.
Drawing	Student does not provide a drawing.	Student's drawing is still at the imagination level.	Student's drawing is moving from imagination to evidence-based realities and includes the bee and flower.	Student's drawing is moving from imagination to evidence-based realities, and words are included with the bee and flower along with arrows or lines pointing to the picture.
Sentence	No words are on the paper.	Words are not organized into a complete sentence.	Words are organized into a complete sentence.	Words are organized into a complete sentence and the information provided describes relevant science content.

References

Carle, E. 1994. *The very hungry caterpillar*. New York: Philomel Books.

Corey, S. 2016. *The secret subway*. New York: Schwarz & Wade.

Drummond, A. 2015. *Energy island: How one community harnessed the wind and changed their world*. New York: Square Fish.

Engle, M. 2010. *Summer birds: The butterflies of Maria Merian*. New York: Henry Holt.

Insect. Encyclopedia Britannica for Kids. *http://kids.britannica.com/comptons/article-285163/insect*.

National Research Council (NRC). 2012. *A framework for K–12 science education: Practices, crosscutting concepts, and core ideas*. Washington, DC: National Academies Press.

NGSS Lead States. 2013. *Next Generation Science Standards: For states, by states*. Washington, DC: National Academies Press. *www.nextgenscience.org/next-generation-science-standards*.

Schwartz, C. V., C. Passmore, and B. J. Reiser. 2017. *Helping students make sense of the world using next generation science and engineering practices*. Arlington, VA: NSTA Press.

FLOWER PATTERN

To create the stem, roll a piece of green paper lengthwise and secure to the flower top.

THE CHRYSALIS PROBE

Chrysalis

Three friends found a monarch butterfly caterpillar. They put it in a jar with a milkweed plant. The next day, they saw that the caterpillar had turned into a chrysalis. They wondered if the chrysalis was alive. This is what they said:

Mac: "I think the chrysalis is alive."

Lila: "I think the chrysalis is no longer a living organism."

Antoine: "I think the chrysalis is dead, but the butterfly that comes out is alive."

Which friend do you agree with the most? _____ Explain why you agree.

4

Planning and Carrying Out Investigations

Many scientists begin their work with observations before they actually conduct their experiments. In some instances, scientists spend many years gathering data and thinking about how to conduct experiments. That was the case for all three scientists in this chapter: Amelia Earhart, Isaac Newton, and Dr. Temple Grandin. These scientists' long-term investigations of airplane flight (Earhart), force and motion (Newton), and the behavior of farm animals (Grandin) changed the way people thought about the world. It is easy to understand how the words *brave, playful,* and *examiner* best define the character traits of these three scientists. We expect that your help in identifying each of these traits will help you to humanize the work and procedures of science for your students while you teach science lessons.

According to the *Next Generation Science Standards* (*NGSS;* NGSS Lead States 2013), planning and carrying out investigations in grades K–2 builds on prior experiences and progresses to simple investigations, based on fair tests, that provide data to support explanations or design solutions. Beginning in kindergarten, students are expected to participate in planning and conducting investigations with their peers. This can be done as a whole class in kindergarten and progress to more independent and complex investigations by grades 1 and 2. As children learn how to plan and conduct observations, they make decisions about steps that need to be taken to answer the question they are trying to answer.

Donna's Personal Story

One of the best examples I can remember about getting my students to plan and conduct experiments is the time I decided (as a very enthusiastic and unseasoned teacher) that I would personally guide each one of my students in planning and conducting their own science fair experiments. I decided to do this in school because I did not want students to do the projects at home and have their parents do it for them. So, I organized my classroom in such a way that I worked with them at every step: forming a question, creating a prediction, testing an idea, and drawing a conclusion. I tried to keep it very simple with a classroom of over 25 students. I set specific deadlines. I "checked in" with each student by conferencing with each individually. I outlined logical checkpoints for progress toward their goal of a completed science fair project. This was in addition to the science I was teaching during the school day. I really, really wanted my students to be responsible for answering their own questions. I was so committed to the process that I did not give up, even when I was pulled in 25 different directions by the ideas. I secured all the materials and talked at length with students about how to plan and conduct their investigations. It was the epitome of individualized instruction—so much so that I could never repeat it again.

I'll never forget how exhausted I was as the students were presenting their final projects to the class. I was worn out; I had spread myself too thin. Eventually, I learned that it was more effective to organize small-group planning experiments. I worried about preparing my students for middle school. I did my best to prepare my students by having them work as a class to figure out what is needed to go about an investigation and what kinds of information and observations are needed to answer questions. As a class, we learned that planning and carrying out investigations is not so much about the "hands-on" part of the activity but more about what leads up to it. After many opportunities, my students gained a sense that doing scientific inquiry was not always a clear, straightforward path.

Key Features of the Practice of Planning and Carrying Out Investigations

- Decide on the question.

- Determine what evidence will answer the question.

- Decide how to interpret the evidence.

- Decide how to use data and revise explanations.

- Ensure that all decisions are motivated by students' questions.

- Encourage testable questions.

- Give students opportunities to make decisions.

- Let students know that observations are collected for a purpose.

- Determine variables.

- Design and manage fair tests.

See Schwartz, Passmore, and Reiser (2017) for more information.

SCIENTISTS AND ENGINEERS ARE
BRAVE

Learning About **Amelia Earhart**

Brave (adj.): bold or courageous

Lesson: Noodle Coaster
Description

In this lesson, students will complete a design challenge and build a roller coaster.

Objectives

Students will consider how the character trait of being brave helped Amelia Earhart to break flying records and prove to the world that women can soar just as high as men.

- In the Predict portion of the lesson, students will complete the Marble Roll assessment probe.

- Students will hear the story *I Am Amelia Earhart* by Brad Meltzer and discuss how it relates to the word *brave*.

- In the Explore portion, students will complete a design challenge using the materials provided to them (a roller coaster with pool noodles and marbles).

- In the Discuss portion, students will describe the motion of the marble on their roller coasters using the terms *balanced* and *unbalanced*.

Learning Outcomes

Students will (1) discuss why being brave is an important trait for scientists and engineers and (2) design a marble roller coaster and be able to discuss the marble's motion in terms of balanced and unbalanced motion.

Connections to the *NGSS*

The following sections make one set of connections between the instruction outlined in this lesson and the *NGSS*. Other valid connections are likely; however, not all possibilities are listed.

Performance Expectation	Connections to Activity
3-PS2-1: Plan and conduct an investigation to provide evidence of the effects of balanced and unbalanced forces on the motion of an object.	• Students participate in an engineering design challenge in which they must plan and conduct an experiment to gather evidence of balanced and unbalanced forces.
Science and Engineering Practice	**Connections to Activity**
Planning and Carrying Out Investigations	• Students use the materials provided to them to plan and conduct the design of their noodle coasters.
Disciplinary Core Idea	**Connections to Activity**
PS2.A: Forces and Motion • Pushes and pulls can have different strengths and directions. • Pushing or pulling on an object can change the speed or direction of its motion and can start or stop it.	• Students will use their experiences with marbles and their noodle coasters to predict and determine motion in terms of balanced and unbalanced motion.
Crosscutting Concept	**Connections to Activity**
Structure and Function	• Students will observe and participate in modifying the structure of the noodle to change the motion of the marble.

Amelia Earhart

Overview

In this lesson, students learn how Amelia Earhart became the first woman to fly and endeavor to break flight records in terms of distance and altitude. She challenged the way people thought about men and women. By reading the featured book, students will learn that men and women from all backgrounds choose careers as scientists. The character attribute of brave refers to Amelia Earhart's attempt to be the first woman to fly across the Atlantic Ocean.

Materials

You will need a copy of the featured book *I Am Amelia Earhart* by Brad Meltzer (2014). You will also need the following materials: several swimming pool noodles with lengths of 4 ft., one roll of duct tape, one roll of masking tape, 5 to 10 marbles of varying sizes, 5 to 10 bouncy balls, three wooden skewers, three station cards provided at the end of this lesson, and safety goggles. *(Teacher Note: To prepare for this lesson, you will need to cut each noodle in half (lengthwise) and glue the two ends together using a hot glue gun to make the noodle 8 ft. long [see Figure 4.1]. A skewer stick in addition to the hot glue connecting the two noodle halves will help strengthen this junction. Reinforce the noodle seam with duct tape or masking tape. If pool noodles are not in season or available, foam insulation for pipes can be found year-round at any home improvement store.)*

Figure 4.1

Attaching the Noodle Halves With a Skewer and a Hot Glue Gun

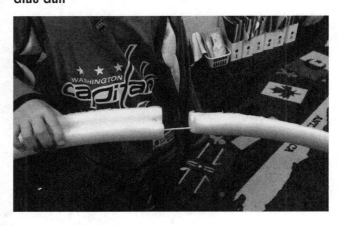

Safety Notes

(1) Remind all students that personal protective equipment should be worn during the setup, hands-on, and takedown segments of the activity. (2) Immediately pick up marbles that have fallen on the floor—these create a slip-and-fall hazard. (3) Use caution when handling skewer sticks. These are sharp and can cut or puncture skin.

Setting the Context
Predict

Use the Marble Roll probe from Page Keeley's *Uncovering Student Ideas in Primary Science, Volume 1* book (p. 86). The purpose of the probe is to get children thinking about motion before they read the book about Amelia Earhart. Just about every student in the class will have had some experience with motion and with toys that look similar to the probe. Post the probe on an Elmo or on a board in front of the whole class and ask children to share their ideas about what they think will happen to the marble. Summarize information from their ideas or comments—for example, "I noticed all of your ideas about the marble included _____. Let's investigate further with this probe."

Guided Reading

Students will be learning about Amelia Earhart, who was brave, by reading *I Am Amelia Earhart*. Students will connect Amelia's efforts to the adventurous part of being an explorer and seeking unknown territory. Introduce the book by asking students, *Can you find the person on the front cover? What seems to be happening on the front cover?* Read the story aloud. Encourage students to notice and think about the challenges Amelia Earhart faced as a woman who was the first to fly during a time when it was not acceptable for women to be pilots.

The following questions may be used to guide children's attention to detail as you read. (Page numbers reference unnumbered book pages, beginning with the title page as page 1.)

1. **Pages 1–12:** Amelia Earhart was a girl who loved adventure and never let anybody stop her from trying new things. What was Amelia trying to do in her backyard that others called "unladylike"? *Amelia was trying to fly. Working with her sister, Amelia set out to build a roller coaster in her backyard. They placed two planks of wood up against the shed and greased the wood with lard so that their wooden box, with newly attached roller skates, would slide down it.*

2. **Pages 12–19:** When Amelia was 23 years old, her dad took her to meet Frank Hawks (a man who eventually set many of his own flight records). Frank Hawks took Amelia up in his plane. What did Amelia realize when she was in an airplane for the first time? *Amelia was certain that she had to fly again.*

3. **Pages 19–20:** Soon after her first flight, Amelia took flying lessons and then eventually purchased her own plane. What did Amelia eventually end up doing that people said could not be done? *She became the first woman to fly across the Atlantic Ocean. (Teacher Note: Show students on a map how big the Atlantic Ocean is.) In those days, people took boats across the Atlantic Ocean because planes were a relatively new means of transportation. On the day Amelia took off to fly alone across the Atlantic, a magazine ran an article saying that a woman would never be able to travel that far by herself. Amelia Earhart was a girl who loved adventure and never let anybody stop her from trying new things—even things that girls had never done before, like flying all the way across the Atlantic Ocean. She broke the record for crossing the ocean in the fastest time.*

Explore

In the story, as a young girl Amelia makes a roller coaster in her backyard. Students will be simulating this type of motion with the pool noodles and marbles. The design challenge is a way to investigate force and motion while asking students to consider the character trait of being brave. Divide students into working groups. Hand out or post the design challenge for all students to read and consider (see p. 87). Have students read the design challenge and create a roller coaster with these three parts (Figure 4.2, p. 82): a slide (Figure 4.3, p. 82), a loop (Figure 4.4, p. 83), and a hill (Figure 4.5, p. 83). Students will then test the marbles and bouncy balls (these should be small enough to fit inside the groove of the pool noodle) to observe motion. Allow students ample time to build and test and rebuild or redesign as necessary. *(Teacher Note: As the students are working, you should walk around and provide guidance by only asking questions. Some questions you should focus on are* What are you thinking? *and* How is your plan coming along? *Some groups will want to use tape to secure their pool noodles together; some will just hold. Either way, let their exploration be their exploration and encourage them to engage in observation and reasoning to improve their designs. Chairs may be used to prop up portions of the track.)*

THE *HOW* OF THE EXPLORE

Go over the design process with students (p. 88). As students learn about making a plan, selecting their own materials, building a prototype, testing their own ideas, and evaluating and revising their own prototypes, they are learning about the design process.

THE *WHY* OF THE EXPLORE

Once you provide the students with materials and tools for exploration, they are responsible for planning and conducting their own investigations. Students test the materials with their ideas by conducting trials. In this process, it will be natural for students to discuss the pros and cons with their group members to help them choose appropriate tools and materials to build their roller coasters, and discussion of design and redesign will likely occur. This lesson focuses on the design and redesign process, so make sure this is part of students' discussions—what might they do differently? How can they modify their roller coasters?

Discuss

Ask students to share their roller coasters with the class. Ask students to discuss how they made decisions when possible. Ask students which part of the roller

Figure 4.2

A Sample Completed Track With All Three Parts (Hill, Slide, and Loop) Attached

Figure 4.3

An Example of a Slide

coaster (hill, loop, or slide) was the easiest to create and which was the hardest to create. *(Teacher Note: Students may notice the difference between the motion of the marble and the motion of bouncy ball—discuss their observations as a class. They may discuss the difference between the shapes and designs of the loop, hill, and slide. All of these are appropriate.)* The overarching question is *Can we get the marble to travel through three different roller coaster designs? (Teacher Note: The best way to secure the noodle roller coaster is to tape the highest points to a desk and then tape [with a loop] the lowest pieces to the floor or rug. The joint [where the noodle is glued] will not be the best place for twisting or looping the pool noodle because it will be stiff; use the other parts of the noodle, which will be more flexible.)* Have students draw the class's roller coaster and label as many parts as they can—slide, loop, and hill—as well as the places where the marble or bouncy ball traveled the fastest and slowest. Discuss the motion of the marble and the motion of the ball. *(Teacher Note: You might ask questions about how the marble behaved differently at different points of the track. Ultimately, you are introducing potential energy [energy in waiting] and kinetic energy [energy in motion] in this lesson [without saying the words]; have students focus on observing motion. Have students draw a picture of the roller coaster they completed in class.)*

Figure 4.4

An Example of a Loop

Figure 4.5

An Example of a Hill
(See Chair Propping Up the Noodle)

Evaluate

Summative evaluation of this lesson will include assessment of students' understanding of (1) the character trait of being brave; (2) the motion of the marble on the class roller coaster as shown in a drawing (labeling the hills, loops, slides, and marble and searching for the fastest and slowest points along the track); and (3) the design and redesign process.

CHARACTER TRAIT

Brave people are able to pursue a dream without being afraid. Therefore, being brave is an important character trait for scientists. Ask students the following question: How does this roller coaster activity relate to Amelia Earhart being brave? *Amelia was brave as a young girl and as an adult. As an adult, she traveled into uncharted territory where no woman had ever dared to travel before. As a young girl, Amelia was brave when she constructed her own roller coaster in her backyard and climbed on board to test it out. Amelia was always asking questions, including important questions such as Why not?*

CONTENT

The idea here is for students to recognize that motion is different (faster and slower) at different points along the track according to the design of the coaster. They should be able to verbalize the likenesses and differences. Encourage students to ask questions throughout this entire process. You might evaluate students' drawings of the class noodle roller coaster for accuracy and expect a minimum of three different points along the track (hill, loop, and slide). Encourage students to repeat the experiment as many times as they need to observe the fastest point of the roller coaster and the slowest point of the roller coaster. You may decide to use a rubric like the one shown in Table 4.1 to evaluate students' drawings.

Table 4.1

Rubric for Assessing the Noodle Coaster Lesson

Content or Skill	Not Yet	Beginning	Developing	Secure
Participation or Observation	Student does not participate.	Student is not able to link his or her reasoning back to the evidence observed in class.	Student is able to link his or her reasoning back to the evidence observed in class.	Student is able to link his or her reasoning back to the evidence observed in class and correctly identify the loop, slide, and hill and where the fastest and slowest points on the track were.
Drawing (on the Design Challenge)	Student does not provide a drawing.	Drawing is still at the imagination level.	Drawing is moving from imagination to evidence-based realities. Drawing includes the hill, loop, and slide.	Drawing is moving from imagination to evidence-based realities and words are included with arrows or lines. Drawing includes the hill, loop, and slide, and the drawing indicates where the marble moved the fastest and the slowest on the track.
Questions	Student does not ask questions.	Student is not able to ask new questions from the Explore phase.	Student is able to ask new questions from the Explore phase, and these new questions are based on evidence. For example, *How does this work and why?*	Student is able to ask new questions from the Explore phase, and these new questions are based on evidence. Student has an idea about how to begin to answer these questions. For example, student understands that at certain points along the track, the marble will stop; therefore, student asks appropriate questions to learn how to position the coaster effectively.
Design and Redesign Process	Student does not analyze data.	Student is not able to analyze data from tests of one or two objects (hill, slide, or loop) designed to solve the same problem to compare the strengths and weaknesses of how each performs.	Student is able to analyze data from tests of three objects (hill, slide, and loop) designed to solve the same problem to compare the strengths and weaknesses of how each performs.	Student is able to analyze data from tests of three objects (hill, slide, and loop) designed to solve the same problem to compare the strengths and weaknesses of how each performs. Student or team is able to redesign the coaster based on this information.

Marble Roll

How will the marble roll on to the floor?

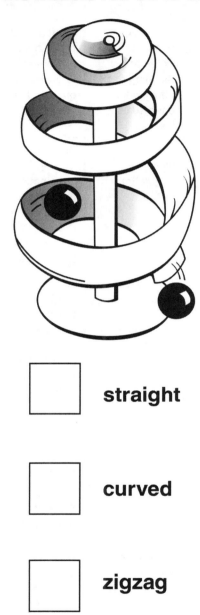

☐ **straight**

☐ **curved**

☐ **zigzag**

What are you thinking?

Name: _____

THE ROLLER COASTER KID

Have you ever been on a roller coaster? If so, what was it like? If you have not been on a roller coaster, have you ever seen one? What do they look like?

Design a roller coaster that will allow a marble or bouncy ball to travel through the track. The roller coaster must include at least one hill, one loop, and one slide. Before you start working with the materials, draw your ideas below.

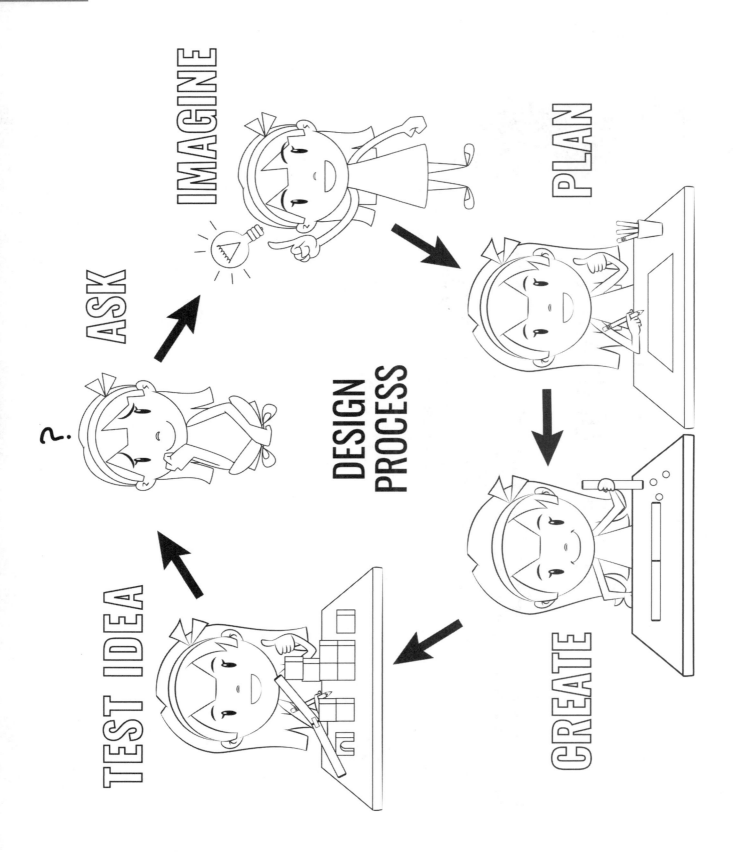

SCIENTISTS AND ENGINEERS ARE
PLAYFUL

Learning About **Isaac Newton**

Playful (adj.): showing that you are having fun and not being serious

Lesson: Newton and Me
Description

In this lesson, students learn motion words and record the meaning with motions using the Seesaw app.

Objectives

Students will consider how the playful character trait helped Isaac Newton investigate motion.

- In the Play portion of the lesson, students will play with items that will be used to define motion.

- Students will hear the story *Newton and Me* by Lynne Mayer and discuss how it relates to the word *playful*.

- In the Explore portion, students will work in teams to record videos with the Seesaw app to define motion words.

- In the Discuss portion, students will discuss if classmates' definitions for motion words are accurate.

Learning Outcomes

Students will (1) discuss what being playful means and why being playful is an important trait for scientists and engineers and (2) create a video or take a picture to explain the motion words.

Connections to the *NGSS*

The following sections make one set of connections between the instruction outlined in this lesson and the *NGSS*. Other valid connections are likely; however, not all possibilities are listed.

Performance Expectation	Connections to Activity
K-PS2-1: Plan and conduct an investigation to compare the effects of different strengths or different directions of pushes and pulls on the motion of an object.	• Students use various recreational toys to investigate specific motion words.
Science and Engineering Practice	**Connections to Activity**
Planning and Carrying Out Investigations	• Students plan and investigate ways to demonstrate motion words.
Disciplinary Core Idea	**Connections to Activity**
PS2.A: Forces and Motion • Pushes and pulls can have different strengths and directions. • Pushing or pulling on an object can change the speed or direction of its motion and can start or stop it.	• Students will show how each demonstrates a push and a pull using the toys provided (skateboard, ball, scooter, and so on).
Crosscutting Concept	**Connections to Activity**
Cause and Effect	• Students will experience cause-and-effect reactions by interacting with objects to define motion words.

Overview

In this lesson, students will plan and conduct an investigation to compare the effects of different strengths or different directions of pushes and pulls on the motion of an object. In the beginning of the lesson, students will read *Newton and Me* by Lynne Mayer. Then, students will go outside to investigate force and motion on the playground. In small groups, students will perform simple tests to gather evidence to support or refute student ideas about motion words. In this way, students are collecting, recording, and sharing observations about their understanding of motion.

Isaac
Newton

Materials

You will need the following materials: the featured
book *Newton and Me* by Lynne Mayer (2010); a skateboard; a wagon; a tennis ball; a wiffle ball; a toy car
(large); a kids' scooter; iPads; a list of motion words
written out on individual sentence strips and then
cut and lamenated (*fast, slow, motion, curved, straight,
gravity, push, pull, force, back, forth, up, down, circular,
zigzag* [see Figure 4.6, p. 92]); and the Seesaw app. *(Teacher Note: The Seesaw app is
free to teachers who sign up at the website www.freetech4teachers.com/2015/01/seesaw-
students-build-digital.html and create a classroom account. As students join the classroom,
they receive their own individual QR code [as do parents for viewing their child's work].
The Seesaw app allows children to take pictures of their work, make a video, or even add
audio to something they create. The teacher can see and sort all the student submissions,*

and students are encouraged to provide feedback to others about their work.)

Safety Notes

(1) Make sure that any fragile materials are out of the way of contact with balls and so on during this activity. (2) Students should wear helmets when riding scooters or skateboards.

Setting the Context
Play

Figure 4.6

Motion Words

Begin by asking students if they have ever wondered why things drop to the ground. In the science center, leave different kinds of balls, skateboards, scooters, and so on so that children can experiment on their own and "play" with motion materials. *(Teacher Note: Students may say the word* gravity, *but probe them for the meaning of the word, such as* How do you know? What if I did … ?*)*

Students are learning about motion and the work of a real scientist named Isaac Newton by reading *Newton and Me.* The purpose of selecting this book is to help students realize that Sir Isaac Newton's laws of motion describe experiences that they have every day and to recognize how forces affect the objects around them. *(Teacher Note: In the story, Newton is a dog. But in history, Sir Isaac Newton was a famous scientist and mathematician. Some of his discoveries include the law of gravity, laws of motion, calculus, the nature of light and color, and the cause of the tides. This book was selected for its developmental appropriateness with young students, as it explains Newton's laws of motion. The first two laws [which are not actually introduced in the NGSS until middle school] have been phrased for age appropriateness. Newton's third law is beyond the scope of this book and is deliberately excluded. The first law states that something will not move until a force makes it move. The second law states that if you push something twice as hard, it will move twice as fast. You may also want to read* Isaac Newton and Gravity *by Yoming S. Lin as a complement to the story or as background information for you.)*

Guided Reading

Introduce the book by asking students, *Can you find the person on the front cover? What does it look like is happening on the front cover?* Then read the story aloud. The following questions may be used to guide children's attention to detail as you read. (Page numbers reference unnumbered book pages, beginning with the title page as page 1.)

1. **Pages 1–6:** How did the boy experience push and pull? *(Teacher Note: A pull is a force that moves something toward you. A push is a force that moves something*

away from you.) While playing with his dog, a young boy discovers the laws of force and motion in his everyday activities. The boy was pushing and pulling a ball and because he pushed it too far, he learned how to push it just right.

2. **Pages 7–8:** How did the boy experience gravity? *(Teacher Note: Gravity is a force that pulls things toward Earth—what goes up will come down.) He was throwing the ball in the air and he learned that it always returned to him—it never stayed in the sky.*

3. **Pages 8–16:** What did the boy notice about his wagon? *He noticed that when he filled it with rocks, it was much harder to move. When it was empty, it was easier to pull.*

4. **Pages 17–24:** How did the boy describe the difference between riding his bike uphill and riding his bike downhill? *He noticed that when the wind pushed at his back when he was riding downhill, it was easy to ride his bike. He also noticed that when the wind pushed against his chest when he was riding uphill, it was harder to ride.*

5. What do you notice about the rhyming patterns of this book? *The book has a clear rhyming pattern. (Teacher Note: This is one of the reasons it is developmentally appropriate.)*

Doing the Activity
Explore
This lesson may take several days. Divide students into groups of four students each.

THE *HOW* OF THE EXPLORE
Encourage them to select three motion words to begin with. It's OK if students select the same words as others, as this will provide for a richer discussion about the varying definitions of the motion words. *(Teacher Note: In our own experience with this lesson, we gave each group a set of 14 words [fast, slow, motion, curved, straight, push, pull, force, back, forth, up, down, circular, zigzag] and sent them on their way to journal on the playground. As it turned out, doing science on the playground was a distraction for the students; therefore, this should only be attempted when the playground is empty. To temper the students' excitement and distractibility, we needed to regroup the students once they had completed their first word. We brought the class inside to check their videos before assigning their second word. This gave students the opportunity to see how other groups met the same challenge. Some students did not have their word visible to the camera or were not speaking loudly enough. We discussed ways to improve the journals, and students were more than happy to redo their first videos. This initial viewing can help students "tweak" their electronic motion journaling. It took several class periods for*

children to have sufficient time to make their videos and discuss their understanding of the definitions.)

Invite students in groups of four to five to select motion words for their group. Each group should have one iPad (with one student assigned to record the video or picture of the motion word). Provide students with the electronic journaling worksheet. *(Teacher Note: Model for students how each motion word should look. For example, if you use the word* gravity, *ask the students how they can best create an action shot to show the meaning of this motion word. Let the group decide whether it should be a picture or a video.)* Set your expectations and communicate the two things you want students to do: (1) decide if a video or a picture will best explain the meaning of their word to their class and (2) decide which activity will best describe the action word. What material will they use: a skateboard (review the safety procedures for using a skateboard correctly), balls, a scooter, or cars? *(Teacher Note: Assign roles to each member of the group: a videographer, an actor for the action, a word holder, and the person describing the definition who helped facilitate the process [see Figures 4.7, 4.8, and 4.9].)*

Figure 4.7

Students Electronic Journaling

Figure 4.8

Students Collecting and Recording Information

Once these roles are set, the students in each group need to plan their activities before going out onto the playground to complete their electronic journaling experience. Each group should then take a picture or record a video and upload it using the Seesaw app. *(Teacher Note: Go over with students questions to think about before they post their work and generate a list, including* What is my purpose? Is this appropriate? *See p. 98 for checklist.)* Invite students to select the other students in their group by clicking on their names so that students can view each other's work. The students can share their learning with their peers and parents on the Seesaw app by showing a video or a picture of their motion words. Seesaw allows students to document their thinking and work by using pictures and videos that then show

Figure 4.9 ————————————————————

Students Planning to Conduct an Investigation

Figure 4.10 ————————————

Classroom Poster Reminding Students How to Work With the Seesaw App

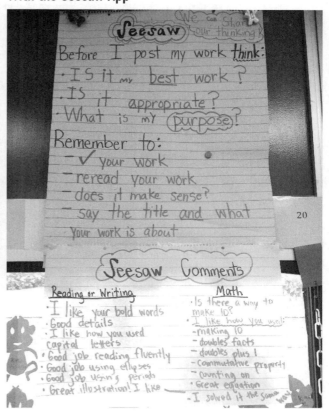

up on the classroom feed. Students are able to observe their peers' work on the classroom feed. Students can then watch videos from other groups and give feedback. Figure 4.10 shows how to prepare students for working with the Seesaw app by setting expectations and providing examples of reminders before posting appropriate modes of feedback. *(Teacher Note: Because these motion words require unusual materials, be sure to set your classroom expectations before the lesson.)*

THE *WHY* OF THE EXPLORE

Allow students to use the props they want to use to provide concrete experiences with pushes and pulls when constructing definitions. The students' active participation in planning and conducting the experiment is critical to their negotiating the meaning of the motion words.

Making Sense
Discuss

Once the class has had a chance to film the definition of their motion word, bring the students together, watch each group's video or view each group's picture, and evaluate the videos or pictures as a group. Later, during class center time, students can watch the videos again on Seesaw (see Figure 4.11) and electronically give feedback to the group, as shown in Figure 4.10. Encourage students to answer the following questions:

Figure 4.11 ────────────

Sharing the Class Journal

1. Did the group define their motion word correctly or not?

2. If so, what did others learn from the video clip or picture? If not, what would make it better?

Have students evaluate their classmates' videos by commenting on others' posts. Establish guidelines as a class on appropriate feedback using other Seesaw app experiences the students had. Encourage discussions that are rich in "science talk." For example, one group might discuss the push and pull of the scooter and hold up the words *push* and *pull.*

Evaluate

Summative evaluation of this lesson will include assessment of students' understanding of (1) the character trait of being playful and (2) videos or pictures for motion words.

CHARACTER TRAIT

The ability to solve problems and invent new ideas is important for scientists and engineers. Therefore, the character trait of being playful for scientists and engineers is central to this way of thinking. How was the boy in the featured book playful? *Isaac Newton was able to ask questions and "play" with his ideas as he experimented with motion.*

CONTENT

Use the electronic journaling rubric shown in Table 4.2 to assess student learning of the first three words before moving on to the remaining words. Having students witness five different versions of the word *circular,* for example, will cause them to expand and strengthen their own definitions. As videos play with other groups' definitions of *circular,* children will be forced to consider their ideas and adjust their original definition, if necessary.

Table 4.2

Electronic Journaling Rubric for *Newton and Me* Lesson

Content or Skill	Not Yet	Beginning	Developing	Secure
Participation	Student does not participate.	Student does not participate as part of a group or team to create electronic journaling experiences of the motion words.	Most students participate as part of a group or team to create electronic journaling experiences of the motion words.	All students participate as part of a group or team to create electronic journaling experiences of the motion words.
Photo or Video	Students do not create a video or take a photo of a motion word.	Students create a video or take a photo of a motion word.	Students create videos or take photos of a motion word, but they are not clear to see and understand.	Students create videos or take photos of a motion word that are clear to see and understand.
Sound and Motion Word Visible	Student does not provide motion.	Neither the sound nor the visibility of the motion is clear.	Either the sound or the visibility of the motion is not clear.	Both the sound and the visibility of the motion are clear.
Scientific Accuracy (Proper Word Labeled)	The motion word is not defined at all.	The motion word is not defined accurately.	The motion word is defined accurately at least once.	The motion word is defined accurately more than once.

Name: _____

ELECTRONIC JOURNALING CHECKLIST

Before I post my work. Check:

_____ Is it my best work?

_____ Is it appropriate?

_____ What is my purpose?

Did I:

_____ Check my work?

_____ Reread my work?

_____ Does it make sense?

_____ Say the title out loud. Does it match what your work is about?

Name: _____

ELECTRONIC JOURNALING CHECKLIST

Before I post my work. Check:

_____ Is it my best work?

_____ Is it appropriate?

_____ What is my purpose?

Did I:

_____ Check my work?

_____ Reread my work?

_____ Does it make sense?

_____ Say the title out loud. Does it match what your work is about?

SCIENTISTS AND ENGINEERS ARE
EXAMINERS

Learning About **Temple Grandin**

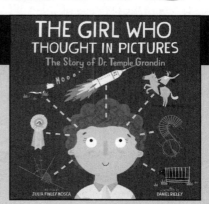

Examiner (n.): one who looks at something closely and carefully to learn more about it

Lesson: A Closer Look
Description

In this lesson, students learn to compare habitats of different plants and animals.

Objectives

Students will consider how Dr. Temple Grandin's examiner character trait helped her discover the details of farm animal's behavior.

- In the Predict portion of the lesson, students will complete the Page Keeley Is It Living? probe.

- Students will hear the story *The Girl Who Thought in Pictures: The Story of Dr. Temple Grandin* by Julia Finley Mosca and discuss how it relates to the word *examiner*.

- In the Observe portion of the lesson, students will record the environment (e.g., land and water) of different kinds of plants and animals in the schoolyard).

- In the Explain portion of the lesson, students discuss their observations of plants and animals to compare the diversity of life in different habitats.

Learning Outcomes

Students will (a) understand what being an examiner means and why being an examiner is an important trait for scientists and engineers and (b) plan and conduct an investigation of diverse plants and animals in the school ground area.

Connections to the *NGSS*

The following sections make one set of connections between the instruction outlined in this lesson and the *NGSS*. Other valid connections are likely; however, not all possibilities are listed.

Performance Expectation	Connections to Activity
2-LS4-1: Make observations of plants and animals to compare the diversity of life in different habitats.	• Students select an area to observe, list the different kinds of plants and animals in the schoolyard, and then, as a class, organize a Diversity of Life chart.
Science and Engineering Practice	**Connections to Activity**
Planning and Carrying Out Investigations	• Students will work in a group to decide where in the schoolyard to plot their square. As a class, students will review the kinds of living things found in their square and organize a Diversity of Life chart.
Disciplinary Core Idea	**Connections to Activity**
LS4.D: Biodiversity and Humans There are many different kinds of living things in any area, and they exist in different places on land and in water.	• Students will demonstrate how a variety of living things can exist in one area.
Crosscutting Concept	**Connections to Activity**
Structure and Function	• The square areas will include diverse features to represent a variety of structures (e.g., water, trees, and grass) to enable students to observe and determine the relationship between structures and functions.

Overview

In this lesson, students learn how one person discovered the intricate details of the study of the behavior of farm animals and used what she learned to improve the way they were treated. By reading the featured book, students will learn that men and women from all backgrounds choose careers as scientists. The scientist character trait of being an examiner refers to Dr. Temple Grandin's ability to notice details. Although Temple has always been careful to point out that not everyone with autism is a visual thinker, she has often described herself as someone who "thinks in pictures."

Temple Grandin

Materials

You will need the following materials: *The Girl Who Thought in Pictures: The Story of Dr. Temple Grandin* by Julia Finley Mosca (2017), iPads, string, and stakes.

Setting the Context
Predict

To start a conversation about the variety of living things in one area, hand out the Page Keeley Is It Living? probe (p. 106). The purpose of this assessment probe is to elicit children's ideas about living and nonliving things. The probe is designed to find out which characteristics children use to find out if something is living or not, and this will help students begin to think about the living things in this lesson. Students will be learning about the work of Dr. Temple Grandin, who was diagnosed with autism at a young age. Her unique mind allowed her to connect with animals in a special way, helping her invent groundbreaking improvements for farms around the globe.

Guided Reading

Introduce the book by showing students the cover. Ask students "What does the front cover tell you about the story we are about to read?" Read the story aloud. Encourage students to notice and think about the challenges Dr. Temple Grandin faced as a scientist with autism.

The following questions may be used to guide children's attention to detail as you read. (Page numbers reference unnumbered book pages, beginning with the title page as page 1.)

1. **Pages 1–12:** Temple showed signs of autism from a young age, and she knew she was different from others. How did she act different from others? *Temple liked many of the same things young children her age liked, such as ice cream and art, but she believed the way she thought about things set her apart from others.*

2. **Pages 13–18:** Temple was sent away to her aunt's farm. Why? *Temple had a hard time at her first school; others teased her, and this made her upset. Her mother decided that she needed time away from school and sent her to her aunt's ranch way out West.*

3. **Pages 19–20:** How did Temple do at her second school? What was different? *Temple did much better at the next school. At this school, she found a teacher who helped her understand that she was good at science. She then used science to invent things. It was here she learned that she was special because her attention to detail was a strength.*

4. **Pages 21–25:** Temple never gave up thinking about and testing her ideas about the animals on the farm. What happened to her at the end of the story? *She went on to earn three college degrees. She became a scientist known all around the world. She now speaks to large crowds about her work and uses her story to encourage others. She spreads the message that each person is unique in how he or she thinks.*

Making Sense
Observe

This is an outdoor lesson that will require some preplanning on your part. Depending on your access to a variety of habitats, you can adjust the activity described here.

THE *HOW* OF THE OBSERVE

First, find a location in your school-yard that will be appropriate for observations of both plants and animals. Make name tags (see Figure 4.12) for the following: *plants* (person responsible for identifying plant to observe), *animals* (person responsible for identifying living animal to observe), *writer* (person responsible for writing observations on the clipboard), and *iPad* (person responsible for taking pictures with the iPad). *(Teacher Note: You will want to preplan and think about cooperative group arrangements so that children are capable of doing their assigned jobs. Create name tags to help students remember their roles and discuss expectations for each role with the students before the lesson. These roles are assigned to help keep each student focused once the class goes outside. Sometimes outside science lessons can be very distracting, so these are intended to help students focus on their "jobs" once they are outside.)* Hand the writer a piece of string (approximately 3 ft. long) that has been tied in a circle. Once outside, direct each group to a particular spot that you have selected for data collection. Create a circle with the string and instruct students to look for living things (or evidence of living things) and plants in their marked-off areas (see Figures 4.13, 4.14 [p. 104], and 4.15 [p. 104]). Once they find a plant or animal to observe, the writer should start recording observations about it on the clipboard, and the iPad person should take a photograph of the

Figure 4.12 ———

Name Tags With Jobs Assigned

Figure 4.13 ———

A Sample of the Schoolyard Area to Be Examined Outlined With String

item. Repeat this process until each group has at least one animal (or evidence of an animal) and one plant (or evidence of a plant). Gather the students and head back to the classroom.

THE *WHY* OF THE OBSERVE

We want students to gain experience with planning and carrying out investigations. It's important to guide students into thinking about how they might gather information about plants and animals in their schoolyard. It is also important that the students notice that if they all place circles in the same area, they will limit the amount of information that can be obtained.

Explain

In the classroom, record all the plants and animals that students have observed in a diversity of life chart on the board. Have students complete a Venn diagram on their own of some of the common environments that plants and animals share (p. 107). Invite students to consider how their observations of plants and animals in different habitats help them to compare the diversity of life in different habitats. Talk with children about Temple's ability to examine what was important for her. Ask students to think about someone who is an examiner or to think of a time when they themselves examined something.

Evaluate

Summative evaluation of this lesson will include assessment of students' (1) understanding of the examiner character trait and (2) creation of a Venn diagram comparing the diversity of life in different schoolyard habitats.

Figure 4.14

A Sample of a Schoolyard Area to Be Explored—We Used Overgrown Planters and Were Able to Find Some Interesting Animals and Plants

Figure 4.15

Children Examining Their Area

CHARACTER TRAIT

Encourage students to discuss what it means to be an examiner. Why is being an examiner an important character trait for scientists to have? *(Teacher Note: Attention to detail is a very important quality of people who examine their work closely.)*

CONTENT

To assess students' observations and photographs taken during the Observe phase of this lesson, use a rubric like the one shown in Table 4.3. Invite students to make a final entry to summarize what they have learned by closely observing the intricate properties of the plants and living species in the schoolyard.

Table 4.3

Rubric for Assessing the Closer Look Lesson

Content or Skill	Not Yet	Beginning	Developing	Secure
Observations or Participation	Student is not able to participate in observations.	Student is not able to observe and record several different kinds of living things in any area with an iPad.	Student is able to observe and record several different kinds of living things in any area with an iPad.	Student is able to observe and record many different kinds of living things in any area with an iPad.
Venn Diagram	Student is not able to complete a Venn diagram.	Venn diagram is still at the imagination level.	Venn diagram contains some evidence-based realities. The diagram includes appropriate plants and animals found in the schoolyard.	Venn diagram contains evidence-based realities. The diagram includes appropriate plants and animals found in the schoolyard with an accurate level of detail and content.

References

Keeley, P. 2013. *Uncovering student ideas in primary science, Volume 1: 25 new formative assessment probes for grades K–2*. Arlington, VA: NSTA Press.

Lin, Y. S. 2011. *Isaac Newton and gravity*. New York: PowerKids.

NGSS Lead States. 2013. *Next Generation Science Standards: For states, by states*. Washington, DC: National Academies Press. *www.nextgenscience.org/next-generation-science-standards*.

Mayer, L. 2010. *Newton and me*. Mt. Pleasant, SC: Abordale.

Meltzer, B. 2014. *I am Amelia Earhart*. New York: Dial Books.

Mosca, J. F. 2017. *The girl who thought in pictures: The story of Dr. Temple Grandin*. Seattle: Innovation Press.

Schwartz, C. V., C. Passmore, and B. J. Reiser. 2017. *Helping students make sense of the world using next generation science and engineering practices*. Arlington, VA: NSTA Press.

Is It Living?

cat

seed

frog

fire

grass

river

rock

tree

cloud

What are you thinking?

VENN DIAGRAM OF PLANTS AND ANIMALS

Animals

Plants

5

Analyzing and Interpreting Data

The practice of analyzing and interpreting data is central to both science and engineering. This chapter will focus on George Washington Carver, Mary Anning, and Rachel Carson: three scientists whose efforts demonstrate the importance of scientific data analysis and interpretation. Their persistent questions about plants (Carver), discovery of the ichthyosaur (Anning), and awareness of harmful pesticides (Carson) all required these scientists to carefully record, review, and understand their data. It is easy to see how the words *diligent*, *curious*, and *persuasive* might be used to describe the character traits of these three individuals.

The *Next Generation of Science Standards* (*NGSS*; NGSS Lead States 2013) describes the importance of analyzing and interpreting data as evidence to support one's conclusions. In science, analyzing data in grades K–2 builds on prior experiences in the natural world arising from collecting, recording, and sharing observations. Therefore, even very young children should be encouraged to share their thoughts and ideas about observations even before they can formally record them. As students share these observations, they should be encouraged to look for patterns and relationships to answer scientific questions. They should also be making predictions—as simple as *yes* or *no*—and comparing these predictions to what

actually occurs. All of these experiences lay the foundation for more complex analysis and interpretation of data. With our youngest learners, this means looking at evidence or facts and deciding if what was supposed to happen did actually occur as expected.

Donna's Personal Story

One simple lesson for teaching students about analyzing and interpreting data is thinking about drops of water on a penny. You can find many variations of this experiment online from The Science Spot (*www.sciencespot.net/media/pennylab.pdf*), TeachEngineering (*www.teachengineering.org/lessons/view/duk_drops_mary_less*), and *PBS Kids* (*http://pbskids.org/zoom/activities/sci/dropsonpennies.html*). Most students will have had experiences with a penny and with water. Simply ask students how many drops of water they think a penny can hold. All you need to do this experiment is water, a penny, and an eyedropper. *(Teacher Note: If you do not have an eyedropper, you can make one by cutting a piece of a plastic straw into 3-in. sections.)* Students will need to move their finger up and down on the top of the straw to restrict airflow so that the water can be drawn up to "drop" onto the penny. Record students' observations about how many drops they think will fit, even if it is in a general way (e.g., "Our class thinks three to five drops

Figure 5.1

Five Senses Student Handouts

(A)

(B)

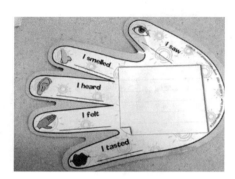

will fit on a penny"). Then ask students how they can find out the number of drops of water that can fit on the penny exactly. Students should provide answers that include actually putting the drops on the penny.

You can then probe further and ask students how many times they should do the experiment. Is one time enough? Twenty times? How do we know? What do scientists do? Do they do science experiments once? From this questioning, students often arrive at a reasonable answer collaboratively as a class—usually the answer is "three times." You can then ask students, *Why do scientists repeat experiments three times? What benefit does this have on the data they collect?* Students' answers will vary but usually include some kind of variation on experimental error and "making sure" they got the experiment correct. Then you can begin the investigation of the question: How many drops can fit on a penny? Ask students to record their data (this can be done informally on scrap paper), which is the number of drops. When I conduct this lesson, I walk around the room to find the children busy with the task, and the joyous noise of children counting fills the classroom. Children soon discover that in some cases they have different numbers for each trial.

We discuss how to arrive at an average in a way that is developmentally appropriate for the grade I am teaching. Then I ask if they used the "heads" side of the penny or the "tails" side. Inevitably, not all children will have used the same side, and we discuss how this could possibly have revealed a *variable* in our experiment, or something that is different. Can we control this variable? Absolutely! Then the entire class agrees which side of the penny to investigate, and the water dropping continues once again. I am never concerned with the data we generate—only with the process with which we generated it. I can use this experiment for the rest of the year to discuss how scientists collect, analyze, and interpret data. Students will come to realize after multiple trials that there is no one answer to the question—that in fact there are many variables, such as the size of the squeeze on the eyedropper, the pressure of the squeeze on the eyedropper, the slant of the desk, and so on.

Eleanor Duckworth (2006) discussed this process of "testing out ideas" as being critical for cognitive development. Her popular essays were consolidated into a book, *The Having of Wonderful Ideas*, and I have never forgotten this book because it is so rich with ideas for children to act like natural scientists to explore their own world.

One of the best ways to do this is by using the senses. I make a point of connecting the idea of being a good scientist with using the five senses. I give students a handout (see Figure 5.1) to help them remember, and they can tape or paste this into their science notebooks. On each finger, children write *What do I see? What do I hear? What did I touch? What do I smell?* I reserve the thumb for taste because we never taste anything in science class. *My Five Senses* by Aliki is also always a great book to read aloud!

What's Important to Remember About the Practice of Analyzing and Interpreting Data

- The process of analyzing and interpreting data should take place in conjunction with other practices.

- There are many ways to analyze and interpret data.

- Scientists have a range of tools to analyze and interpret data.

- Scientists work with data (evidence) toward the goal of answering a question.

See Schwartz, Passmore, and Reiser (2017) for more information.

SCIENTISTS AND ENGINEERS ARE

DILIGENT

Learning About **George Washington Carver**

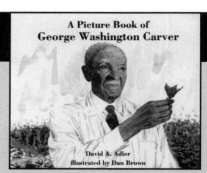

A Picture Book of
George Washington Carver

David A. Adler
Illustrated by Dan Brown

Diligent (adj.): putting forth constant effort to accomplish something; attentive and persistent in doing anything

Lesson: Plant Needs
Description

In this lesson, students use observations to describe patterns of what plants need to survive.

Objectives

Students will consider how the character trait of being diligent helped George Washington Carver pursue his questions about plants and plant products.

- In the Predict portion of the lesson, students will complete the formative assessment probe Seeds in a Bag by Page Keeley.

- Students will hear the story *A Picture Book of George Washington Carver* by David A. Adler and discuss how it relates to the word *diligent*.

- In the Observe portion, students will analyze their observations to determine what seeds need to germinate (light, water, temperature).

- In the Explain portion, students will describe their findings after placing seed bags in three different locations throughout the classroom.

Learning Outcomes

Students will (1) discuss why being diligent is an important trait for scientists and engineers and (2) analyze and interpret patterns to determine what seeds need to germinate.

Connections to the *NGSS*

The following sections make one set of connections between the instruction outlined in this lesson and the *NGSS*. Other valid connections are likely; however, not all possibilities are listed.

Performance Expectation	Connections to Activity
2-LS2-1: Plan and conduct an investigation to determine if plants need sunlight and water to grow.	• Students decide where to place seeds in a bag in their classroom.
Science and Engineering Practice	**Connections to Activity**
Analyzing and Interpreting Data	• Students analyze what happens in each of the three locations and interpret what that means for seed germination.
Disciplinary Core Idea	**Connections to Activity**
LS2.A: Interdependent Relationships in Ecosystems • Plants depend on water and light to grow. • Plants depend on animals for pollination or to move their seeds around.	• Students learn that seeds depend on water and light to germinate.
Crosscutting Concept	**Connections to Activity**
Cause and Effect	• Water, temperature, and location determine whether seeds germinate or not.

Overview

In this lesson, students learn how one person discovered many uses for peanuts that are important today. By reading the featured book, students will learn that men and women from all backgrounds choose careers as scientists. The scientist character trait of being diligent refers to George Washington Carver's consistent determination to investigate plants and plant products.

Materials

For this lesson, you will need the following materials: a copy of *A Picture Book of George Washington Carver* by David A. Adler (2000), a bag of large lima beans (from the grocery store), water, a stapler with staples, tape, a ruler, the worksheets associated with this lesson, resealable plastic bags (sandwich size), and the Seeds in a Bag formative assessment probe.

George
Washington
Carver

Safety Notes

(1) Some seeds contain herbicides and pesticides. Make sure that students wash their hands with soap and water after completion of the activity. (2) Never eat food (seeds) used in a classroom activity.

Setting the Context
Predict

Use Page Keeley's Seeds in a Bag assessment probe (p. 119) to help students make a prediction about what will happen to seeds that are kept in a bag. The purpose of this probe is to elicit children's ideas about the germination needs of seeds. The probe is designed to find out if students recognize that when seeds are planted in soil, they need to take in water from the soil to sprout. *(Teacher Note: As the teacher, your role should be to facilitate the experiment and focus on letting the students gather, analyze, and interpret data as much as possible.)* The questions that follow are provided to guide the investigation that students design.) Invite students to gather as a large group to listen to the story.

Guided Reading

Students will be learning about plants and plant parts and the life work of a scientist who was especially diligent by reading *A Picture Book of George Washington Carver*. Introduce the book by asking, *Can you find the person on the front cover? What does it look like is happening on the front cover?* Read the story aloud. Encourage students to notice and think about the challenges George Washington Carver may have faced as an African American scientist.

1. **Pages 6–11:** George Washington Carver was not raised by his mother and father but by two kind families who saw to his early learning. How did George become interested in plants as a young boy? *His owners did not make him work as hard as other slaves, so he had time to learn about flowers in the nearby woods. When he went to the African American school, he learned about medicinal plants and herbs from his "Aunt" Mariah.*

2. **Pages 4–5 and 10–11:** As a slave born sometime near the end of the Civil War, George experienced considerable prejudice. What prejudicial tragedies marked George's young life? *Night raiders separated him from his mother when he was an infant. Later he witnessed a mob of masked white men hang and burn a black prisoner they had pulled out of jail. This later memory haunted George for the remainder of his life.*

Figure 5.2

Place the Lima Bean on a Damp Towel and Fold the Towel Up

3. **Pages 14–17:** George graduated from high school and wanted to go to college. Why did George have trouble getting into college? *He was accepted at Highland University, but when he arrived he was told he couldn't attend the school because he was black. Later he was accepted at Iowa State College, where he studied agriculture. He was the school's first African American student and became the school's first African American teacher.*

4. **Pages 18–22:** When he moved to Alabama, George devoted his life to improving the lives of Southerners, especially African Americans. When

Figure 5.3 ────────────

Place the Lima Bean Wrapped in the Damp Paper Towel in a Plastic Bag That Can Be Sealed

Figure 5.4 ────────────

Place One Bag in a Closet

cotton production began to fail, George discovered the benefits of growing peanuts and sweet potatoes—and identified 300 peanut by-products and more than 100 products from sweet potatoes. Why did George Washington Carver not accept money for these ideas? *He believed in the goodness of all people and that successful black people should become models who can transform others' racial prejudices.*

5. **Pages 26–29:** George Washington Carver won many awards for his research. He is known for saying "Know science and science shall set you free because science is truth." How was asking questions important to George's work? *From the time he was young boy, George wanted to learn—even when his only book was a spelling book he had memorized. His persistent questions about plants encouraged him to keep trying to find a way to go to school. His questions about how to improve the lives of Southern cotton farmers led to notable discoveries that are still respected today.*

Observe

Ask students if they would like to try to do some experiments with plants like George Washington Carver. They will most likely be enthusiastic to do a science experiment! They can study how lima bean seeds react to different locations within the classroom. Ask students how they can find out if a lima bean will grow in three different places throughout the classroom. As they are thinking and deciding where to place the lima beans, remind them that there should only be one thing different about each location they select in the classroom.

THE *HOW* OF THE OBSERVE

As the groups begin planning, soak the lima beans overnight before "planting them" during the next science session. Once the class has decided where to place the lima beans in the classroom (e.g., someplace sunny, someplace shady, and someplace dark) and how long to let them sit, you are ready to begin the experiment. Place each lima bean on a damp paper towel and fold it up tightly (see Figure 5.2, p. 115). Fold the paper towel with the seed inside it into fourths so that it will fit into the plastic bag (see Figure 5.3). Repeat this two more times until you have three bags with lima beans inside a damp paper towel. Then place or tape these in three different locations. *(Teacher Note: A previous class picked inside a closet [see Figure 5.4], on the window [see Figure 5.5], and on the radiator [see Figure 5.6]).* After a week or two, check the bags.

THE *WHY* OF THE OBSERVE

The purpose of this activity is for students to analyze how the seeds germinate in different places in the classroom with and without light. Temperature could also be a possible variable. Try to keep it to one variable—either temperature (maybe place a thermometer at each station) or light—so as not to confuse students.

Explain

Encourage students to summarize their observations and questions prompted by this investigation—for example, what are the differences they noticed in the lima beans? Encourage them to draw their observations and write sentences based on what they see. Can the plants sprouting off each lima bean be measured? How are they alike? How are they different? Students should observe that the lima bean placed in darkness did not grow because plants need light. Depending on where the other two were placed, the lima bean in the shady spot is less likely to sprout plants than the bean in the sunny spot.

Ask students, *How does this science activity help you think about George Washington Carver's diligent nature? When planning and carrying out investigations, what considerations do you think George Washington Carver had to think about?*

Evaluate

Summative evaluation of this lesson will include assessment of students' understanding of (1) the character trait of being diligent and (2) how to plan and conduct an investigation to determine what lima bean seeds need to germinate.

Figure 5.5

Place One Bag on the Window (Variable)

Figure 5.6

Place One Bag on the Radiator (Variable)

CHARACTER TRAIT

Encourage students to answer the following questions:

1. If George Washington Carver had not discovered uses for sweet potatoes or peanut by-products, do you think someone else would have? *Yes, of course someone might have eventually thought of these ideas. But George Washington Carver was diligent and couldn't rest until his persistent questioning produced results. (Teacher Note: The point here is to review George's agricultural discoveries while keeping in mind this one specific character trait.)*

2. Why is being diligent an important attribute for scientists to have? And how was George Washington Carver diligent? *Diligent people are hardworking, persistent people who keep working until they find answers. In George Washington Carver's case, he overcame considerable personal tragedies as an African American by studying and working hard to improve the lives of Southerners, especially African Americans. (Teacher Note: Encourage students to work in pairs and discuss a time in their lives when they might have been diligent or to identify a person they might think of as being diligent. Students may identify Barack Obama as someone who displayed characteristics of being diligent because he was our first African American president. Invite students to write in their science notebooks to explain why being diligent is an important trait for scientists and engineers.)*

CONTENT

Students will complete a worksheet on their observations of the lima beans (p. 121). Observations may be evaluated by a rubric like the one shown in Table 5.1. To conclude this lesson, revisit students' questions about the locations of the lima beans and plan some investigations to answer their new questions.

Table 5.1

Rubric for Assessing Plant Needs Activity

Content or Skill	Not Yet	Beginning	Developing	Secure
Participation in Planning and Carrying Out Investigations	Student is not able to participate in planning or conducting the experiment.	Student is able to participate in either the planning or the conducting of the experiment.	Student is able to participate in some of the planning or conducting of the experiment.	Student is able to participate in all parts of planning and conducting the experiment.
Drawing	Student does not provide a drawing.	Drawing is still at the imagination level.	Drawing is moving from imagination to evidence-based realities.	Drawing is moving from imagination to evidence-based realities, and words are included with arrows or lines.

Seeds in a Bag

What will happen when the bag of seeds is put in soil?

 **All** of the seeds will sprout.

 **Some** of the seeds will sprout.

 **None** of the seeds will sprout.

What are you thinking?

Name: _____

LIMA BEAN DATA

QUESTION: What happens to a lima bean when it is placed in different places?

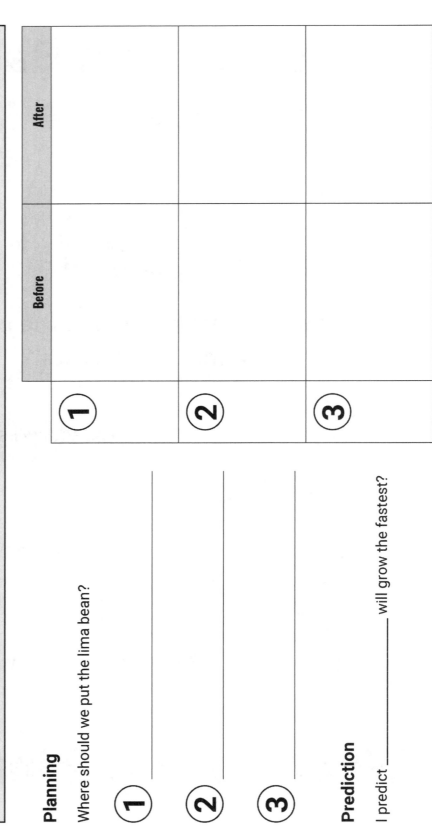

	Before	After
①		
②		
③		

Planning

Where should we put the lima bean?

① _____

② _____

③ _____

Prediction

I predict _____ will grow the fastest?

LIMA BEAN OBSERVATIONS

The location of your lima bean is the variable for this experiment. Find three locations where you can place the three plastic bags. Record your observations. You can write out your observations or draw them.

Location A _____

Location B _____

Location C _____

CONCLUSION: I learned that

SCIENTISTS AND ENGINEERS ARE
CURIOUS

Learning About **Mary Anning**

Curious (adj.): having a desire to learn or know more about something or someone

Lesson: Fossil Fun
Description

In this lesson, students will learn about the history of Earth through the discovery of fossils.

Objectives

Students will consider how the curious character trait refers to Mary Anning's ability to find and identify fossils.

- In the Play portion of the lesson, students will complete a KWL chart.

- Students will hear the story *The Fossil Girl: Mary Anning's Dinosaur Discovery* by Catherine Brighton and discuss how it relates to the word *curious* as a character trait.

- In the Explore portion of the lesson, students will make a trace fossil.

- In the Discuss portion of the lesson, students will compare fast and slow changes as processes that shape Earth.

Learning Outcomes

Students will (1) discuss what being curious means and why being curious is an important trait for scientists and engineers and (2) distinguish between fast and slow changes that shape Earth.

Connections to the *NGSS*

The following sections make one set of connections between the instruction outlined in this lesson and the *NGSS*. Other valid connections are likely; however, not all possibilities are listed.

Performance Expectation	Connections to Activity
2-ESS1-1: Use information from several sources to provide evidence that Earth events can occur quickly or slowly.	• Students watch videos of fast and slow changes.

Science and Engineering Practice	Connections to Activity
Analyzing and Interpreting Data	• Students analyze what makes a fast change and what makes a slow change.

Disciplinary Core Idea	Connections to Activity
ESS1.C: The History of Planet Earth Some events happen very quickly; others occur very slowly, over a time period much longer than one can observe.	• Students make a fossil that represents a slow change.

Crosscutting Concept	Connections to Activity
Stability and Change	• In the KWL chart at the end of the lesson, students are able to articulate examples of fast and slow changes.

Overview

In this lesson, students learn how one curious person used mathematical thinking to estimate the size of an ichthyosaur. Mary Anning used scientific methods to collect objects that she called "curiosities." By reading the featured book, students will learn that men and women from all backgrounds choose careers as scientists. The trait of being curious refers to Mary Anning's unique desire to find objects (fossils) and attempt to estimate their size by solving mathematical problems. As a young girl who discovered the first complete ichthyosaur, Mary astonished the scientific world of her time with evidence that Earth is millions of years old. Mary lived in a time when scientists were working on a new idea—that the world was much older than they had always thought. Mary's discoveries helped provide the evidence that scientists needed to support their new ideas. Mary went on to be highly regarded

Mary Anning

as a fossil expert, finding two complete plesiosaurs and the first ever pterodactyl. Fossils provide evidence about the plants and animals that lived long ago and the nature of the environment at that time.

Materials

You will need a copy of the featured book *The Fossil Girl: Mary Anning's Dinosaur Discovery* by Catherine Brighton (1999). Individual students will need an empty (and cleaned out) 6-oz milk carton, a craft stick, an object for fossil prints (e.g., leaves, grasses, shells), and safety goggles. The teacher will need a package of plaster of paris, an old bucket to mix the plaster of paris in, water (as much as described in the directions for the plaster of paris), and petroleum jelly in a tube.

Safety Notes

(1) Remind all students that personal protective equipment should be worn during the setup, hands-on, and takedown segments of the activity. (2) Use caution when handling sticks—these can be sharp and can puncture or cut skin. (3) Wash hands with soap and water upon completing this activity.

Setting the Context
Predict

Have the class create a KWL chart about the age of Earth (see Table 5.2). In this approach, students document their learning with what they Know (K), what they Want to know about the age of Earth (W), and what they have Learned about the age of Earth (L). To begin, focus only on the K and W sections (what students know about the history of Earth and what they want to know) as an introduction to this lesson; students will fill in the Learn (L) section during the Explain phase. Keep this chart in a central location that is visible throughout the lesson so that students can fill in the KWL chart during and after the lesson.

Guided Reading

Students will be learning about Mary Anning, a woman who found evidence that changed scientists' ideas about the age of Earth. Students will learn that Mary was especially curious by reading *The Fossil Girl: Mary Anning's Dinosaur Discovery*. Introduce the book by asking, *Can you find the person on the front cover? What does it look like is happening on the front cover?* Read the story aloud. Encourage students to notice and think about the challenges Mary Anning faced as a woman who enjoyed finding "curiosities."

The following questions may be used to guide children's attention to detail as you read. (Page numbers reference unnumbered book pages, beginning with the title page as page 1.)

Table 5.2

Sample KWL Chart

What Do We *Know* About the Age of Earth?	What Do We *Want* to Know About the Age of Earth?	What Have We *Learned* About the Age of Earth?
• Earth is old, but we are not sure how scientists know this. • Volcanoes and earthquakes are on Earth.	• How do scientists know exactly how old Earth is? • What makes a volcano erupt? • What makes an earthquake happen?	• We've learned that sometimes Earth changes quickly and sometimes it changes slowly. • Fossils document slow changes on Earth.

1. **Pages 1–5:** Mary Anning and her brother Joe were forced to collect fossils after their father died to help her mother keep her curiosity shop open. One evening, all their curiosities were swept away. How did the Annings lose all their curiosities? *A bad storm came through their house, and a flood washed all the curiosities away.*

2. **Pages 6–9:** One of Mary's curiosities was the biggest they had ever seen. How did Mary and her brother use math to estimate the size of the curiosities? *They were able to estimate the size by examining the size of the creature's head. They used their arms to estimate the size of the creature to be 20 ft. or more.*

3. **Pages 10–14:** Mary looked in a book called *Strange Creatures of the World*. She asked herself questions—Is it a giraffe? A gorilla? How did Mary figure out what the name of the creature was? *Henry Henley, the lord of the manor, came by and told her that it was not a gorilla or a giraffe but an ichthyosaur (a type of dinosaur). The age of the dinosaur gave scientists clues about the age of Earth.*

4. **Pages 14–16:** The ichthyosaur was on the side of a cliff. How did Mary solve the problem of digging up (excavating) the dinosaur on the side of the cliff? *Mary brought flowers to a family friend, Mr. Arkwright, and asked him if he would build her a tower up the cliff. He was intrigued, so he said yes.*

5. **Pages 17–20:** How did Mary and Joe make money from finding the dinosaur? *They were able to charge one penny for locals to climb the tower Mr. Awkright had built to see the ichthyosaur. This gave them enough money to buy a warm meal. Eventually they would sell the fossil to Henry Henley and make a profit.*

Making Sense
Explore

In this lesson, students will explore how Earth, over time, slowly changes. One process for creating fossils involves shells, bones, and plant materials that leave an impression in mud or in a bed of sand. The organic materials decay, but the impression is preserved and then slowly hardens into rock. *(Teacher Note: Fossils can also be created by the very slow decay of things such as flesh or skin. These fossils help scientists determine the types of plants or animals that lived in a location [and whether they lived on land or in water]. There are four types of fossils: molds, casts, trace fossils, and true-form fossils. In this lesson, you will focus on trace fossils [i.e., fossils formed by a plant or animal in soft clay or silt that is buried by silt over time and preserved] as an example of a "slow" change on Earth.)* This Explore phase will last for approximately two days.

THE *HOW* OF THE EXPLORE

On the first day, make sure that all desks being used for the work area are covered with newspaper or scrap paper. Hand out one cleaned-out milk carton (or wax paper cups) to each student. Have students trim the sides so about half the original carton remains. *(Teacher Note: Depending on the age of the students, you may want to do this for them.)* Mix the plaster of paris and then have students come up to the work area and fill their milk cartons halfway. Let the plaster sit for five to eight minutes. During this time, ask students to select an object with which they can create a trace fossil. This object, once selected, will need to be covered in petroleum jelly so it does not adhere to the plaster. Once the plaster appears to be solidifying, instruct students to gently press their fossil object into the plaster and leave it there for 24 hours. The second day, students will use their craft sticks to pry out their fossil object (this is why the petroleum jelly is important) and see the shape it leaves behind (see Figure 5.7).

Figure 5.7

Sample Dinosaur Fossil Using a Milk Carton and Plaster of Paris

THE *WHY* OF THE EXPLORE

I have never met a class that did not love doing this activity because, unlike so many science experiments, it produces something they can take home and keep for as long as they want. Although the fossil print will be a relatively fast change, be sure to mention how fossils are an example of slow changes on Earth. Students are asked to predict (and analyze) what the fossil will look like in a few days.

Discuss

Although these fossils will only take about 24 hours to set, it is important that you take the time to discuss slow changes on Earth over time and discuss fast changes on Earth during the Discuss portion of the lesson. Ask students if these fossils are formed quickly or slowly in nature. You should explicitly state that you have just made a replica in this lesson but that it would take many, many years for a fossil to form in real life. Ask students to think about fast changes on Earth. *(Teacher Note: Students can more easily identify fast changes once they have a frame of reference for the "slow" changes [fossils]. For example, children may be able to identify a landslide as an example of a fast change. National Geographic has a video called "Landslides 101" [https://video.nationalgeographic.com/video/landslides]. By watching this video, students can see a fast change on Earth. Have students watch "Earthquakes 101" from National Geographic [https://video.nationalgeographic.com/video/101-videos/earthquake-101] and ask them to decide what kind of change an earthquake is (fast or slow). You can also discuss "Volcanoes 101" from National Geographic* [https://video.nationalgeographic.com/video/101-videos/volcanoes-101] *with students.)*

As a class, decide which changes are fast and which changes are slow. Revisit the KWL chart from the beginning of the lesson by answering the following questions:

1. What is our prior knowledge about the age of Earth? (K)

2. What do we still wonder about? (W)

3. What have we learned? (L)

Evaluate

Summative evaluation of this lesson will include assessment of students' understanding of (1) the character trait of being curious and (2) the relationship between fast and slow changes on Earth.

CHARACTER TRAIT

1. Why is being curious an important character trait for scientists to have?
   Being curious allows scientists to generate new ideas from ordinary experiences. For example, Mary Anning loved to question and wonder about things.

2. Describe a time when you were curious.

Ask students to work in groups to tell each other about a time when they were curious and to discuss their experiences as a class.

CONTENT

Evaluate the class's responses on the KWL chart. To evaluate how well students understand the fast and slow changes of Earth over time, have them complete a Venn diagram (see Figure 5.8, p. 130) that includes examples of fast and slow changes from the resources (National Geographic videos) and the fossil lesson. Label one side *Fast* and one side *Slow*. How can students quantify a fast change? How would they quantify a slow change? *(Teacher Note: Earthquakes occur as a result of a sudden release of stored energy. This energy builds up over a long period of time. Therefore, earthquakes are both slow and fast changes in Earth's shape, and it would be most appropriate to list this in the middle of the Venn diagram. Landslides [the movement of a mass of rock, earth, or debris down a slope] can occur anywhere. Sometimes they are caused by human activities such as deforestation and construction. Landslides can move quickly or slowly. In terms of this lesson and comparing this change with fossil creation, landslides move quickly. Therefore, these quantitative comparisons are relative, just to give students an idea about Earth and how it can change quickly or slowly. Volcanoes would be a slow change and evolve slowly over many years.)* Evaluate the Venn diagram for correct responses (see Figure 5.8).

Figure 5.8

Venn Diagram of Fast and Slow Changes of Earth

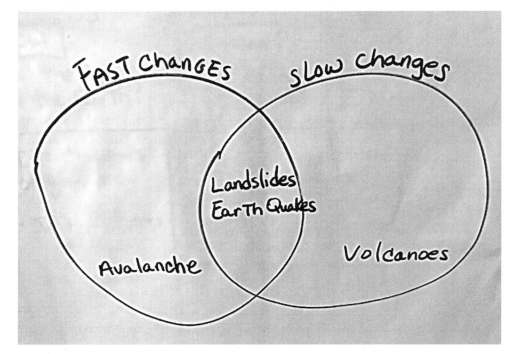

SCIENTISTS AND ENGINEERS ARE
PERSUASIVE

Learning About **Rachel Carson**

Persuasive (adj.): having the power or ability to convince others

Lesson: **Walk and Wonder**
Description

In this lesson, students will collect observations on a walk outdoors to look for living creatures in their natural habitats.

Objectives

Students will consider how the character trait of being persuasive helped Rachel Carson convince others that habitats are important.

- Students will hear the story *Rachel Carson: Preserving a Sense of Wonder* by Thomas Locker and Joseph Bruchac and discuss how it relates to the word *persuasive*.

- In the Predict portion of the lesson, students will complete the formative assessment Is It a Plant? and Is It an Animal? probes by Page Keeley (pp. 138–139).

- In the Observe portion of the lesson, students will take a walk outside to use their senses, find living animals, and identify the animals' habitats.

- In the Explain portion of the lesson, students will describe the habitats of the animals they observed with their senses.

Learning Outcomes

Students will (1) discuss why being persuasive is an important trait for scientists and engineers and (2) analyze and interpret the data they collected on their walk.

Connections to the *NGSS*

The following sections make one set of connections between the instruction outlined in this lesson and the *NGSS*. Other valid connections are likely; however, not all possibilities are listed.

Performance Expectation	Connections to Activity
2-LS4-1: Make observations of plants and animals to compare the diversity of life in different habitats.	• Students will make observations of plants and animals.

Science and Engineering Practice	Connections to Activity
Analyzing and Interpreting Data	• Students will analyze the attributes of plants and animals on their walk and interpret the diversity of habitats.

Disciplinary Core Idea	Connections to Activity
LS4.D: Biodiversity and Humans There are many different kinds of living things in any area, and they exist in different places on land and in water.	• Students will see during their walk that there are many different kinds of living things in one area.

Crosscutting Concept	Connections to Activity
Patterns	• Students will begin to observe patterns of living things in different habitats (e.g., plants and animals that need to be constantly hydrated live near water).

Overview

In this lesson, students will be introduced to a scientist who was persuasive in her communication about the risks of chemical applications. Rachel Carson argued that citizens had the right to know how pesticides were being used on their private property. By reading the featured book, students will learn that men and women from all backgrounds choose careers as scientists. The character trait of being persuasive refers to Rachel Carson's ability to convey her passion about the environment through her writing. As an advocate for the environment, Rachel often argued in such a way that everyday people would be able to understand scientific research. In this way, she communicated what the scientific community understood to common people. In doing so, Rachel, the citizen-scientist, spawned a revolution. Rachel believed that people would protect only what they loved, so she worked to establish a "sense of wonder" about nature.

Rachel Carson

Materials

You will need a copy of the featured book *Rachel Carson: Preserving a Sense of Wonder* by Thomas Locker and Joseph Bruchac (2009). For the Predict portion of the lesson, students will need Page Keeley's formative assessment probes Is It a Plant? and Is It an Animal? (pp. 138–139). For the Observe portion of the lesson, students will need the Walk and Wonder worksheet (p. 140), clipboards, and pencils.

Safety Notes

(1) Caution students about touching poisonous plants, insects, trash, and so on. They can have an allergic effect. Trash containing broken glass and other sharps

can cut or puncture skin. (2) Wash hands with soap and water upon completing this activity.

Setting the Context
Predict

To prepare students for their walk outside, complete one or both of the formative assessment probes about plants and animals. They are likely to see one or both on their walk. Begin by asking students what they think they will see on the walk. Most likely they will start saying types of plants and animals. They will make predictions on their Walk and Wonder worksheets, but for now ask them to complete the plant and/or animal formative assessments. The purpose of the probes is to elicit students' ideas about plants and animals before the experience—this will help identify misconceptions and misunderstandings.

Guided Reading

Rachel Carson was revolutionary in her persuasive nature toward educating people about critical science issues. Students will be learning about a scientist who was especially persuasive when they read *Rachel Carson: Preserving a Sense of Wonder.* Introduce the book by asking, *Can you find the person on the front cover? What does it look like is happening on the front cover?* Read the story aloud. Encourage students to notice and think about the challenges Rachel Carson might have faced as a woman who was an environmental advocate.

The following questions may be used to guide children's attention to detail as you read. (Page numbers reference unnumbered book pages, beginning with the title page as page 1.)

1. **Pages 3–5:** As a child, Rachel Carson was a curious and determined little girl who spent a lot of time exploring the woods, orchards, and fields around her home. However, she knew early on that she would be a writer. As a writer, she combined two things she loved: nature and writing. In what ways did she use her love of nature to influence her writing? *She wrote about birds singing and ocean waves. (Teacher Note: The book says on page 16: "Rachel followed the creatures of the ocean shore throughout the seasons." It is important to point out to children that they can love two subjects and use one to enhance the other as Rachel did.)*

2. **Pages 18–20:** Rachel eventually moved to live close to the ocean and write books. How did Rachel's hometown change in her time away? *Rachel returned home to find that the air was choked with smoke and that the rivers were polluted. These things left her sad and worried about the environment and her own future—and may have influenced Rachel's decision to become a biologist.*

3. **Pages 21–25:** Rachel began to explore the heavy use of chemicals to kill insects. What motivated Rachel's concern about chemical sprays? *Rachel was concerned about the declining bird populations and worried that chemical sprays (insecticides) were deadly to birds, insects, fish, and other animals—and people too. She wanted to let people know about the effects of these chemicals so they could fight for clean air and water.*

4. **Pages 26–30:** How did Rachel use her skill of writing to help the animals in nature that were dying due to chemical sprays? *Rachel wrote persuasive books, which means that she was able to convince people through her choice of words that spraying chemicals was not good for animals.*

Making Sense
Observe

Students will be going outside for a walk to look for living creatures in their natural habitats. *(Teacher Note: You should scope out an appropriate area around your school for such a walk. You may be struggling to find living creatures, but remember that squirrels and ants count. You can leave out some bait [e.g., something sweet along the trail a few hours before the walk] to increase the likelihood of observing ants. It is not the species of the living animals or insects that is important but rather the process of getting students outside and asking them to use their senses to make observations.)*

THE *HOW* OF THE OBSERVE

Pass out the Walk and Wonder worksheets and clipboards. Remind students that they will need to bring their pencils. Review the five senses in each box on the worksheet and encourage them to make as many observations as possible. Discuss the components of a habitat (food, water, and shelter) and encourage them to think not only about how to identify the living creature but also about how that creature lives (i.e., how it finds food, water, and shelter). Review expectations for behavior as students prepare to journey outside the classroom. Set an appropriate time limit that fits with your school schedule. Wander outside ! Have students record words or pictures of living animals they find in each of the blocks on the Walk and Wonder worksheet (see Figure 5.9, p. 136). A great follow-up, depending on what you see, is to supplement the activity with books. For example, if you find a log that looks like it could have life on it but does not at the time of the observation and walk, you could read either *A Log's Life* by Wendy Pfeffer or *Who Lives Here?* by Rozanne Lanczak Williams. If you find ants, you could read *If I Were an Ant* by Amy Moses. If you see a squirrel, you could read *Squirrels All Year Long* by Melvin Berger. These books will help augment the ideas that students have already included on their worksheets.

THE *WHY* OF THE OBSERVE

It is important to get students out in nature observing because the more they hone their observation and reasoning skills, the better science students they will be.

Explain

The focus of this lesson is on analyzing and interpreting data. Therefore, after the walk is complete, collect everyone's papers from their clipboards and begin to look for trends in the data they collected. *(Teacher Note: It's a good idea to look over their papers first to anticipate trends so you can better facilitate discussions with students in the coming days. This way, you can prepare and decide which kinds of questions will lead them as they analyze the data of living animals.)* You may find, for example, that all students saw a squirrel with their eyes. As much as possible (and developmentally appropriate), allow students to analyze data and encourage pattern thinking. This can sound really intimidating if you are a K–2 teacher who has never attempted this before, but you can simply ask, *What* true *statements can you make from the information we collected? (Teacher Note: If it's your first time doing this with your students, you can ask for three true statements and then build to more as students become more comfortable with analyzing and interpreting data.)*

Evaluate

Summative evaluation of this lesson will include assessment of students' (1) understanding of the character trait of being persuasive and (2) ability to analyze and interpret the data collected on their walk to observe diverse living things near their school.

CHARACTER TRAIT

Have students answer the following question:

1. Why is being persuasive an important character trait for scientists? *Being persuasive is important because scientists who are knowledgeable about any one particular area, such as biology and environmental science, can inform people like us how to make good decisions that help our environment. Rachel Carson was persuasive and became famous for her ability to convince others to alter the use of pesticides. (Teacher Note: Helping students think about Rachel Carson's persuasive skills will encourage them to think about how scientists improve the lives of many people.)*

2. Describe a time when you were persuasive.

Figure 5.9

Students Filling Out Their Walk and Wonder Worksheets

CONTENT

Evaluate students' ability to analyze and interpret the data collected on their walk using their Walk and Wonder worksheets. You can use a rubric like the one shown in Table 5.3.

Table 5.3

Rubric for Assessing Walk and Wonder Activity

Content or Skill	Not Yet	Beginning	Developing	Secure
Observations	Student is not able to make observations.	Student is not able to link his or her reasoning back to the evidence observed during the Walk and Wonder activity.	Student is able to link some of his or her reasoning back to the evidence observed during the Walk and Wonder activity.	Student is able to link all of his or her reasoning back to the evidence observed during the Walk and Wonder activity.
Interpreting Data	Student is not able to interpret data.	Student is able to interpret the data from the Walk and Wonder activity but is only able to make a few statements that are not connected to each other and/ or not necessarily true (more like an opinion).	Student is able to interpret one or two true statements from the data from the Walk and Wonder activity.	Student is able to interpret three or more true statements from the data from the Walk and Wonder activity.

References

Adler, D. A. 2000. *A picture book of George Washington Carver.* New York: Holiday House.

Aliki. 2015. *My five senses.* New York: HarperCollins.

Berger, M. 1993. *Squirrels all year long.* New York: Doubleday.

Brighton, C. 1999. *The fossil girl: Mary Anning's dinosaur discovery.* London: Frances Lincoln.

Duckworth, E. R. 2006. *"The Having of Wonderful Ideas" and other essays on teaching and learning.* New York: Teachers College Press.

Keeley, P. 2013. *Uncovering students' ideas in primary science, Volume 1: 25 new formative assessment probes for grades K–2.* Arlington, VA: NSTA Press.

Locker, T., and J. Bruchac. 2009. *Rachel Carson: Preserving a sense of wonder.* Golden, CO: Fulcrum.

Moses, A. 1993. *If I were an ant.* Chicago, IL: Children's Press.

NGSS Lead States. 2013. *Next Generation Science Standards: For states, by states.* Washington, DC: National Academies Press. www.nextgenscience.org/next-generation-science-standards.

Pfeffer, W. 2007. *A log's life.* New York: Aladdin.

Schwartz, C. V., C. Passmore, and B. J. Reiser. 2017. *Helping students make sense of the world using next generation science and engineering practices.* Arlington, VA: NSTA Press.

Williams, R. L. 1994. *Who lives here?* Cypress, CA: Creative Teaching Press.

Is It a Plant?

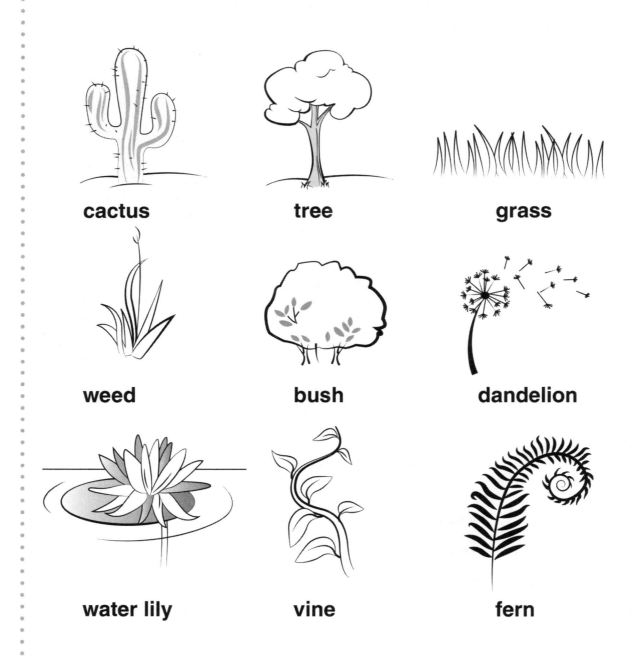

cactus   tree   grass

weed   bush   dandelion

water lily   vine   fern

What are you thinking?

Is It an Animal?

mouse

fish

ant

puppy

flower

worm

person

snail

tree

What are you thinking?

Name: _____

WALK AND WONDER

Predict what things you might notice on the walk.

Record the things you notice below.

Things I hear	
Things I touch	
Things I see	
Things I smell	

6

Using Mathematics and Computational Thinking

The practice of using mathematics and computational thinking is central to both science and engineering. This chapter will focus on three scientists—Eugenie Clark, Margaret Hamilton, and Marie Curie—who all used mathematical and computational thinking in their work. The first person who said that sharks should be admired instead of feared (Clark), the first woman to write the code for computer commands on Apollo missions (Hamilton), and a scientist who discovered two chemical elements (Curie) improved the lives of many people. It is easy to see how the words *curious, explorer,* and *imaginative* best define the character traits of these three scientists. We believe that helping your students to identify each of these traits will allow you to humanize the work and procedures of science and engineering while you teach science lessons to your students.

The *Next Generation of Science Standards* (*NGSS;* NGSS Lead States 2013) suggest that mathematical and computational thinking in grades K–2 builds on prior experience and progresses to helping students recognize that mathematics can be used to describe the natural and designed world. In K–2 classrooms, children are encouraged to use counting and numbers to identify and describe patterns. This begins with them describing, measuring, and comparing the quantitative attributes of different objects and displaying the data using simple graphs. As children mature, they build on the framework of the relationship between mathematics and science to answer their questions in the field of science.

Mathematical thinking is about relationships, whereas computational thinking is about processes. Both of these ways of thinking are examples of how one represents, shares, or tests ideas about how or why something happens. The most important thing is that students think about and use mathematical representations and see the connections to science.

Donna's Personal Story

At the K–2 level, it is easy to believe that the practice of mathematical and computational thinking is the integration of math and science. It is, but it is not limited to the integration of math and science; it's using mathematical thinking to "do" science or understand science. For example, one simple lesson I frequently teach is the building and launching of paper airplanes. This is a kids' favorite at any age. Varying flight features create simple engineering challenges wherein the collected data provide immediate information and feedback about the engineering design. In this activity, students investigate how the design of a paper airplane affects the flight in terms of hang time, height achieved, and distance traveled. In this activity, students create planes with different variables and test them out after making a prediction about which one will fly the farthest. Students become intently involved in test trials and redesigns of their planes. The mathematical thinking becomes almost natural, and it's in those moments—when students barely realize they are doing mathematical and computational thinking—that this practice is most beneficial. For example, when students simply want to make their plane fly farther, they are easily able to make adjustments in the paper folds and continue testing to recognize the relationship between the design variables and the distance traveled. Thus, repeated processes such as this help students to understand the relationship between computational thinking and science.

What's Important to Remember About the Practice of Mathematical and Computational Thinking

- Mathematical thinking is about relationships.

- Computational thinking is about processes.

- Both of these are powerful ways to represent, share, and test our ideas about how or why something happens.

- Not all models can be expressed mathematically or computationally, and not all mathematical expressions are models.

See Schwartz, Passmore, and Reiser (2017) for more information.

SCIENTISTS AND ENGINEERS ARE

FEARLESS

Learning About **Eugenie Clark**

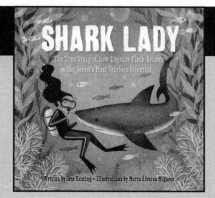

Fearless (adj.): not afraid; very brave

Lesson: Shark Cages
Description

In this lesson, students use straws to create an appropriately sized shark cage for the shark of their choice: a whale shark, a nurse shark, a tiger shark, or a lemon shark.

Objectives

Students will consider how the character trait of being fearless helped Eugenie Clark learn all she could about sharks and will create a cage for a shark with correct mathematical proportions.

- In the Play portion of the lesson, students will pretend that they are underwater scientists and will select a shark for their design challenge.

- Students will hear the story *Shark Lady: The True Story of How Eugenie Clark Became the Ocean's Most Fearless Scientist* by Jess Keating and discuss how it relates to the word *fearless*.

- In the Explore portion of the lesson, students will create a shark cage to fit one type of shark.

- In the Discuss portion of the lesson, students will share the shark cages they build with the class and discuss whether the cage will fit their shark or not.

Learning Outcomes

Students will (1) discuss what being fearless means and why being fearless is an important trait for scientists and engineers and (2) create a cage for a shark with correct mathematical proportions.

Connections to the *NGSS*

The following sections make one set of connections between the instruction outlined in this lesson and the *NGSS*. Other valid connections are likely; however, not all possibilities are listed.

Performance Expectation	Connections to Activity
K-2-ETS1.1: Ask questions, make observations, and gather information about a situation people want to change to define a simple problem that can be solved through the development of a new or improved object or tool.	• Working in teams, students will select a type of shark they would like to catch and design a cage (a new tool) based on information provided about that particular shark.

Science and Engineering Practice	Connections to Activity
Using Mathematics and Computational Thinking	• Students use straws to create a three-dimensional cage for a shark in nonstandard units of measurement.

Disciplinary Core Idea	Connections to Activity
ETS1.A: Defining and Delimiting Engineering Problems • A situation that people want to change or create can be approached as a problem to be solved through engineering. Such problems may have many acceptable solutions. • Asking questions, making observations, and gathering information are helpful in thinking about problems. • Before beginning to design a solution, it is important to clearly understand the problem.	• Students work as a team to plan and design a cage from straws for shark of their choice.

Crosscutting Concept	Connections to Activity
Structure and Function	• Students learn about structure and function as they design their cage.

Eugenie Clark

Overview

In this lesson, students learn how one fearless person became a prominent and compelling advocate for sharks. When Eugenie Clark shared her knowledge about and observations of sharks, she changed the way people thought about them. By reading the featured book, students will learn that men and women from all backgrounds choose careers as scientists. The character trait of being fearless refers to Eugenie Clark's brave attempt to learn as much as she could about sharks.

Materials

You will need a copy of the featured book *Shark Lady: The True Story of How Eugenie Clark Became the Ocean's Most Fearless Scientist* by Jess Keating (2017). For the Play and Explain portions of the activity, use the shark cards and shark sizes for scale (pp. 150–151; the teacher will need card stock or cardboard to mount [glue] the shark cutouts). For the Explore portion of the lesson, each group of students will need soda straws and glue.

Setting the Context
Play

Ask students if they have ever wondered what it would be like to be a scientist studying animals in the ocean. Tell students that they are going to learn about a scientist who spent a lot of time doing just that. Ask them to work in groups to select a shark they would like to use for this engineering design challenge. Have each team draw a picture of what their shark cage will look like (Figure 6.1). *(Teacher Note: Children's drawings at this level will most likely be very basic. Help students include details on their shark cage by asking questions about the shark cage they are drawing. Encourage them to add detail when necessary. As they move from drawing to actually building, they will need reminders to build what they have drawn.)*

Guided Reading

Students will be learning about sharks by reading *Shark Lady: The True Story of How Eugenie Clark Became the Ocean's Most Fearless Scientist.* Introduce the book by asking, *Can you find the person on the front cover? What seems to be happening on the front cover?* Read the story aloud. Encourage students to notice and think about the challenges Eugenie Clark faced as a female scientist.

The following questions may be used to guide children's attention to detail as you read. (Page numbers reference unnumbered book pages, beginning with the title page as page 1.)

1. **Pages 1–6:** The first few pages of the book describe Eugenie, a girl who liked sharks. What were some of the things she wondered about sharks? *She had many questions about sharks, so she decided to learn everything about them: how they swam, where they lived. She kept notebooks of notes on sharks and learned everything she could about them. She thought sharks were beautiful creatures. She wanted everyone to think sharks were beautiful and not ugly or scary.*

2. **Pages 7–13:** When Eugenie decided to go to college, what did her professors say about a girl wanting to be a scientist? *Her professors thought women were not smart enough or brave enough to explore the oceans. They thought she should be a secretary or a housewife. This only increased Eugenie's desire to be a scientist.*

Figure 6.1

Sample Drawing

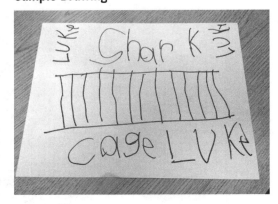

Figure 6.2

Students Realizing That Their Shark Cage Idea Might Need Revisions

3. **Pages 13–23:** Eugenie continued to study and learn about sharks despite some people's belief that a woman could not be a scientist. Eventually she became the first scientist in the world to do what? *She trained sharks like a person would train a dog. She learned that sharks can remember what they have learned for up to two months after the training.*

Explore

Set up materials in a special place in the classroom. Invite students to the carpet.

THE *HOW* OF THE EXPLORE

Each group should have a cut-out shark on card stock or cardboard. Tell students that their job is to create a three-dimensional cage to fit around the shark that was given to their group (see Figure 6.2; cut outs are available on the Extras page at *www.nsta.org/EurekaAgain*). The size of the cage should be proportional to the size of the cut out. They can use only the materials provided. Encourage them to use their drawings as a blueprint. Allow enough time for students to be able to create their cage. *(Teacher Note: Note that the students shown in the photo are starting to create a shark cage based on their design and find it difficult to complete. They need to add more materials than they originally thought. This is OK because scientists and engineers often need to revise their illustrations or blueprints when they come up against unforeseen challenges.*

Figure 6.3 ───────────────────────────────────────

Sample Revised Shark Cage Design

(A)  (B)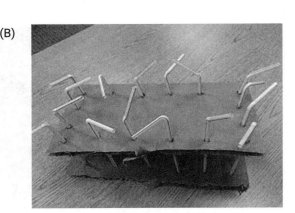

Discuss this process with students and encourage them to write about or illustrate their revisions and observations [including basic reasoning] in their science notebooks.)

THE *WHY* OF THE EXPLORE

This practice is about using mathematical skills to answer science questions. Having students create a physical model to answer a question helps them to think mathematically. See Figure 6.3 for an example of a model cage.

Discuss

Guide students' consideration of the evidence as they make decisions about how to design their shark cage. Encourage students to listen to each other's mathematical thinking in their design challenge. Encourage students to consider different design strategies for different sharks.

Evaluate

Summative evaluation of this lesson will include assessment of students' understanding of (1) why being fearless is an important trait for scientists and engineers and (2) how to create a cage for a shark with correct mathematical proportions.

CHARACTER TRAIT

Encourage students to answer the following questions:

1. If Eugenie Clark had not become an advocate for sharks when she did, how might people view sharks today? *Eugenie Clark was fearless and passionate about the study of sharks which eventually improved people's perceptions of sharks. Once people had a better understanding of sharks and less fear of them, they began to view this animal differently. Eugenie showed people that she was not afraid to get close to them and helped others not to be afraid either. In this way, she was an*

advocate for sharks. If she had not shown people another side of sharks, they might still fear them today. (Teacher Note: The point here is to review Eugenie's consistent pursuit of studying sharks, which meant studying them underwater and getting up close to living sharks.)

2. Why is being fearless an important attribute for scientists to have? And how was Eugenie Clark fearless? *Fearless people are willing to take risks when others might be afraid or cautious. In Eugenie's case, she set out to know all she could about sharks, even when it meant putting herself in danger.*

CONTENT

Encourage students to summarize their beginning sketch and the final outcome of their shark cage. Ask students to reflect on what they are learning about the importance of the design process when it comes to solving a problem. Use the rubric shown in Table 6.1 to evaluate students' work during this lesson.

Table 6.1

Rubric for Assessing Shark Cages Activity

Content or Skill	Not Yet	Beginning	Developing	Secure
Sketch (Plan)	Students do not provide a sketch.	The sketch is at the imaginary level.	The sketch is present but does not resemble the cage that was constructed.	The sketch is present and resembles the cage that was constructed.
Cage Structure	Students do not provide a cage.	The cage is not properly secured.	The cage is properly secured but not level.	The cage is properly secured and level.
Does the Shark Fit Inside the Cage?	No	It fits inside the cage but extends outside the straw walls.	It fits inside the cage with lots of room left over.	It fits inside the cage to the exact proportions.
Revision Process	Students do not develop a revised plan.	Students recognize that their original idea would not work but do not develop a revised plan.	Students recognize that their original idea would not work and develop a revised plan with either a picture or a sample cage.	Students recognize that their original idea would not work and develop a revised plan with both a picture and a sample cage.

SHARK CARDS

Nurse Shark

- Bottom-dwelling shark

- Uses thin, fleshy, whisker-like organs on the lower jaw in front of the nostrils to touch and taste

- Sleeps during the day and hunts at night

- Commonly featured at aquariums

Lemon Shark

- Can live in aquariums, giving scientists the opportunity to learn a lot about them

- Has a unique bright-yellow or brown color

- Not aggressive toward humans and avoids fighting other animals

- Often found in shallow waters

Whale Shark

- Biggest shark and biggest fish

- Not a whale (whales are mammals, not fish)

- Can grow to 45 feet long and weigh up to 30,000 pounds, but average length is 25 feet

- Filters plankton from the water using gill rakers

Tiger Shark

- Has extremely sharp teeth and a strong jaw

- Second-most dangerous shark to humans

- Eats anything, including debris found in the water

- Has tiger-like stripes when young

SHARK MODELS

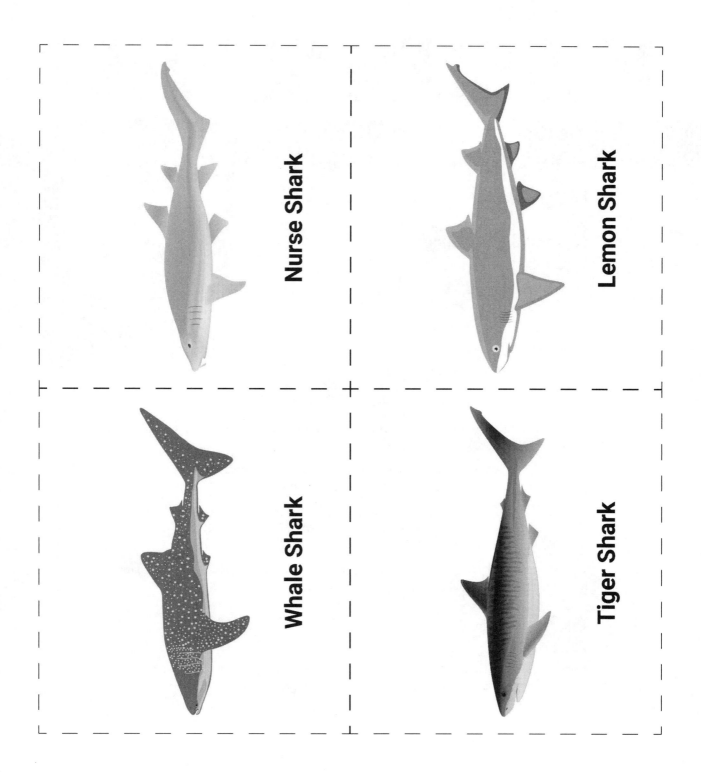

Nurse Shark

Lemon Shark

Whale Shark

Tiger Shark

SCIENTISTS AND ENGINEERS ARE
PROBLEM SOLVERS

Learning About **Margaret Hamilton**

Problem solver (n.): one who solves difficulties

Lesson: Sky Watching
Description

In this lesson, students will use observations of the Sun, Moon, and stars to describe patterns that can be predicted.

Objectives

Students will consider how the character trait of being a problem solver helped Margaret Hamilton teach herself to observe the patterns of the motion of the Sun, Moon, and stars in the sky.

- In the Predict portion of the lesson, students will complete Page Keeley's probe When Is the Next Full Moon?.

- Students will hear the story *Margaret and the Moon: How Margaret Hamilton Saved the First Lunar Landing* by Dean Robbins and discuss how it relates to the term *problem solver*.

- In the Observe portion of the lesson, students will compare the motion of the Sun, Moon, and stars through interactive journal writing.

- In the Explain portion, students will describe the motion of the Sun, Moon, and stars and how they are alike and different.

Learning Outcomes

Students will (1) discuss what being a problem solver means and why being a problem solver is an important trait for scientists and engineers and (2) describe the motion of the Sun, Moon, and stars and how they are alike and different.

Connections to the *NGSS*

The following sections make one set of connections between the instruction outlined in this lesson and the *NGSS*. Other valid connections are likely; however, not all possibilities are listed.

Performance Expectation	Connections to Activity
1-ESS1-1: Use observations of the sun, moon, and stars to describe patterns that can be predicted.	• Students will record daily observations in their journals.
Science and Engineering Practice	**Connections to Activity**
Using Mathematics and Computational Thinking	• Students use nonstandard measurements for distances to describe how far away the Sun, Moon, and stars are from Earth.
Disciplinary Core Idea	**Connections to Activity**
ESS1.A: The Universe and Its Stars Patterns of the motion of the sun, moon, and stars in the sky can be observed, described, and predicted.	• Students describe the patterns of the Sun, Moon, and stars in their journals.
Crosscutting Concept	**Connections to Activity**
Patterns	• Students recognize and compare the patterns of the Sun, Moon, and stars.

Overview

In this lesson, students will learn how Margaret Hamilton used her mathematical and computational skills to create a code for several missions of Project Apollo. By reading the featured book, students will learn that men and women from all backgrounds choose careers as scientists. The character trait of being a problem solver refers to Margaret Hamilton's quick thinking as she observed the patterns of the Sun, Moon, and stars.

Materials

You will need one copy of the featured book *Margaret and the Moon: How Margaret Hamilton Saved the First Lunar Landing* by Dean Robbins (2017). For the Play portion of the lesson, you will need Page Keeley's probe When Is the Next Full Moon? (p. 157); the set of interactive journal prompts for the Sun, stars, and Moon for the Observe and Explain portions (pp. 160–163); pencils; and drawing tools.

Margaret Hamilton

Setting the Context
Predict

Ask students if they have ever seen a full Moon. Ask them to describe the full Moon or where they were when they saw it. Then ask them how often we have a full Moon. Students' answers will vary, so putting these on the board may help you to identify some misconceptions prior to the lesson. Hand out or place the probe on an Elmo so the entire class can see it. The purpose of this probe is to elicit children's ideas about the lunar cycle.

Guided Reading

Students will be learning about how Margaret Hamilton used mathematical and computational thinking by listening to *Margaret and the Moon: How Margaret Hamilton Saved the First Lunar Landing*. Introduce the book by asking student, *Can you find the person on the front cover? What seems to be happening on the front cover?* Read the story aloud. Encourage students to notice and think about the challenges Margaret Hamilton faced as a female coder at NASA.

The following questions may be used to guide children's attention to detail as you read. (Page numbers reference unnumbered book pages, beginning with the title page as page 1.)

1. **Pages 1–9:** The first few pages of the book describe a girl who liked to ask questions. What were some of the things she wondered about? *She wondered why more girls did not grow up to become doctors or scientists. She wondered about the Moon and space, and she read everything she could about addition and subtraction.*

2. **Pages 10–14:** When Margaret discovered computers, what did she do with them? *She wrote instructions for the computer. She started with asking the computer to add, subtract, multiply, and divide and then moved on to more difficult calculations. The code she wrote was software. She called herself a "software engineer."*

3. **Pages 13–23:** Margaret became the director of software programming for NASA's Project Apollo. Name something she accomplished in that position. *She helped* Apollo 8 *orbit the Moon 10 times. She helped* Apollo 9 *connect two ships in space. She also helped* Apollo 10 *get within 9 miles of the Moon's surface.*

Observe

Invite students to help you put together an interactive writing journal on the sky called "My Sky Watching Journal."

THE *HOW* OF THE OBSERVE

Print out the observation journal at the end of this chapter (pp. 158–163). Start with one object a day (e.g., the Sun). Have students observe the Sun, record their observations, bring their journals back to class, and discuss their observations.

THE *WHY* OF THE OBSERVE

As students start to learn about the Sun, Moon, and stars independently, they can consider how each affects the others in the sky. Factors such as the Moon's phases should be taken into account.

Explain

It is best to discuss each object in the sky—the Sun, Moon, and stars—independently. Then as students gain an understanding of each, have them work on their writing prompts to compare the objects in their journals. Ask students, *How does this science journal help you think about Margaret Hamilton's problem-solving nature? When thinking about mathematics and computations, what considerations do you think Margaret Hamilton had to think about?*

Evaluate

Summative evaluation of this lesson will include assessment of students' understanding of (1) the character trait of being a problem solver and (2) how to describe and compare the patterns of the Sun, Moon, and stars.

CHARACTER TRAIT

Encourage students to answer the following questions:

1. What made Margaret Hamilton a problem solver? *Margaret had questions about the stars in the sky. She wanted answers so she sought them out herself. In this way, she was a problem solver—thinking through difficult problems and not giving up until she tried many solutions. (Teacher Note: Encourage students to think about how motivated they are to write or keep a journal. How difficult do they believe it was for Margaret?)*

2. Why is being a problem solver an important character trait of scientists and engineers? *Scientists and engineers rarely come across the right answer or perfect solution the first time they try to solve a problem. Solving a problem takes patience and the ability to think about one question for a long time and come up with many solutions. It was Thomas Edison who once said, "I have not failed; I just know 99 ways a light bulb does not light." (Teacher Note: Ask students to think about a time when they were problem solvers.)*

CONTENT

You will need to evaluate the students' sentences and pictures in their Sky Watching journals. You can use a rubric like the one shown in Table 6.2.

Table 6.2

Rubric for Assessing Sky Watching Journals

Content or Skill	Beginning	Developing	Secure
Sentences	Student writes sentences that are still forming and are not complete.	Student writes some complete thoughts about the Sun, Moon, or stars.	Student writes complete thoughts that were turned into sentences about the Sun, Moon, and stars.
Drawing	Student's drawing is still at the imagination level.	Student's drawing is moving from imagination to evidence-based realities.	Student's drawing has moved from imagination to evidence-based realities, and words are included with arrows or lines.
Questions	Student is not able to ask new questions in his or her journal.	Student is able to ask new questions in his or her journal, but these new questions are not based on evidence.	Student is able to ask new questions that are based on evidence. Student has an idea about how to begin to answer these questions.

When Is the Next Full Moon?

What are you thinking?

MY SKY WATCHING JOURNAL

BY: _____

Three things I have seen in the sky before are:

1. _____

2. _____

3. _____

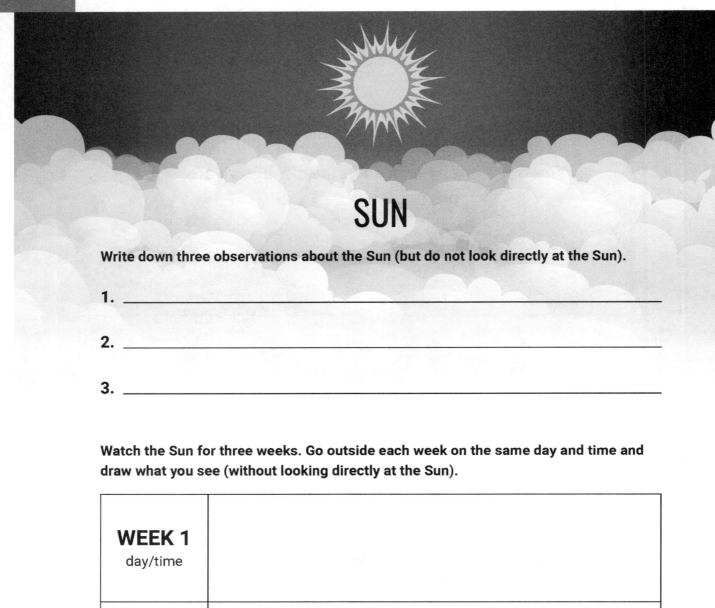

SUN

Write down three observations about the Sun (but do not look directly at the Sun).

1. _____

2. _____

3. _____

Watch the Sun for three weeks. Go outside each week on the same day and time and draw what you see (without looking directly at the Sun).

WEEK 1 day/time	
WEEK 2 day/time	
WEEK 3 day/time	

STARS

Write down three observations about stars.

1. _____

2. _____

3. _____

Watch stars for three weeks. Go outside each week on the same night and time and draw what you see.

WEEK 1 day/time	
WEEK 2 day/time	
WEEK 3 day/time	

MOON

Write down three observations about the Moon.

1. _____

2. _____

3. _____

Watch the Moon for three weeks. Go outside each week on the same day and time and draw what you see.

WEEK 1 day/time	
WEEK 2 day/time	
WEEK 3 day/time	

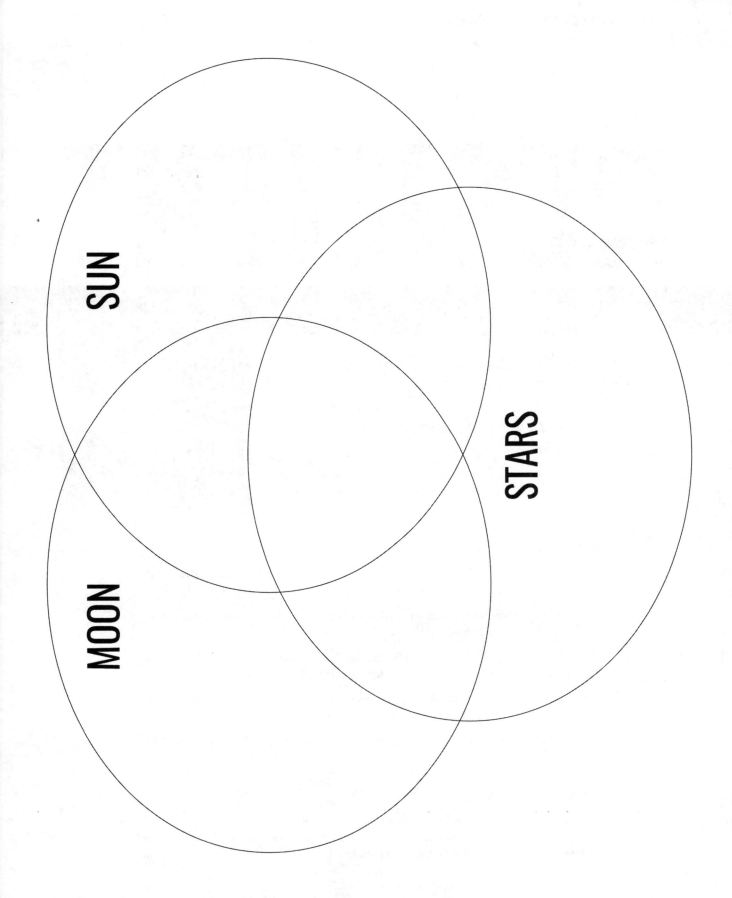

SUN

STARS

MOON

SCIENTISTS AND ENGINEERS ARE

RESILIENT

Learning About **Marie Curie**

Resilient (adj.): able to become strong, healthy, or successful again after something bad happens

Lesson: All Kinds of Matter
Description

In this lesson, students will plan and conduct an investigation to describe and classify different kinds of materials based on their observable properties.

Objectives

Students will consider how the character trait of being resilient helped Marie Curie as they plan and conduct a sort of properties of materials.

- In the Play portion of the lesson, students will participate in a scavenger hunt (Matter Bingo) in the classroom.

- Students will hear the story *Little People, Big Dreams: Marie Curie* by Isabel Sánchez Vegara and discuss how it relates to the word *resilient*.

- In the Observe portion of the lesson, students will classify different materials based on their observable properties.

- In the Explain portion of the lesson, students in small groups will explain how they sorted materials.

Learning Outcomes

Students will (1) discuss why being resilient is an important trait for scientists and engineers and (2) plan and conduct an investigation to describe and classify different kinds of materials based on their observable properties.

Connections to the *NGSS*

The following sections make one set of connections between the instruction outlined in this lesson and the *NGSS*. Other valid connections are likely; however, not all possibilities are listed.

Performance Expectation	Connections to Activity
2-PS1-1: Plan and conduct an investigation to describe and classify different kinds of materials by their observable properties.	• Students describe and classify different items in the classroom.

Science and Engineering Practice	Connections to Activity
Using Mathematics and Computational Thinking	• Students will use mathematical thinking to describe the items they find and classify.

Disciplinary Core Idea	Connections to Activity
PS1.A: Structure and Properties of Matter • Different properties are suited to different purposes. • A great variety of objects can be built up from a small set of pieces. • Different kinds of matter exist and many of them can be either solid or liquid, depending on temperature. Matter can be described and classified by its observable properties.	• Students will observe objects with different properties of matter and decide how to classify the objects.

Crosscutting Concept	Connections to Activity
Energy and Matter	• Students will learn that objects may break into smaller pieces and be put together into larger pieces or change shapes.

Overview

In this lesson, students learn how Marie Curie became the first woman to win the Nobel Prize (with her husband, Pierre). She and her husband discovered two chemical elements: radium and polonium. Marie Curie challenged the way people thought about women and science. By reading the featured book, students will learn that men and women from all backgrounds choose careers as scientists. The character trait of being resilient refers to Marie Curie's attempt to carry on with her experiments after her husband died during a time in history when women could not become scientists without a male influence.

Marie Curie

Materials

You will need a copy of the featured book *Little People, Big Dreams: Marie Curie* by Isabel Sánchez Vegara (2017). Use the Matter Bingo worksheet (p. 170) for the Play portion of the lesson. It depends what you want to include in the activity, but the following are some ideas of materials you might want to gather for your students to classify (in enough quantity to fill a bowl or a small container): wood-chip mulch, rocks, pieces of paper (of any kind), felt, leaves, milk, hand sanitizer, glue, balloons, sand-paper, salt, dish detergent, uncooked pasta, yarn, fur, or cotton balls. Students will also need safety goggles.

Safety Notes

(1) Remind all students that personal protective equipment should be worn during the setup, hands-on, and takedown segments of the activity. (2) Any food used during the activity should not be eaten. (3) Immediately wipe up any liquid spilled on the floor—it creates a slip-and-fall hazard. (4) Wash hands with soap and water upon completing this activity.

Setting the Context
Play

Gather students in a central location in your classroom. Ask if they have ever participated in a bingo game before. Explain that bingo is fun and that they will work in teams to locate items listed on the bingo card. Show students the Matter Bingo worksheet (p. 170) and review the items they will look for; you can also provide suggestions of where they might look.

Guided Reading

Students will be learning about Marie Curie, who was resilient, by reading *Little People, Big Dreams: Marie Curie*. Students will connect Marie's efforts to not giving up when it may have been easy to give up. Introduce the book by asking, *Can you find the person on the front cover? What seems to be happening on the front cover?* Read the story aloud. Encourage students to notice and think about the challenges Marie Curie faced as a female scientist during a time when it was not acceptable for women to become scientists.

The following questions may be used to guide children's attention to detail as you read. (Page numbers reference unnumbered book pages, beginning with the title page as page 1.)

1. **Pages 1–2:** Marie Curie was a girl who was determined and never let anybody stop her from trying new things. What vow did Marie make to herself as a young girl? *From a young age, Marie promised herself that she was going to be a scientist and not a princess. (Teacher Note: Students may not be aware that a vow is a promise. Discuss what they think might have prompted her to make this promise to herself. Did the world she lived in expect girls to be princesses and not scientists? Where or how might she have gotten this message as such a young girl? Discuss gender-specific toys and gender-neutral toys, as all kids will have had experiences with toys "for boys only" and toys "for girls only.")*

2. **Pages 4–6:** Marie was from a poor family, but she was very smart—she even won a gold medal for her studies. Why wasn't she allowed to go to the same university as her brother? *She was not allowed to go to the same university because only boys could go to certain universities, and girls had to attend other universities.*

(Teacher Note: Ask the students if they think this is fair. Why or why not? What might today's classrooms look like if we separated boys and girls in grades K–2? Are there schools that do that? What might the benefits and disadvantages of doing this be?)

Figure 6.4

How the Observe Portion Might Look in Your Classroom

3. **Pages 20–26:** Marie was very successful in her career as a scientist. She even earned the highest honor for scientists—the Nobel Prize—with her husband, Pierre. At the end of the book, what was Marie's valuable advice to others? *Her advice to others was "There is nothing to be afraid of, only many things to learn, and many, many ways to help those in need."*

Observe

Divide students into working groups. Hand out or post the Matter worksheet for all students to read and consider (see p. 171). Have students read the worksheet with you so they understand the directions. They will be observing the different properties of matter and classifying them in a way that makes sense to them. Therefore, there are many possible ways to go about this activity. For example, students may select three or four items and classify them as "soft" or "hard." Students will then need to provide evidence as to why and how they selected this classification.

THE *HOW* OF THE OBSERVE

Set up containers of each type of matter around the room. Allow students enough time to complete their investigation. Each team will need a copy of the Matter worksheet. Discuss what working as a team means in your class.

THE *WHY* OF THE OBSERVE

By providing the students with materials for exploration, you are allowing the students to be responsible for planning and conducting their own investigation and testing their ideas by group consensus. During this process, it is natural for students to discuss the pros and cons with their group members to help them choose an appropriate method of classifying objects. See Figure 6.4 for an example of how this section of the Observe portion might work.

Explain

Ask students to share their classification thinking with the class. Ask students to discuss the decisions they made and why, when possible. Discuss the properties of matter and how they are relevant to each group's examples. *(Teacher Note: You might ask questions about how the matter was classified and what information or knowledge students used to classify objects.)*

Evaluate

Summative evaluation of this lesson will include assessment of students' understanding of (1) the character trait of being resilient and (2) how to conduct an investigation to describe and classify different kinds of materials based on their observable properties.

CHARACTER TRAIT

Resilient people are able to pursue a dream after something terrible happens. Therefore, resiliency is an important character trait for scientists. Encourage students to answer the following question:

1. How was Marie resilient? *Marie was resilient because she continued to focus on studying science even after her husband died. They had studied science together and even won the Nobel Prize. After her husband's death, it would have been easy for her to give up studying science because at that time it was not acceptable for women to become scientists. The fact that she continued to focus on her work is what makes her resilient.*

2. Describe a time when you were resilient.

CONTENT

The idea here is for students to recognize that the properties of matter can be different. They should be able to verbalize the differences and likenesses. Students should be asking questions throughout this entire process.

References

Keating, K. 2017. *Shark lady: The true story of how Eugenie Clark became the ocean's most fearless scientist.* Naperville, IL: Sourcebooks Jabberwocky.

Keeley, P. 2013. *Uncovering student ideas in primary science, Volume 1: 25 new formative assessment probes for grades K–2.* Arlington, VA: NSTA Press.

NGSS Lead States. 2013. *Next Generation Science Standards: For states, by states.* Washington, DC: National Academies Press. www.nextgenscience.org/next-generation-science-standards.

Robbins, D. 2017. *Margaret and the moon: How Margaret Hamilton saved the first lunar landing.* New York: Knopf Books for Young Readers.

Schwartz, C. V., C. Passmore, and B. J. Reiser. 2017. *Helping students make sense of the world using next generation science and engineering practices.* Arlington, VA: NSTA Press.

Vegara, I. S. 2017. *Little people, big dreams: Marie Curie.* London: Frances Lincoln.

Name: _____

MATTER BINGO WORKSHEET

Matter is anything that takes up space and can be seen or touched. Use a crayon to mark off any examples of these kinds of matter in your classroom.

Crayon	Paper	Hardcover Book
Paper Clip	Paperback Book	Magazine
Metal	Plastic	Tissue

Name: _____

MATTER WORKSHEET

List three kinds of matter you found.

_____   _____   _____

How were they alike? Different?

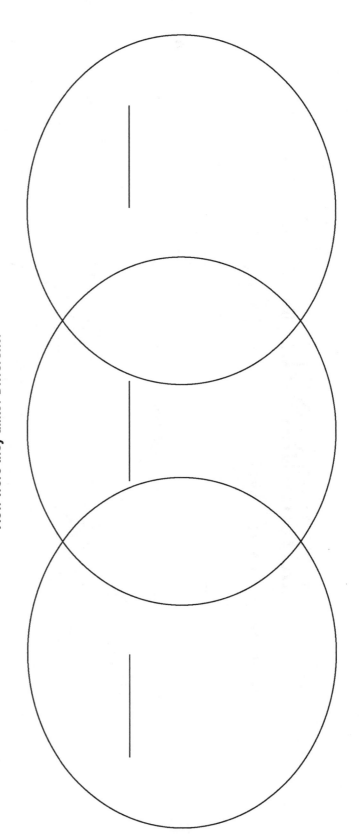

MATTER WORKSHEET (CONTINUED)

List three kinds of matter your friend found.

_____

How were they alike? Different?

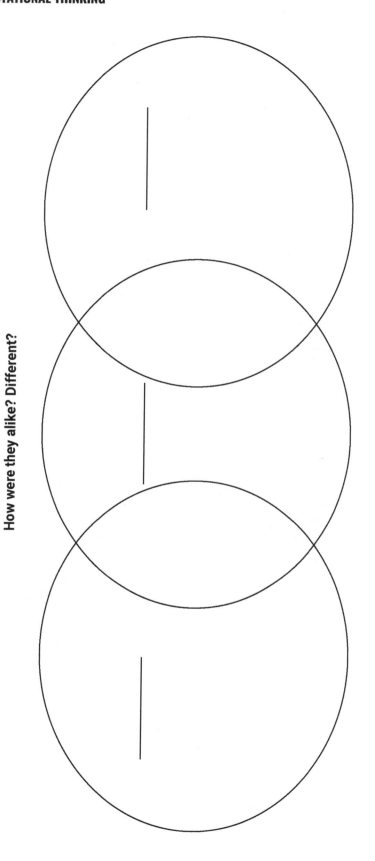

7

Constructing Explanations (Science) and Designing Solutions (Engineering)

The practice of constructing explanations and designing solutions is very important in both science and engineering. This chapter will focus on three engineers—Thomas Edison, Isatou Ceesay, and John Muir—who all ended up designing solutions based on the science explanations they developed. These engineers' development of electricity for common use (Edison), recycling as engineering (Ceesay), and preservation of land into what we know today as national parks (Muir) improved the lives of many people. It is easy to see how the character traits of being inspiring, being a catalyst, and being dedicated define the personalities of these three scientists. We believe that helping your students to identify each of these traits will allow you to humanize the work and procedures of science and engineering while you teach science lessons to your students.

Constructing explanations and designing solutions in grades K–2 involves children writing down and drawing their observations. At this level, for engineering the goal is to design rather than to provide an explanation. The goal of engineering is to solve problems. Likewise, asking students to provide evidence for their observations needs to be consistent and continuous.

Donna's Personal Story

I really appreciate this practice—constructing explanations (science) and designing solutions (engineering)—because it helps me as a science teacher understand the connection between science and engineering. I have to be honest: When the national science standards changed in 2013

Key Features of Teaching the Practice of Constructing Explanations and Designing Solutions

- Explanations address a question about an occurrence.

- Explanations include a *how* or a *why* of the occurrence that draws on a scientific model or generalized principles that use disciplinary core ideas.

- Explanations are based on evidence by either fitting the data we have about the occurrence or by providing support for the steps in the evaluation (i.e., when evidence may be included to provide support for the steps in an evaluation).

See Schwartz, Passmore, and Reiser (2017) for more information.

to include engineering, I was cautious. In theory, I thought it was a great idea, but in terms of practice, I had little pedagogical experience to actually include engineering in my elementary classes. I struggled. I tried many lessons I thought had to do engineering—then I realized they did not. I found three simple questions that helped me tie together science and engineering within just about any lesson, and then I used these questions as a framework moving forward. The three guiding principles I use are (1) asking a question about the occurrence (this could be as simple as *What is occurring?*), (2) determining the how or the why of the occurrence, and (3) determining the basis for evidence (in other words, *How do you know?*). Teaching children to think in terms of these three simple questions helps them investigate the science and the solution (see Table 7.1 for examples of explanations and solutions from this chapter).

Table 7.1

Three Guiding Principles in This Chapter

Feature	Edison	Ceesay	Muir
Question About Occurrence	How is sound made?	Which plastic bag is the strongest?	How do wildfires destroy trees?
How or Why of Occurrence	Why does an object vibrate? What causes vibrations?	What affects the strength of the plastic bag? Dampness? Stretching?	Why do wildfires occur?
Basis for Evidence	Students test several different objects that can fit into a brown paper bag and construct an explanation about sound and vibrations.	How can you determine which bag will be the strongest? When?	What kinds of human solutions can affect wildfires and save forests?

SCIENTISTS AND ENGINEERS ARE
INSPIRING

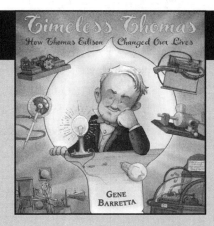

Learning About **Thomas Edison**

Inspiring (adj.): to have the effect of encouraging others

Lesson: Timeless Thomas
Description

In this lesson, students will observe vibrations and provide evidence that vibrating materials can make sound and that sound can make materials vibrate.

Objectives

Students will consider how the character trait of being inspiring helped Thomas Edison while engaging in an experiment to observe.

- In the Play portion of the lesson, students will experiment with metal forks and hear and feel vibrations.

- Students will hear the story *Timeless Thomas: How Thomas Edison Changed Our Lives* by Gene Barretta and discuss how it relates to the word *inspiring*.

- In the Explore portion, students will collect and test items that fit in their brown paper bags based on the items' ability to vibrate.

- In the Discuss portion, students will compare the items they found with those of their classmates based on the loudness of sound produced.

Learning Outcomes

Students will (1) discuss what being inspiring means and why being inspiring is an important trait for scientists and engineers and (2) plan and conduct investigations to provide evidence that vibrating materials can make sound and that sound can make materials vibrate.

Connections to the *NGSS*

The following sections make one set of connections between the instruction outlined in this lesson and the *NGSS*. Other valid connections are likely; however, not all possibilities are listed.

Performance Expectation	Connections to Activity
1-PS4-1: Plan and conduct investigations to provide evidence that vibrating materials can make sound and that sound can make materials vibrate.	• Students plan and conduct an investigation to experience that sound is a vibration.
Science and Engineering Practice	**Connections to Activity**
Constructing Explanations and Designing Solutions	• Students plan and conduct investigations collaboratively to produce data to serve as the basis for evidence to answer questions about vibration.
Disciplinary Core Idea	**Connections to Activity**
PS4.A: Wave Properties Sound can make matter vibrate, and vibrating matter can make sound.	• Students make items vibrate and experience wave properties.
Crosscutting Concept	**Connections to Activity**
Cause and Effect	• Students observe the cause-and-effect relationships between vibrating matter and sound.

Overview

In this lesson, students learn what record players, batteries, and movie cameras have in common. All of these devices were created by Thomas Edison. Students may already be familiar with the name Thomas Edison. However, despite his popularity, many of his experiments failed, yet he still inspired others to create. When Thomas shared his inventions and failures with others, it drastically changed the way people lived—it would be very difficult to go through a day without using one of his life-changing inventions.

By reading the featured book, students will learn that men and women from all backgrounds choose careers as scientists. The character trait of being inspiring refers to Thomas Edison's encouragement of others to come up with new inventions. In this lesson, students will share their ideas about whether scientists are inventors and whether inventors are scientists.

**Thomas
Edison**

Materials

You will need a copy of the featured book *Timeless Thomas: How Thomas Edison Changed Our Lives* by Gene Barretta (2012). For the Play portion of the activity, groups of students will need one metal fork and one piece of string approximately 12 in. long. For the Explore portion, students will need a brown paper bag, a letter to parents (see p. 183), a ruler, and one rubber band per child.

Safety Note

Make sure no hazardous materials are used for this activity.

Figure 7.1

Students Experimenting With Vibrations in the Play Portion of the Lesson

(A)  (B)

Setting the Context
Play

Ask students if they have ever wondered how sound is made. *(Teacher Note: Children's answers may vary—some might know that sound is a vibration, but most will not.)* Allow students to "toss around" several possibilities and then ask them to place two fingers on their Adam's apple and sing. They should feel the vibrations from their vocal cords. This observation should guide them to the correct answer that sound is a vibration. Next, hand out one fork per four or five students tied to a string. Ask students to hold the two ends of the string up to each ear and bang the dangling fork onto the end of the table (see Figure 7.1). Ask students what they hear. End the lesson by handing out the brown paper bags and the note to parents (see p. 183). Students will need these items for the next part of the Explore portion of the lesson.

Guided Reading

Students will be learning about sound and about the work of an inventor who was especially inspiring by reading *Timeless Thomas: How Thomas Edison Changed Our Lives.* Introduce the book by asking "Can you find the person on the front cover? What does it look like is happening on the front cover?" Read the story aloud. Encourage students to notice and think about the challenges Thomas Edison faced as an inventor.

The following questions may be used to guide children's attention to detail as you read. (There are no page numbers because they are general questions about the entire story. This book is written differently from the others in that it is not a typical story with a beginning, middle, and end.)

1. This book has a unique format; most of the pages from page 4 onward are written in "present day" versus "Edison's lab." Ask students to name three things mentioned in these pages that we might not have today if it were not for Edison. *(Teacher Note: There are many things students may recall or mention. For example, batteries might be an easy answer because nearly all children have had experience with batteries in their toys. Other examples, including music from record players and movies, may also be relevant to young children.)*

2. Throughout the story, Edison's failures and the improvements he made to his designs are mentioned. How are failures part of science? Why are improvements necessary? *Edison remarked that he learned more from his failures than he did from his successes. Improvements are necessary because we do not always get the correct answer the first time. (Teacher Note: It is important for children to understand that we learn things through failures. For example, if we begin a science experiment and what happens is what we think will happen, then we have not learned anything at all. The learning is in the discovery of what we did not think would happen.)*

3. The book mentions that Edison worked in a laboratory. Thumb through the illustrations one more time and ask students to describe the laboratory in the book. Did the laboratory have beakers and chemicals? Did he work alone or with others? Did Edison wear a laboratory coat? *The laboratory in the pictures did have glass bottles and beakers. In most of the pictures, he is working alone and without a lab coat. (Teacher Note: These questions prompt children to address some of the stereotypes they may have about scientists. It is important to explicitly teach children about what scientists look like, where they work, and what they do. Although Thomas Edison was an older Caucasian man, he did not have crazy hair or a laboratory coat, which is commonly how children visualize scientists.)*

Making Sense
Explore
Invite students to form groups of four to five students.

THE *HOW* OF THE EXPLORE
Gather the brown paper bags filled with items that the the students have brought from home. Give students who did not bring a bag a few minutes to gather a few items from around the classroom. Begin by asking students to identify various items around their classroom and homes that vibrate and would fit inside the paper bag. Assist the students with some ideas in the brainstorming process as they look around the room. Have them start collecting and testing different items for their ability to vibrate. If students test an item and it vibrates, have them place it in their brown paper bags. If they test an item and it does not vibrate, have them leave

it out of their brown paper bags. Ask students if they have any questions about this procedure, and encourage them to make predictions before they test different items in the classroom as well as at home. Once the students bring back their bags, have them share the contents with other students. Keep a running chart at the front of the room that lists how many similar and different items were collected. *(Teacher Note: Depending on the age of your students, you may want to put a limit on the number of items to bring back to school. Most children will be successful with three to five.)* Ask students, *What did you find out? How does this relate to Thomas Edison's experiments and inventions? What items allowed you and your classmates to observe vibrations the most? What items allowed you and your classmates to observe vibrations the least?* Encourage students to write about or illustrate their observations and reasoning in their science notebooks.

THE *WHY* OF THE EXPLORE

Students should be gathering and testing different items for vibration. They should be learning through their observations that sound is made by vibrations. Providing many opportunities to try this idea out and test it will help students gain confidence as they learn about this phenomenon.

Discuss

Encourage students to construct an explanation for what they observed. This could happen individually, in pairs or in small groups, and/or as a class. It is beneficial to do all three in sequence to allow students to modify their ideas as new ones are shared. Encourage students to summarize their observations and pose questions prompted by this investigation on the chalkboard or on an Elmo. Students should directly compare the results of the different items vibrating and describe how each item produced a sound. Discussion should focus on two questions: *What did the students observe? How was sound produced?* Introduce a discussion about vibration. *(Teacher Note: Some students will notice that certain sounds are louder or softer than others. Try as a class to categorize these sounds as loud or soft as a means of classifying them. This portion of the lesson would also fit nicely with a discussion about instruments. You can make simple instruments with an empty tissue box or a can and several rubber bands. Ask students how this science activity helps them think about Thomas Edison's clever inventions. This discussion is likely to remind students about the invention of the telephone, the phonograph, and so on.)*

Evaluate

Summative evaluation of this lesson will include assessment of students' understanding of (1) the character trait of being inspiring and (2) how to plan and conduct investigations to provide evidence that vibrating materials can make sound and that sound can make materials vibrate.

CHARACTER TRAIT

Encourage students to answer the following questions:

1. If Thomas Edison had not invented the electric lightbulb, the phonograph, or the motion picture, do you think someone else would have? Can we figure out how it is possible that Edison invented so many items? Is there some relationship between these inventions? *Of course someone might have eventually thought of all these ideas about ways to use electricity, but it is unusual that all of these things were developed by the same person. In this case, Thomas Edison was inspiring to others and thought of these things before anyone else did. (Teacher Note: The point here is to review Thomas Edison's lightbulb and other electrical engineering inventions in terms of one scientist's character trait.)*

2. Why is being inspiring an important attribute for scientists to have? How was Thomas Edison inspiring? *Inspiring people are clever and dedicated to thinking of innovative ideas. In this case, Thomas Edison was first inspired by his mother's encouragement to ask questions, read, and dream about his next experiment. Although he sold newspapers on the train, he usually carried a book about his next experimental idea in his pocket. He even set up a laboratory at the back of the railway station so he could experiment during his off-hours. (Teacher Note: Encourage students to work in pairs and tell each other about a time when they were "inspiring.")*

CONTENT

Summative evaluation of this lesson might focus on students' predictions and observations according to the worksheet provided on page 184.

1. **Prediction:** Did students make a prediction about which items may vibrate? *(Teacher Note: Accuracy is not important here. Although predictions often rely on some observational data, these may come from prior experiences. Therefore, any prediction indicates that some thought went into what students thought might happen. Take this opportunity to talk with students about some common, daily predictions [e.g., when they look at the cover of a book to anticipate the story inside]. The point here is to encourage children to think a bit about what they already know before engaging in the experiment phase.)*

2. **Observation:** Students are prompted to respond to their observations by placing items that vibrate into their brown paper bags to share with the class. *(Teacher Note: As you evaluate students' oral observations, look for true statements that can be backed up by evidence versus opinions that cannot be backed up by evidence.)*

3. **Conclusion:** Students are summarizing what they learned and then tying together their predictions and observations by testing items. Look for indications of student learning and understanding of the scientific method (i.e., recognition of data to evidence new understanding).

LETTER TO PARENTS

Dear Parents,

We have started investigating sound in class. Please use this brown paper bag (attached) to collect items around your house that students can use for a science lesson about vibration. Please make sure the items can all fit inside the brown paper bag. You may want to discuss with students predictions about the items as you help them select appropriate items. We will use these items for approximately a week and then your child will bring them home.

Thank you,

_____

Dear Parents,

We have started investigating sound in class. Please use this brown paper bag (attached) to collect items around your house that students can use for a science lesson about vibration. Please make sure the items can all fit inside the brown paper bag. You may want to discuss with students predictions about the items as you help them select appropriate items. We will use these items for approximately a week and then your child will bring them home.

Thank you,

_____

Name: _____

EDISON WORKSHEET

QUESTION: Do these objects vibrate?

How can I find out? First, I will _____.

Second, I will _____.

Third, I will _____.

Object	Prediction: Will This Object Vibrate?	Observation (Circle One)	Observations
	Yes or No	Yes Some No	
	Yes or No	Yes Some No	
	Yes or No	Yes Some No	
	Yes or No	Yes Some No	
	Yes or No	Yes Some No	
	Yes or No	Yes Some No	
	Yes or No	Yes Some No	
	Yes or No	Yes Some No	

SCIENTISTS AND ENGINEERS ARE
CATALYSTS

Learning About **Isatou Ceesay**

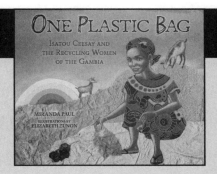

Catalyst (n.): a person or event that quickly causes change or action

Lesson: Engineering a Solution
Description

In this lesson, students test different types of plastics for strength and create a new design just as Isatou Ceesay did with the families in her community.

Objectives

Students will consider being a catalyst as the character trait that helped Isatou Ceesay do something about the quality of her environment and create new uses for old plastic bags.

- In the Play portion of the lesson, students will arrange plastic bags from strongest to weakest based on their observations and predictions.

- Students will hear the story *One Plastic Bag: Isatou Ceesay and the Recycling Women of The Gambia* by Miranda Paul and discuss how it relates to the character trait of being a catalyst.

- In the Explore portion of the lesson, students will keep a running tally of how many bags they use at their house in a week. Students will observe several items that can be made from plastic bags.

- In the Discuss portion, students will observe several items that can be made from plastic bags and attempt to make a new item from the materials.

Learning Outcomes

Students will (1) discuss what being a catalyst means and why being a catalyst is an important trait for scientists and engineers and (2) ask questions, make observations, and gather information about a situation people want to change to define a simple problem that can be solved through the development of a new or improved object or tool.

Connections to the *NGSS*

The following sections make one set of connections between the instruction outlined in this lesson and the *NGSS*. Other valid connections are likely; however, not all possibilities are listed.

Performance Expectation	Connections to Activity
K-2-ETS1-3: Analyze data from tests of two objects designed to solve the same problem to compare the strengths and weaknesses of how each performs.	• Students analyze data from testing plastic bags and design a new tool from the plastic using the data collected.
Science and Engineering Practice	**Connections to Activity**
Constructing Explanations and Designing Solutions	• Students construct a new design from plastic bag strips that will solve a problem they have identified.
Disciplinary Core Idea	**Connections to Activity**
ESS3.C. Human Impacts on Earth Systems Things that people do to live comfortably can affect the world around them. But they can make choices that reduce their impacts on the land, water, air, and other living things.	• Students will learn about and observe different types of plastic bags in a fair test. They will consider how one plastic versus another would best solve a problem.
Crosscutting Concept	**Connections to Activity**
Structure and Function	• The structure and function of the plastic bag affects the new design.

Overview

In this lesson, students learn how one woman addressed the overwhelming challenge of cleaning up garbage and plastic debris in the form of plastic bags in her community in The Gambia, West Africa. By reading the featured book, students will learn that men and women from all backgrounds choose careers as scientists. The character trait of being a catalyst refers to Isatou Ceesay's determination to solve the problem she encountered in her community. Students will share their

Isatou
Ceesay

ideas about scientists as engineers and will discuss how problems are solved. Students will explore multiple solutions for recycling plastic bags and learn why Isatou Ceesay decided to recycle plastic bags and transform her community.

Materials

You will need a copy of the featured book *One Plastic Bag: Isatou Ceesay and the Recycling Women of The Gambia* by Miranda Paul (2015). For each small group (or the class as a whole), you will need approximately 50 plastic bags from grocery stores (send the letter on p. 193 home with students, asking parents to help them collect plastic bags to bring to class). You will need three different kinds of bags (resealable plastic bags, trash bags, and store bags) to test the strength of each in the Explore portion of the lesson.

Safety Notes

(1) Remind students not to place the plastic bags over their heads or mouths during the activity. (2) Use caution when working with scissors or sharps—these can cut or puncture skin.

Setting the Context
Play

Ask students if they have ever noticed that not all plastic bags are alike. There are some that we put our groceries in, some that we put our trash in (trash bags), and some that we put our sandwiches in (resealable plastic bags). Ask students what other kinds of plastic bags they can think of. Discuss these observations with the entire class and make a list in the classroom of the different types of plastic bags. Bring in samples for students to observe, and have the class work together to line up the bags from strongest to weakest. *(Teacher Note: Plastics are used for all sorts of purposes in our lives today. The scientists that study and make new plastics are called engineers [chemical engineers]. Plastics are often used because they are less expensive to make and more durable than other materials, but they are not always good for the environment if they are not disposed of properly or if they are overused, as students will learn from the story you read.)*

Guided Reading

Students will be learning about Isatou Ceesay and her attempt to solve a problem and clean up her community. Find The Gambia on a map and explain to students that it is part of West Africa. Introduce the book by holding up the cover and asking, *What do you think this story is about?* Read the story aloud.

1. **Pages 1–5:** What clues in the first few pages tell you that this story does not take place in America? *(Teacher Note: Some students may notice Isatou's clothing, which is traditional African clothing, or the fact that she carries a basket on her head. If students notice her carrying a basket on her head, you might ask, Why would she carry a basket on her head? [If people are carrying loads long distance, it makes it easier if they carry these loads on their heads.] Other students might notice a goat being near Isatou. A goat is not uncommon, but having a goat at your house may seem strange to some students.)*

2. **Pages 5–9:** Isatou is carrying fruit back home in her basket and the basket breaks. What does she notice floating around outside? Why do people seem to let their bags float away? *She notices plastic bags in different colors either floating in the wind or piled up in the dirt. They become part of the scenery until she decides to do something about them as a grown woman.*

3. **Pages 12–14:** The plastic bags tossed out into the open caused many problems for the villagers and the animals. Name at least two problems caused by the piles of plastic bags all around Isatou's village. *One problem was the smell of dirty trash. Animals such as goats would scavenge for food, and they risked eating the bags and dying. Mosquitoes also swarmed near the trash piles.*

4. **Pages 15–17:** Isatou asked her friends one important question that began a positive change in behavior. What was that question? And how did this question solve a problem? *The question Isatou asked was* What can we do? *Isatou and her friends began problem solving to find solutions. They began to wash the bags and then laid them out on the clothesline. Isatou's sister was crocheting as the bags were drying, and they came up with the idea to make "thread" from the bags hanging on the clothesline.*

5. **Pages 20–26:** Isatou teaches the other women to crochet by candlelight, and they design a purse. How did the people in the village react to the women "who believed they were doing something good by crocheting the plastic"? *Some people laughed at the women. Some people said they were dirty for working with those old, ripped, and stinky plastic bags. But many people also wanted to pay for the purse, and Isatou soon had enough money for a new goat. The new plastic purses she engineered not only brought her financial wealth—but also did something very important: They reduced the amount of trash and rubble in the streets.*

Making Sense
Explore

In the story, the plastic bags are able to be recycled and used in a different way because of the plastic they were made from. The bags, once cut and woven together, are actually stronger than before. In this portion of the lesson, students will explore the properties of plastic.

THE *HOW* OF THE EXPLORE

Select three types of plastic bags for students to experiment with. Ask them to record their predictions in the prediction portion of Table 7.2 (p. 191). Ask students to develop a way to test these ideas. Discuss how a "fair test" is conducted. *(Teacher Note: A "fair test" controls for variables and uses a number of trials. For example, I typically ask my students to identify what will be the thing that is different in testing the strength of the plastic bags. The one thing that will be different is the type of plastic bag to be tested. This is the variable. Then I ask students how many times scientists do experiments— for example, do they just do them once and get an answer? Most students are aware that a scientist must test something more than once to arrive at a conclusion that will be respected by the science community. Usually we arrive at a "three and done" rule for testing any kind of science experiment. We end by asking the students if they think this is fair or not because we are trying to conduct a "fair test.")* In this portion of the lesson, students will also have to determine the size of the plastic bag to test. For example, a trash bag is much larger than a plastic bag from the store, so how can they make three different bags the same size, and how can you make this lesson about the material versus the size of the bag? Select an appropriate amount of weight to test. Books are usually readily available and easy to manage with younger children. Gather students around and test out the number of books each piece of plastic can hold before breaking. Have students design a new product from the bags if time allows.

THE *WHY* OF THE EXPLORE

In the featured book, the plastic bags are able to be recycled and used in a different way because of the plastic they were made from. The bags, once cut and woven together, are actually stronger than before. In this portion of the lesson, students will explore different ways plastic bags can be recycled and will be challenged to make a new creation from recycled plastic parts. *(Teacher Note: There are many items that can be made from plastic bags, including flowers [www.sillysimpleliving.com/2012/01/17/use-plastic-bags-to-make-your-own-flowers], shoes, and coats. You may want to share some websites with students, such as "12 Amazing Things Made from Plastic Bags" [www.oddee.com/item_97040.aspx]).* You may have an example to show your students (see Figure 7.2 for an example of

Figure 7.2

A Purse Made From Recycled Plastic Bags

Figure 7.3

Trim the Handles Off the Bag

a purse). You can also easily make a jump rope. Challenge students to create a new item from recycled bags. Begin by cutting off the top of a recycled bag (Figure 7.3) and then cutting the remaining bag into 1-in. circular strips (see Figure 7.4) . This will take some preparation on your part, and child or parent volunteers could be very helpful.

Discuss

Hand out the plastic bags students have brought to school and allow students to imagine, create, and design items however they wish. Ask them to bring items into class and share these with other students once they have created a new item from an old bag as a way to solve a problem. Students should receive a checklist about asking questions, making observations, and gathering information about a situation people want to change to define a simple problem that can be solved by developing a new or improved object or tool (see p. 194).

Figure 7.4

Fold the Remainder of the Bag into a 1-in. Strip and Then Cut

Table 7.2

Data Collection Log for the Engineering a Solution Activity

Plastic Type	Prediction	Size		Strength Test
		Length	Width	Books
Plastic A: Grocery Store Bag				
Plastic B: Trash Bag				
Plastic C: Resealable Plastic Bag				

Note: A larger version of this table is available at *www.nsta.org/EurekaAgain*.

Evaluate

Summative evaluation of this lesson will include assessment of students' understanding of (1) the character trait of being a catalyst and (2) how to ask questions, make observations, and gather information about a situation people want to change to define a simple problem that can be solved through the development of a new or improved object or tool.

CHARACTER TRAIT

Encourage students to answer the following questions:

1. If Isatou Ceesay had not developed a solution for her village, how might it look today? *Her village may still have trash bags all around if no one motivated and inspired others to clean up the trash. Of course, someone might have eventually thought to pick up plastic bags, but would they have thought of using the bags in such a creative way for financial gain? Isatou Ceesay was the catalyst who envisioned and initiated this engineering feat before anyone else did. (Teacher Note: The point here is to review Isatou Ceesay's effort to help her village and do something about the plastic bags when others just looked the other way. It is important that children understand that the change started with her.)*

2. Why is being a catalyst an important character trait for scientists and engineers? *Oftentimes, people see problems but no solution, so they don't try to make the world a better place. Isatou Ceesay saw the problem and developed a solution on her own. This character trait reinforces the idea that one person can make a difference for many others.*

CONTENT

Once the class has completed their new designs, evaluate these according to the graphic organizer on asking questions, making observations, and gathering information about a situation people want to change to define a simple problem that can be solved through the development of a new or improved object or tool. A new design from a recycled bag should accompany students' journal illustrations. A model of the jump rope they created in class might look like the one shown in Figure 7.5.

Figure 7.5

Weaving From Plastic Bags to Make a Jump Rope

LETTER TO PARENTS

Dear Parents,

We have started investigating plastic in class, and students are learning how one woman, Isatou Ceesay, addressed the overwhelming challenge of cleaning up garbage—especially plastic bags—in The Gambia, West Africa. In the book *One Plastic Bag: Isatou Ceesay and the Recycling Women of The Gambia* by Miranda Paul (2015), Ceesay discovers that these bags are able to be recycled and used as purses and in many other ways because of the plastic they are made from. Once cut and woven together, the purses are actually stronger than when they were simply plastic bags! In our classroom lesson related to this book, we will discuss the properties of plastic. Students will explore multiple solutions for recycling plastic bags and learn why Ceesay decided to recycle plastic bags and transform her community.

Please collect as many plastic grocery bags as possible for your child to bring into class. We will use them to create new products, just like Ceesay did. Over the next several weeks, be sure to discuss with your child what he or she is learning about plastic and how humans can impact the environment.

Thank you,

_____

Name: _____

GRAPHIC ORGANIZER

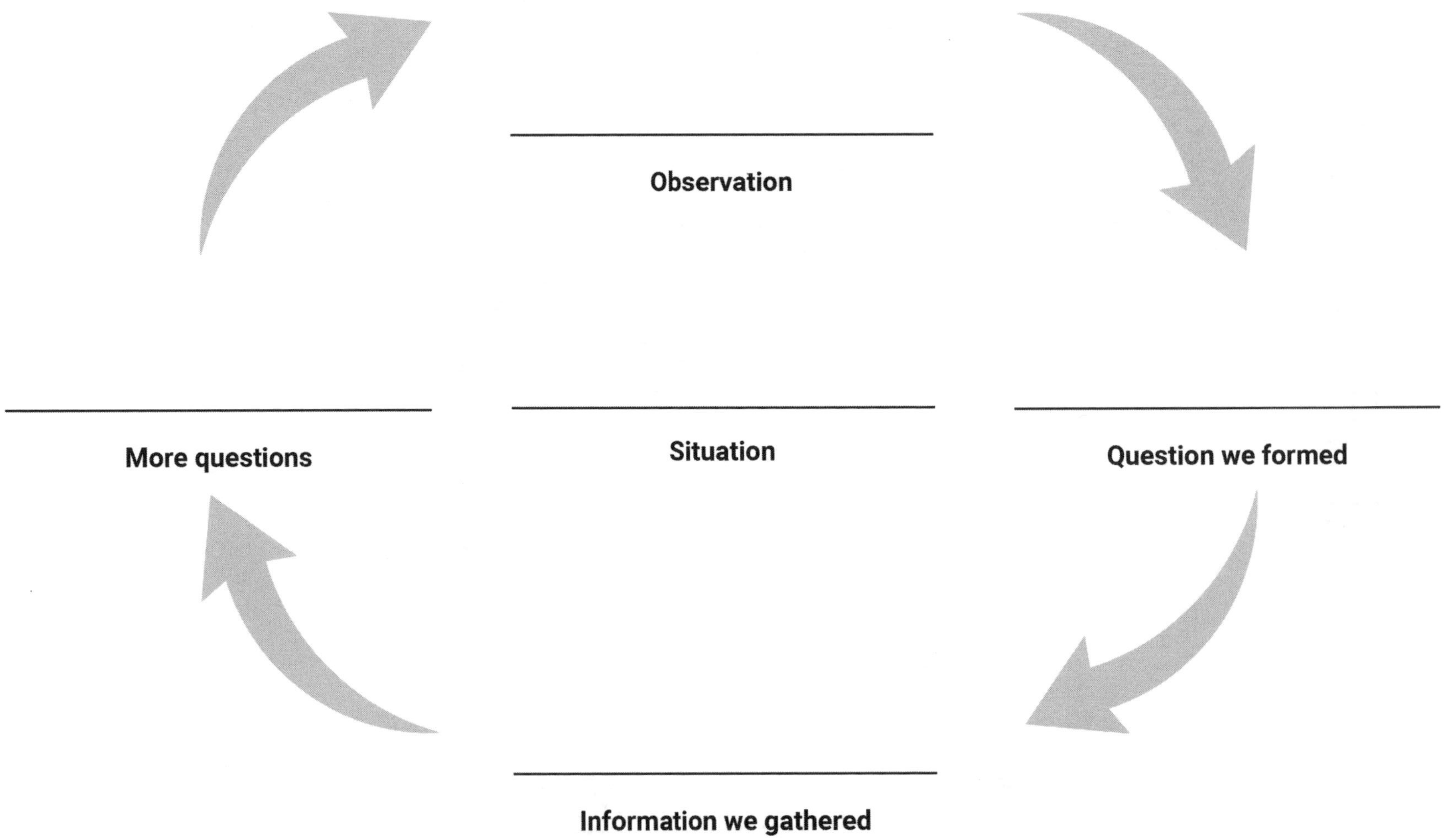

Question we formed

Information we gathered

More questions

Observation

Situation

SCIENTISTS AND ENGINEERS ARE
DEDICATED

Learning About **John Muir**

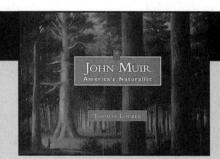

Dedicated (adj.): devoted to a task or purpose; having single-minded loyalty or integrity

Lesson: Adopt a Tree
Description

In this lesson, students use their seasonal observations about trees to develop a solution for forest wildfires.

Objectives

Students will consider how the character trait of being dedicated helped John Muir preserve nature.

- In the Play portion of the lesson, students will play 20 Questions and select a tree to observe throughout the year.

- Students will hear the story *John Muir: America's Naturalist* by Thomas Locker and discuss how it relates to the word *dedicated*.

- In the Explore portion of the lesson, students will observe and record data about their adopted tree and develop solutions for forest wildfires.

- In the Discuss portion, students will explain patterns of what a tree needs to survive throughout the year and discuss solutions to minimize the impact of wildfires.

Learning Outcomes

Students will (1) discuss what being dedicated means and why being dedicated is an important trait for scientists and engineers, (2) use their observations to describe patterns of what a tree needs to survive throughout the year, and (3) communicate solutions to help stop the spread of wildfires.

Connections to the *NGSS*

The following sections make one set of connections between the instruction outlined in this lesson and the *NGSS*. Other valid connections are likely; however, not all possibilities are listed.

Performance Expectation	Connections to Activity
K-ESS3-3: Communicate solutions that will reduce the impact of humans on the land, water, air, and/or other living things in the local environment.	• Students will develop a solution for preventing the spread or start of forest wildfires.

Science and Engineering Practice	Connections to Activity
Constructing Explanations and Designing Solutions	• Students will use their seasonal observations about trees to develop a solution for preventing forest wildfires.

Disciplinary Core Idea	Connections to Activity
ESS3.C. Human Impacts on Earth Systems Things that people do to live comfortably can affect the world around them. But they can make choices that reduce their impacts on the land, water, air, and other living things.	• Students will use their observations to describe patterns of what a tree needs to survive through the year.

Crosscutting Concept	Connections to Activity
Patterns	• Students will learn that trees have patterns and develop in cycles.

Overview

In this lesson, students are introduced to a person who devoted himself to the study and importance of nature. By reading the featured book, students will learn that men and women from all backgrounds choose careers as scientists. The scientist character trait of being dedicated refers to John Muir's confidence and willingness to take a risk with exploring new territories and preservation efforts.

Materials

You will need a copy of the featured book *John Muir: America's Naturalist* by Thomas Locker (2010). Each student will need tree observation journal pages (see pp. 203–207) and wildfire information (map, videos, and so on).

John Muir

Safety Note

Remind students to stay clear of poisonous plants, insects, and trash. These can produce allergic effects, and trash can contain sharps that can cut or puncture skin.

Setting the Context
Play

Invite students to sit in a circle. Ask students if they know what the word *adopted* means. Tell them that the class is getting ready to "adopt" something for the entire year so they can study it for science. Play a game of 20 Questions to engage the students and arrive at the answer of a tree. Their job will be to ask you questions, one at each time, that require a "yes" or "no" answer. Each child gets to guess after he or she asks a question about what the class will be adopting. Give the students some clues to begin—some possible ideas are "It's living," "It needs water often," and "It requires food and sunshine." This should be enough to get their imaginations going. Each student should be provided the opportunity to ask you a "yes" or "no" question about the adoption and then a guess as to what it might be. Keep this going around the circle until the students figure out that the answer is a tree. If students have trouble, you can give more specific clues as the game progresses, such as "It has bark," "It needs soil," and "It can hibernate." *(Teacher Note: This circle talk with students is intended to stimulate the children's thoughts about living and nonliving things and generate some excitement about the long-term process of conducting a scientific investigation.)* Tell students that the purpose of the scientific study of a tree is to learn about how it grows and changes over time. This will require careful observations and measurements throughout the entire school year. Tell students that they will need to select a tree to adopt after reading a story about a man who thought trees were pretty important.

Guided Reading

Students will be learning about the work of a person who shared his love of nature in a new way that had never been done before. *(Teacher Note: You might want to show children the Sierra Club website [www.sierraclub.org]. The Sierra Club, which was started by John Muir, is now the nation's largest and most influential grassroots environmental organization, with more than 2 million members and supporters. Its successes range from protecting millions of acres of wilderness to helping pass the Clean Air Act, the Clean Water Act, and the Endangered Species Act.)* Introduce the featured book by showing students the cover and asking, *What does the front cover tell you about the story we are about to read?* Read the story aloud. The following questions may be used to guide children's attention to detail as you read. (Page numbers reference unnumbered book pages, beginning with the title page as page 1.)

1. **Page 4:** This story takes place in a valley in the Sierra Mountains called Yosemite National Park. *(Teacher Note: Show students a map of the United States.)* Ask students, *Can you find Yosemite National Park on the map? Has anyone ever visited Yosemite National Park? Has anyone ever heard of it?*

2. **Pages 8–12:** John Muir was born in Scotland in 1838. When he was 11 years old, his family sailed across the Atlantic Ocean to come to the United States. He grew up on a farm and took a job in a factory to make ends meet. What happened to John at his factory job that caused him to devote his life to the study of nature? *John was in an accident at work that caused him to temporarily lose his eyesight. While recovering, he made the decision to leave the factory and devote his life to the study of nature. Once his eyesight returned, he set off and walked 1,000 miles from Indiana to the Gulf of Mexico, observing nature and journaling about his experiences.*

3. **Pages 14–18:** John found himself in California in the Yosemite Valley. He took a variety of odd jobs to stay there and take hikes in all the beautiful locations. Name some things he discovered while he was there. *John discovered how beautiful the skyline was. (Teacher Note: Show students what a skyline is and describe how a skyline from a city and from a forest might appear.) He observed giant sequoia trees that were thought to be thousands of years old. He also studied squirrels, bears, deer, and even tiny ants.*

4. **Pages 19–24:** John married and had two children. He ran a farm in the valley and returned to the Yosemite Valley whenever he could. What did his friends ask him to write letters about, and why do you think he wrote them? *John Muir and his friends became upset when lumber interests and ranchers began to cut down trees in the forest for their own financial gain. This is when John started to communicate his desire to preserve the wilderness. Although his friends urged him to write the letters, he did so because he was trying to convince others of the beauty that existed in the wilderness and tell them that this land should be protected.*

5. **Pages 24–27:** How did people respond to John's letters? *John's letters helped convince others that the wilderness should be preserved. Eventually John started the Sierra Club, which was one of the first organizations devoted to preserving the wilderness. The national parks were a result of his tireless effort. National parks are designated land that people can visit to appreciate the beauty of nature; however, no one can build on this land or cut down any trees. The purpose of the National Park Service is to preserve the wilderness for many generations to come.*

Making Sense
Explore

After reading the story, discuss why trees are an important part of nature. *(Teacher Note: Answers from children will vary.)* Ask students how the class should go about selecting a tree to adopt. Let them develop a plan as part of them learning how to investigate in scientific ways from the youngest of ages. For example, the class could go outside and find a tree they like as a group, they could vote on a tree, or they could use cameras to take pictures of a tree and then present to the class why they think a particular tree would be interesting to watch and observe throughout the year.

THE *HOW* OF THE EXPLORE

Once a tree has been selected, plan a day and time to visit (for the first time) the tree the class will adopt. Talk to the students about what they might observe and how they might describe their tree. Encourage them to use their senses as their journal page suggests. *(Teacher Note: They might mention bark, branches, buds, leaves or needles, the trunk, what surrounds the tree, the roots, and so on.)* Prepare students by bringing their tree observation journals (see pp. 203–207), clipboards, and pencils, and review appropriate behavior during science outside of school. Use an iPad or camera to take photos of the tree, and display these in the classroom. Set expectations for the students appropriate for their age group. For example, if the students are in kindergarten (and it's the beginning of the year), perhaps one observation per child is best. Encourage students to use their senses and write down or draw their observations. Consider children's abilities to make observations.

THE *WHY* OF THE EXPLORE

Watch children as they observe—this is most likely a new skill for them. Encourage the students to make observations. Listen to children as they verbalize their descriptions, and encourage them to draw what they see. Encourage detail in their illustrations. For example, if a child shows you a picture of a tree with no definition in the bark, ask him or her to approach the tree and place a hand on it. Is it smooth, as the illustration suggests? Return to class after students have finished recording their observations. *(Teacher Note: John Muir loved nature so much that he would go outside in nature and just sit and write and enjoy. Try to have students sit and enjoy this assignment, which is very different from normal assignments inside the classroom. This way they can begin to develop an appreciation for nature and its beauty.)*

Now that students have a good understanding of the details associated with trees from their observations, guide them to understand the destructive nature of forest fires. Use videos and current maps to help students understand what wildfires are, how they destroy trees, and where wildfires occur. Ask students to work in groups to develop a solution to stop wildfires.

Discuss

During the next science time, gather children with their tree observations for a class discussion. Listen to students as they offer their observations of the tree. Explain to children how the class will be watching this tree throughout the year. Have students make a prediction about how they think the tree might change over time. Is it a type of tree that stays green all year (evergreen) or a type of tree that loses its leaves (deciduous)? Ask students to provide evidence for how they know. Remember that the purpose of this chapter is to get students to start thinking about the best way to plan and conduct experiments, so you'll want them to decide *when* to observe next and how to observe. Students could decide to do a tree inventory: How many trees are in the schoolyard, and how many of those trees are like the tree that the class adopted? What does the tree's root system look like? How can we figure out how it gets water? Does it bear any fruit? Make a plan for the school year in terms of how and when to observe your adopted tree. Predict what changes you will observe as a class and keep a running log all throughout the year.

Evaluate

Summative evaluation of this lesson will include assessment of students' understanding of (1) how the character trait of being dedicated might benefit scientists and engineers and (2) how to use observations to describe patterns of what a tree needs to survive throughout the year.

CHARACTER TRAIT

Encourage students to answer the following questions:

1. What if John Muir had not led the fight for the protection of national park areas? *Someone might have eventually thought to save some wilderness for parks, but how many more forests would have been destroyed before this idea came to light? (Teacher Note: The point here is to review John Muir's effort to preserve nature in terms of one scientist's character trait.)*

2. Why is being dedicated an important trait for scientists? *John's dedication enabled his continuous and focused agenda. John clearly won others over and was convincing in his arguments that we should preserve nature.*

CONTENT

Evaluate students' science journals as each observation occurs. You should expect more detailed and more comprehensive evaluations as the year progresses. Use a rubric like the one shown in Table 7.3 to evaluate students' observations in their journals.

Table 7.3

Log for the Adopt a Tree Activity

Date of Observation	Beginning	Developing	Secure
	Observations and descriptions often reflect the characteristics of imagination versus actual characteristics or events. Descriptions of observations are inaccurate.	Observations and descriptions reflect actual characteristics or events but lack detail. Only one sense was used to observe.	Observations and descriptions are accurate and detailed. More than one sense was used to observe the tree.
Fall			
Winter			
Spring			
Summer			

Note: A larger version of this table is available at www.nsta.org/EurekaAgain.

References

Barretta, G. 2012. *Timeless Thomas: How Thomas Edison changed our lives*. New York: Henry Holt.

Locker, T. 2010. *John Muir: America's naturalist*. Golden, CO: Fulcrum.

Paul, M. 2015. *One plastic bag: Isatou Ceesay and the recycling women of The Gambia*. Minneapolis, MN: Millbrook.

Schwartz, C. V., C. Passmore, and B. J. Reiser. 2017. *Helping students make sense of the world using next generation science and engineering practices*. Arlington, VA: NSTA Press.

Resource

Holiday, S., P. J. Baker, and J. Frezzo. 2014. Hands-on activity: Stretching to compare properties: The plastic test. TeachEngineering. *www.teachengineering.org/activities/view/nyu_plastic_activity1*.

TREE OBSERVATION JOURNAL

NAME: _____

Draw a picture of the tree your class selected in the

FALL

Draw a picture of the tree your class selected in the

WINTER

Draw a picture of the tree your class selected in the

SPRING

Draw a picture of the tree your class selected in the

SUMMER

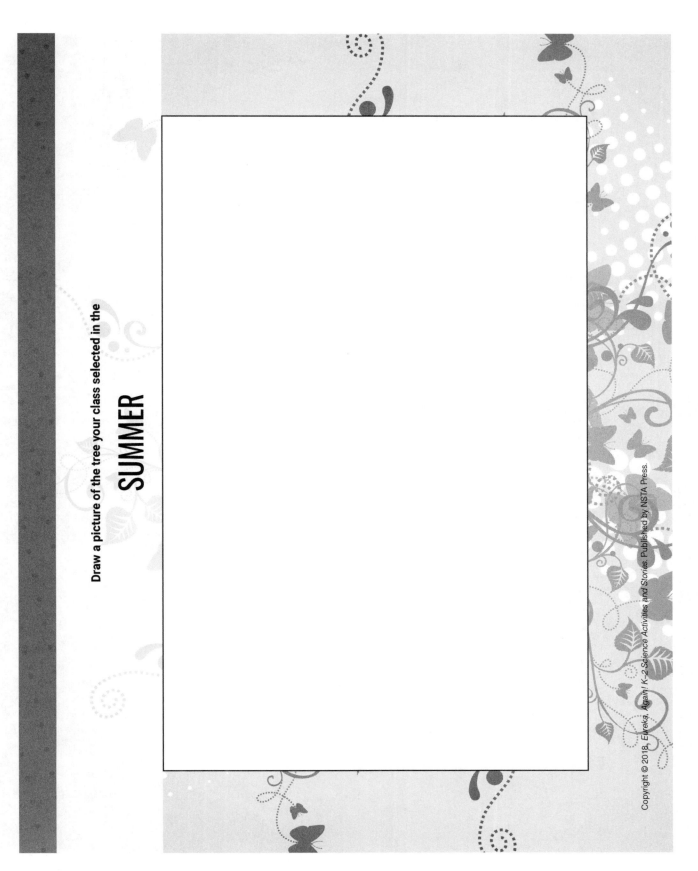

8

Engaging in Argument From Evidence

The practice of constructing explanations and designing solutions is very important in both science and engineering. This chapter will focus on three individuals—Cynthia Moss, Helen Martini, and Michael Faraday—who all engaged in arguments from evidence during their work as it relates to science. Our understanding of how elephants communicate (Moss); our understanding of the need to protect the delicate ecosystem of animal babies (Martini); and our understanding of changes in solids, liquids, and gases (Faraday) can all be credited to the practice of arguing from evidence. These scientists had to compare and refine their arguments based on the evaluation of evidence they presented. It is easy to see how the words *passionate, caring,* and *experimenter* might describe the character traits of these three scientists.

The claim, evidence, and reasoning (CER) framework will be used to describe the argumentation lessons throughout this chapter and is adapted for the youngest of learners. The adaptation includes three questions to ask students beginning in kindergarten: (1) What do you think is going on here? (the claim); (2) How do you know? (the evidence); and (3) What makes you think that? (the reasoning). Beginning science talk in classrooms from the youngest ages provides insight into how young scientists are thinking

and contemplating the world. Children may surprise you when you start asking them for more answers than you provide. Although it may seem strange to "facilitate arguments" with young students, you are actually setting the stage for science talk and scientific reasoning. Therefore, in each of these three lessons, it is important to create a situation and then let the students respond and talk as a means of developing their scientific reasoning skills.

It is your job to facilitate arguments based on evidence when teaching children how some explanations get replaced by other, more acceptable explanations in both science and engineering. This "science talk" helps students think through scientific explanations while communicating with others. Importantly, researchers have found that children also develop language and literacy skills when they have opportunities to use these skills in authentic situations.

Donna's Personal Story

One of my favorite science lessons for getting young children to engage in "science talk" is an activity that accompanies *Little Blue and Little Yellow* by Leo Lionni. The story is a simple one about two friends—Little Blue and Little Yellow—and the adventures they share. One day, they can't find one another. When they finally meet, they hug and something magical happens: They turn green. The hands-on science lesson that I use with this book is also a simple one, but it is still valuable. All you need is a straw cut into 3-in. pieces, a 5 in. × 5 in. piece of wax paper, cups, water, food coloring, and toothpicks. Place a couple drops of blue food coloring into a cup of water. Place a couple drops of yellow food coloring into another cup of water. Use the straw pieces to act as an eyedropper (by covering one end and lifting your finger to release the waterdrops). Release each color separately on the wax paper. The drops will stay in a rounded, dome-like form due to the interaction of the waterdrop with the surface of the wax paper. Use the toothpick to "carry" over each color until the colors meet—what happens? You should observe that once the little blue drop touches the little yellow drop, both drops become green. Children *love* this moment and *ooh* and *ahh* over the dramatic and instant change. This promotes science talk because children are making sense of what just happened. I always challenge my students to tell me not only what they observed (claim), how they know (evidence), and why it happened (reasoning) but also whether they can make green become yellow and blue again. I typically do the experiment before reading the story, but I have also done it the other way around—it just depends on the students and the experience I want them to have.

Key Features of Teaching the Practice of Engaging in Argument From Evidence

- Engaging in "argument from evidence" does not mean that students argue with each other; rather, it means they discuss differing interpretations of data, which model might be best, or why a question might be important to investigate.

- There are three components of scientific argumentation: claim, critique, and reconciliation.

- There are several possible ways to evaluate or critique arguments. Students can make a comparison, make an evaluative statement ("I disagree because …"), ask a question, make a counterargument, or refute the counterargument.

- Argumentation can occur in small groups or large groups, and these sort of back-and-forth conversations take time to have in a classroom setting. It's important to allow time for a verbal dialogue among students.

See Schwartz, Passmore, and Reiser (2017) for more information.

PASSIONATE

Learning About **Cynthia Moss**

Passionate (adj.): having or showing strong feelings

Lesson: Take a Close Look
Description

In this lesson, students observe three different pictures of elephants and debate whether these are from the same species (mother and baby) or from different species.

Objectives

Students will consider how the character trait of being passionate helped Cynthia Moss learn about elephants.

- In the Play portion of the lesson, students will immerse themselves in imaginative play with a partner, pretending they are scientists out in the wild studying an animal of their choice.

- Students will hear the story *A Passion for Elephants: The Real Life Adventure of Field Scientist Cynthia Moss* by Toni Buzzeo and discuss how it describes Cynthia as being passionate.

- In the Explore portion of the lesson, students will argue the evidence they gather from observation of the elephants as to whether they come from the same family or not.

- In the Discuss portion of the lesson, students will gain experience with the process of making an argument from evidence by using their "science talk."

Learning Outcomes

Students will (1) discuss what being passionate means and why being passionate is an important trait for scientists and engineers and (2) engage in student-driven discussion using the adapted CER framework.

Connections to the *NGSS*

The following sections make one set of connections between the instruction outlined in this lesson and the *NGSS*. Other valid connections are likely; however, not all possibilities are listed.

Performance Expectation	Connections to Activity
1-LS3-1: Make observations to construct an evidence-based account that young plants and animals are like, but not exactly like, their parents.	• Students will read books about elephants and watch videos to learn about elephants' parents and their offspring.

Science and Engineering Practice	Connections to Activity
Engaging in Argument From Evidence	• Students discuss the CER framework, observe three different pictures of elephants, and debate whether these are from the same species (mother and baby) or from different species.

Disciplinary Core Idea	Connections to Activity
LS1.B: Growth and Development of Organisms Adult plants and animals can have young. In many kinds of animals, parents and the offspring themselves engage in behaviors that help the offspring to survive.	• Students will read books about elephants and watch videos to learn about elephants' parents and their offspring.

Crosscutting Concept	Connections to Activity
Patterns	• Students look for patterns in elephants' body parts to explain the animals' behaviors.

Overview

In this lesson, students learn how one passionate person became a prominent and compelling advocate for elephants. When Cynthia Moss shared her knowledge and observations of elephants, she changed the way people thought about them. By reading the featured book, students will learn that men and women from all backgrounds choose careers as scientists. The scientist disposition of being passionate refers to Cynthia Moss's brave attempt to learn as much as she could about elephants.

Materials

You will need a copy of the featured book *A Passion for Elephants: The Real Life Adventure of Field Scientist Cynthia Moss* by Toni Buzzeo (2015). For the Play and Explain

**Cynthia
Moss**

portions of the activity, use a variety of books and videos of elephants for students to observe. For the Explore portion of the lesson, each group of students will need one set of Elephant Pictures A, B, and C.

Setting the Context
Play

Ask students if they have ever wondered what it would be like to be a scientist studying animals out in the wild. Tell students that you are going to learn about a scientist who spent a lot of time doing just that. Ask them to imagine an animal they would like to study and think of things they might find in the wild if they spent two weeks studying that animal. Once each child has selected his or her animal for imaginative play, have students act out a scene from their two-week pretend trip in groups of two.

Allow seven minutes for each student to engage in imaginative play about being a scientist in the wild. Encourage them to focus on three questions: (1) What is the animal? (2) Where is the animal? and (3) What is it doing?

Guided Reading

Students will be learning about elephants and what it means to engage in argument from evidence by reading *A Passion for Elephants: The Real Life Adventure of Field Scientist Cynthia Moss* by Toni Buzzeo. Introduce the book by asking, *Can you find the person on the front cover? What seems to be happening on the front cover?* Read the story aloud. Encourage students to notice and think about the challenges Cynthia Moss faced as a female scientist.

The following questions may be used to guide children's attention to detail as you read. (Page numbers reference unnumbered book pages, beginning with the title page as page 1.)

1. The first few pages of the book explain that Cynthia liked BIG things. What prompted Cynthia to want to travel to Africa? *Cynthia's college friend Penny Naylor was in Africa and wrote Cynthia letters describing the climate and culture of Africa. These letters made Cynthia want to go to Africa and see the continent for herself. She was not afraid to travel alone.*

2. **Pages 7–9:** Within weeks of arriving in Africa, Cynthia felt "home." How was she able to find a job to support herself while she was there? *Cynthia met a zoologist, Iain Douglas-Hamilton, who was studying African elephants, and she worked for him taking pictures until she began her own research project.*

3. **Pages 9–10:** Cynthia took many pictures of elephants. At first they all looked alike. How did she learn to tell the elephants apart? *She focused on their tusks and discovered that the differences in the tusks helped her identify the elephants. Some had long ivory tusks; others were curved or straight. The elephants that had broken or even missing tusks were easy to identify.*

4. **Pages 11–15:** Before long, Cynthia fell in love with elephants. What is something Cynthia loved about elephants? *Cynthia loved how big elephants are, and she loved their dusty homes. She began to give the elephants human names, and she learned about their family dynamics—which one was the mother, father, sister, and brother—by watching them. Cynthia said that elephants are like our friends because they defend each other, they care for each other, and they cooperate with each other.*

5. **Pages 20–22:** Not all humans loved elephants as much as Cynthia. Why didn't people love elephants as much as Cynthia? *Some people wanted to kill elephants just so they could profit from their ivory. Elephant tusks can be carved into statues or jewelry, and people were willing to pay others for items made from*

elephants' tusks. What did Cynthia try to do about this? *She tried to educate people about ivory and tell them that ivory is really the tooth of the elephant and therefore should not be made into other items for sale. (Teacher Note: In 1990, a global ban was passed on the sale of ivory.)*

Explore

Invite students to the carpet. Share some background information about this critically endangered species. *(Teacher Note: Africa's elephants are currently in critical danger. There are two websites you should look at with your students for the most up-to-date information: Save the Elephants* [www.savetheelephants.org] *and Elephant Voices* [www.elephantvoices.org]. *You can also view pictures of elephants on National Geographic's website* [www.nationalgeographic.com/animals/photos/elephants]*).*

THE *HOW* OF THE EXPLORE

Show students Picture A of the elephants (see p. 218). Tell students that their job is to answer the first question: *What do you think is going on here?* This is the *claim. (Teacher Note: This question prompts students to develop a claim based on evidence.)* Encourage students to summarize their observations and evidence prompted by this debate. Prompt students to use the SCUMPS (size, color, use, materials, parts, shape) model to encourage them to pay attention to detailed similarities and differences between the two elephants as they form their claim.

When students seem to have developed their claim (or a statement that answers the original question or problem), ask those students who believe that these elephants might belong to the same family to stand at the right side of the room. Invite those students who believe that the elephants are from two different families to stand at the left side of the room.

Tell students you have a second question for them: *How do you know?* This is the *evidence.* Begin by asking students to state their ideas (predictions) about the elephants and why they believe that the elephants are or are not from the same family. As they share their evidence or observations, encourage students to move from one side of the room to the other if something a classmate says causes them to change their mind about their original belief. *(Teacher Note: Students are now focused on the evidence that supports their claim).* Encourage students to point to detailed observations of the pictures to support their claim. Keep going several rounds to encourage students to continue to weigh arguments and evidence throughout the activity.

Tell students you have one last question for them: What makes you think these elephants are from the same family or not? This is the *reasoning* phase of the lesson, where students are called to justify or connect evidence to their claim. Finally, encourage students to write down or illustrate their observations and reasoning in their science notebooks.

THE *WHY* OF THE EXPLORE

This practice is about listening to each other's arguments and reasoning while making a claim based on evidence. This "science talk" helps students think through scientific explanations while communicating with others. Importantly, researchers have found that children also develop language and literacy skills when they have opportunities to use these skills in authentic situations.

Discuss

Guide students' consideration of the evidence as they make their decision about the two elephants. Encourage students to listen to each other's arguments and to feel free to change sides of the room if another student provides an argument that causes them to change their mind. *(Teacher Note: Encourage students to stick to factual evidence and to follow the SCUMPS guide [see Figure 8.1]. For example, examining the shape and size of an elephant's body—particularly the ears—provides important evidence. The two elephants in Picture A differ in terms of the length and shape of their ears. A fair argument might be, "Hold on—I noticed that the elephants each have two ears." This is one of the common characteristics. Another student might say, "Yes, they have two ears, but the shape is different, so they are different elephants." So, although students might initially assume that these elephants are parent and child, there is one important difference: the shape of the ears.)* The correct answer is that these elephants are not from the same family and are not parent and child. Hand out Elephant Pictures B and C (see pp. 219–220) and have students work in pairs to decide if the elephants in the pictures are related or not. Show videos of elephants and review books in class about elephants. You can also discuss as a class what students have learned about parent and offspring behavior.

Evaluate

Summative evaluation of this lesson will include assessment of students' understanding of (1) why being passionate is an important trait for scientists and engineers and (2) how to make an argument from evidence in science using the modified CER framework.

CHARACTER TRAIT

Encourage students to answer the following questions:

Figure 8.1

"SCUMPS" Acronym, Which Can Help Students Make Good Observations While They Gather Data to Determine Whether the Elephants Are Related

1. If Cynthia Moss had not become an advocate for elephants at the time she did, how might elephant populations be different today? *Cynthia Moss was passionate and it may be that if someone did not advocate for elephants when she did, they might have become extinct. (Teacher Note: The point here is to review Cynthia's awareness of elephants as unique, important animals in terms of one scientist's character trait.)*

2. Why is being passionate an important attribute for scientists to have? And how was Cynthia Moss passionate? *Passionate people are willing to take risks when others remain doubtful or cautious. In Cynthia's case, she set out to know all she could about elephants (even moving to a different country far away from her family and friends) when others did not even think about elephants or know enough to care about endangered animals like elephants.*

CONTENT

Encourage students to summarize their observations and evidence prompted by the elephant debate. Help students realize how the SCUMPS model helped them note similarities and differences between the two elephants. Ask students to reflect on what they are learning about the importance of evidence when it comes to scientific knowledge. Use the rubric shown in Table 8.1 to evaluate students' interactions.

Table 8.1

Assessing the CER Rubric

Criteria	Not Yet	Beginning	Developing	Secure
Claim	Student does not provide a claim.	Student provides an inaccurate claim.	Student provides a claim, but it is either inaccurate or incomplete.	Student provides a complete and accurate claim.
Evidence	Student does not provide evidence.	Student provides inaccurate evidence.	Student provides evidence, but it does not support the claim.	Student provides appropriate evidence suitable to support the claim.
Reasoning	Student does not provide reasoning.	Student provides inaccurate reasoning.	Student provides reasoning, but it is not connected to evidence.	Student offers reasoning that connects evidence to the claim.

ELEPHANT PICTURE A

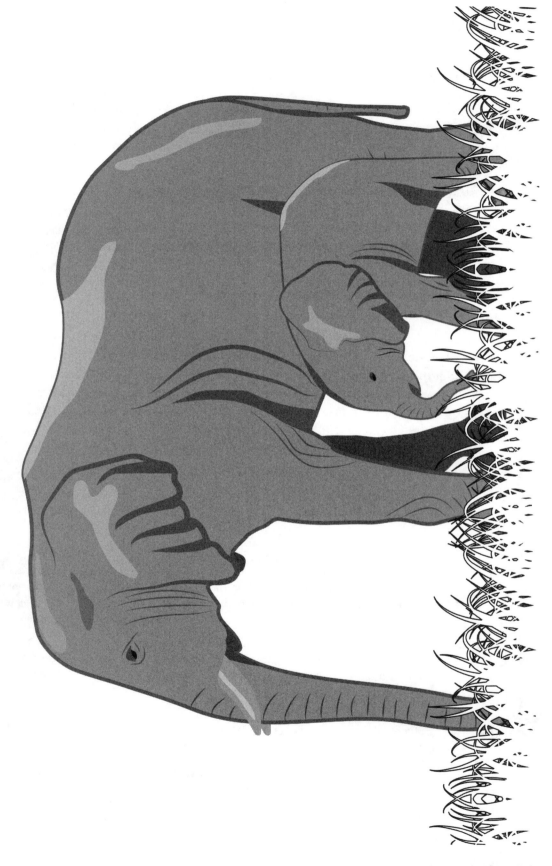

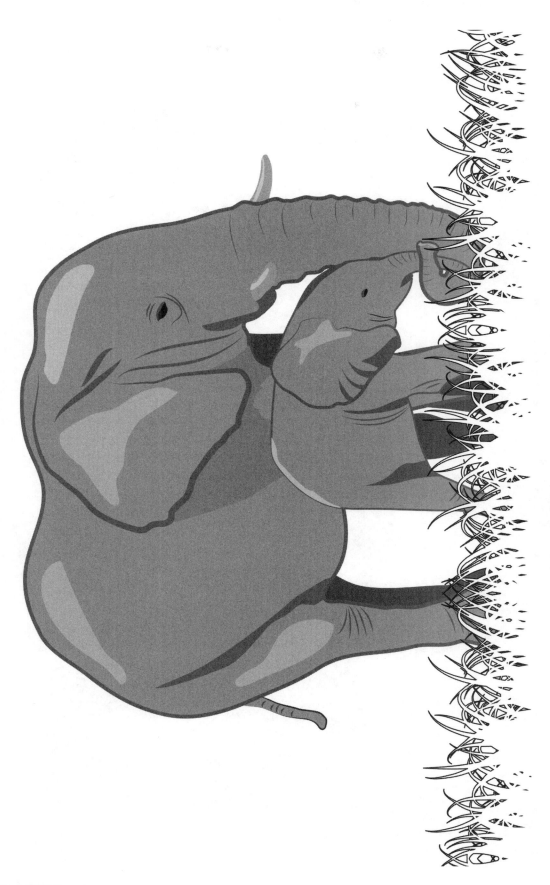

ELEPHANT PICTURE B

ELEPHANT PICTURE C

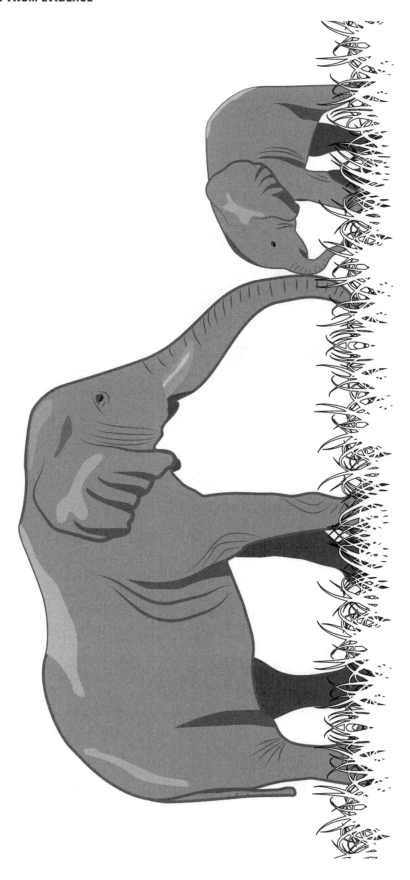

SCIENTISTS AND ENGINEERS ARE

CARING

Learning About **Helen Martini**

Caring (adj.): feeling or showing concern for other people or animals

Lesson: Worms Alike and Different
Description

In this lesson, students observe two types of worms and debate whether they are living or nonliving using the modified CER framework.

Objectives

Students will consider how the character trait of being caring helped Helen Martini to rescue baby animals and provide adequate spaces to care for them in zoos.

- In the Play portion of the lesson, students will immerse themselves in imaginative play with a partner, pretending they are caring for a wild baby animal that they have found.

- Students will hear the story *Mother to Tigers* by George Ella Lyon and discuss how it describes Helen Martini as being caring.

- In the Explore portion of the lesson, students will argue the evidence they gather from their observations of worms as to whether they are living or not.

- In the Discuss portion of the lesson, students will gain experience with the process of making an argument from evidence by using their "science talk."

Learning Outcomes

Students will (1) discuss what being caring means and why being caring is an important trait for scientists and engineers and (2) engage in student-driven discussion using the adapted CER framework to engage in argument from evidence.

Connections to the *NGSS*

The following sections make one set of connections between the instruction outlined in this lesson and the *NGSS*. Other valid connections are likely; however, not all possibilities are listed.

Performance Expectation	Connections to Activity
K-LS1-1: Use observations to describe patterns of what plants and animals (including humans) need to survive.	• Students make observations about living worms and gummy worms.

Science and Engineering Practice	Connections to Activity
Engaging in Argument From Evidence	• Students use the CER framework to compare living worms and gummy worms.

Disciplinary Core Idea	Connections to Activity
LS1.C: Organization for Matter and Energy Flow in Organisms • All animals need food in order to live and grow. They obtain their food from plants or from other animals. • Plants need water and light to live and grow.	• Students identify the need for food as one of the differences between living and nonliving animals.

Crosscutting Concept	Connections to Activity
Systems and System Models	• Students learn that living things have systems and nonliving things do not.

Overview

In this lesson, students learn how one person with a caring spirit created a way for zoos to take care of baby animals. Helen Martini shared her ideas with others and challenged the way people thought about caring for young animals. By reading the featured book, students will learn that men and women from all backgrounds choose careers as scientists. The character trait of being caring refers to Helen Martini's attempts to solve a problem. In the hands-on activity portion of this lesson, students will observe worms and gather evidence to determine if they are living or nonliving.

Helen Martini

Materials

You will need a copy of the featured book *Mother to Tigers* by George Ella Lyon (2003); one package of gummy worms; one container of real worms (night crawlers) from your local pet store (they range in price from $2.50 to $4.99); two of the same containers with lids for each student group; a small bag of soil; scissors; and safety goggles.

Safety Notes

(1) Remind all students that personal protective equipment should be worn during the setup, hands-on, and takedown segments of the activity. (2) Use caution when working with scissors—they are sharp and can cut or puncture skin. (3) Never eat

food that is used in a class activity. (4) Wash hands with soap and water upon completing this activity.

Setting the Context
Play

Ask students how they know if an animal is living or not. *(Teacher Note: Create a cube from a square tissue box by covering each side with paper or wrapping it like a present. Find pictures of both living and nonliving things and paste or tape these to each side. Laminate the entire cube if possible.)* **Ask** students to sit in a circle on the carpet. Roll the cube to one student at a time and ask them to tell you what they see on the cube and whether it is living or nonliving (see Figure 8.2).

Figure 8.2

Living/Nonliving Cube for the Play Portion of the Activity

Dialogue with students about what processes scientists might follow to make the educated guesses they make. Start to keep a class list of how to tell if something is living (e.g., it moves from place to place) in a central location in your classroom.

Guided Reading

Students will be learning about engaging in argument from evidence and about the work of a scientist who was especially caring by reading *Mother to Tigers.* Introduce the book by asking, *Can you find the person on the front cover? What does it look like is happening on the front cover?* Read the story aloud. Encourage students to notice and think about the challenges Helen Martini might have faced as an activist and scientist.

The following questions may be used to guide children's attention to detail as you read. (Page numbers reference unnumbered book pages, beginning with the title page as page 1.)

1. **Pages 1–4:** The book asks the reader to imagine that he or she is an abandoned cub. What was unusual in how Helen Martini took care of the young tiger cub she found? *Helen cared for the cub as if it were a small baby, fixing it warm milk and putting the cub on a pillow on her lap. These are not "normal" human–tiger interactions. (Teacher Note: Ask students how their mothers care for them when they are sick. You should get a variety of answers.)*

2. **Pages 5–17:** Helen and her husband Fred never planned on caring for animals. They found themselves unable to have a baby. They were drawn to learning and caring for all kinds of animals, and soon their apartment filled up with animals. Where did Helen's husband find the perfect job? *Helen's husband became a zookeeper at the Bronx Zoo. Each night he would take home animals, and Helen would research that particular type of animal. She would then read to her husband about the proper care for each animal.*

3. **Pages 18–20:** After Helen cared for the tigers and they grew healthy and strong, she could no longer keep them in her apartment. What did Helen decide to do for zoo babies that needed special care? *Even though the tiger babies Helen and Fred cared for grew up healthy and strong, Helen felt that there ought to be a place where other zoo babies could go to receive special care away from the adult animals. She asked for a room at the zoo and agreed to do all the work to set up the space for the baby animals. The book says that "she begged, borrowed, and bought everything she needed"—this was a display of her caring for baby animals. (Teacher Note: In 1932, Helen married Fred Martini. Fred was hired by the Bronx Zoo in 1940, and in 1942 he brought home MacArthur the tiger cub. Word spread quickly about the woman raising tiger cubs in her apartment, and the news media published several stories and photographs.)*

4. **Pages 22–24:** Before Helen arrived, no tiger born at the zoo had ever survived. How did Helen become the first female zookeeper in the history of the Bronx Zoo? *At first Helen did not get paid, but her nursery filled up quickly. Helen did not mind not getting paid at first because she was following her passion to care for sick baby animals. Eventually, however, the zoo paid her for her work. (Teacher Note: In August 1944, the first year of the Bronx Zoo opening, Helen was put on the payroll as the first female zookeeper. She said of her work, "Every day is just like Christmas. Anything can happen.")*

5. **Pages 24–26:** Helen's cubs had cubs that were sent to zoos all around the world. The idea of a nursery soon spread, too. How did Helen change the way zoos cared for their young? *More and more zoos started including a nursery on site. (Teacher Note: After she began the zoo nursery in June 1944, the loving care she gave her baby cats was extended to everything from addaxes to yapoks.)*

Making Sense
Explore

Invite students to remain seated at their tables. Clear their tables off completely so they will not have any distractions.

THE *HOW* OF THE EXPLORE

Tell students you will be placing two containers at each table. Their job is to answer the question, *Which one is living and which one is nonliving?* See Figures 8.3 and 8.4. *(Teacher Note: This question prompts students to develop a claim based on evidence. For this activity, it will be very easy for students to distinguish which container has the living worms, but the lesson will become more challenging when they have to provide evidence for their claim.)* Encourage students to summarize their observations and evidence prompted by this debate. Place both containers (which should both have breathing holes on their covers) on each student table. Instruct students to remove the covers and observe the containers when the entire class is ready.

When students seem to have developed their claim (*Which one is living and which one is nonliving?*), ask students how they know. Begin by asking students to state their ideas (predictions) about the worms and how they can tell whether the worms are living or nonliving (see Figure 8.5). As they share their evidence or observations, encourage students to give you as many pieces of evidence as possible. *(Teacher Note: Students are now focused on the* evidence—*the data that support their claim.)* Tell students that you have one last question for them: What makes you think these worms are living or nonliving? This is the *reasoning* phase of the lesson, where students are called to justify or connect evidence to their claim. Finally, encourage students to write about or illustrate their observations and reasoning in their science notebooks.

THE *WHY* OF THE EXPLORE

The more opportunities you can provide to students to engage in science talk, the more likely they will be to engage in this kind of talk independently later on. Using the CER framework allows students to engage in this kind of dialogue when presented with a challenge—in this case, living and nonliving worms.

Figure 8.3

How to Prepare the Two Containers So They Seem Identical to Students' Containers

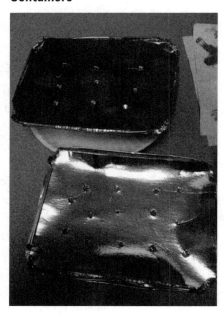

Figure 8.4

Bird's-Eye View of Two Containers

Discuss

Encourage students to summarize their *reasoning*—their observations and questions prompted by this investigation. *(Teacher Note: Young children often have difficulty characterizing things as living or nonliving. For example, they tend to describe anything that moves as alive. They also do not yet understand the cycle of life [birth, growth, death] and often hold the misconception that anything that has died is nonliving. In science, living is used to describe anything that is or has ever been alive [e.g., a puppy, a plant seed, a dead skunk, a log]; nonliving is used to describe anything that is not now nor has ever been alive [e.g., a rock, a pencil, a glass, a hill]. Over time, students will begin to understand that all living things grow, breathe, reproduce, excrete, respond to stimuli, and have similar basic needs such as nourishment. In time, students will come to understand that all living things are made up of cells.)*

Students' reasoning should be a justification that connects their points of evidence to a claim. Reasoning shows why the data count as evidence by using appropriate and sufficient scientific principles. Introduce discussion about how scientists know whether things are living or not. Record traits of living things on the board and make a class poem or song to help students remember this experience (see Figure 8.6).

Evaluate

Summative evaluation of this lesson will include assessment of students' understanding of (1) why being caring is an important trait for scientists and engineers and (2) evidence and how to make an argument in science using the CER modified framework.

Figure 8.5

Students Making Observations About the Living Worms During the Explore Portion of the Lesson

Figure 8.6

Poem/Song Created During the Discuss Portion of the Lesson

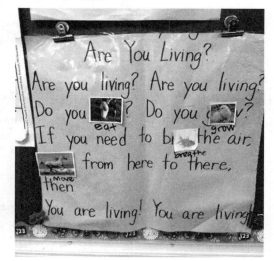

CHARACTER TRAIT

Encourage students to answer the following questions:

1. If Helen Martini had not created a nursery for animal babies, do you think someone else would have? *Someone might have eventually thought of these ideas, but Helen Martini was especially caring and thought of these things before anyone else did. (Teacher Note: The point here is to review Helen's caring personality and her ability to visualize and build a place to help young animal babies thrive and grow.)*

2. Why is being caring an important attribute for scientists to have? And how was Helen Martini caring? *Caring people are passionate about their work. They find a way to achieve a solution if presented with one. Helen nurtured and cared for the tigers at her home until a place was created for them at the zoo (or, nursery). Because she cared for the tigers, she found a way to solve the problem of being responsible for them before there was a designated place to do so.*

CONTENT

Encourage students to find ways to explore the characteristics of living things. Have students find two or three pictures of living and nonliving things and identify their common features. Ask students to record their claims, evidence, and reasoning about the worms in their science notebooks. Use the rubric shown in Table 8.2 to evaluate their CER frameworks.

Table 8.2

Assessing the CER Rubric

Criteria	Not Yet	Beginning	Developing	Secure
Claim	Student does not provide a claim.	Student provides an inaccurate claim.	Student provides a claim, but it is either inaccurate or incomplete.	Student provides a complete and accurate claim.
Evidence	Student does not provide evidence.	Student provides inaccurate evidence.	Student provides evidence, but it does not support the claim.	Student provides appropriate evidence suitable to support the claim.
Reasoning	Student does not provide reasoning.	Student provides inaccurate reasoning.	Student provides reasoning, but it is not connected to evidence.	Student offers reasoning that connects evidence to the claim.

EXPERIMENTERS

Learning About **Michael Faraday**

Experimenter (n.): a person who tries out new ideas, methods, or activities

Lesson: Reverse Me Not
Description

In this lesson, students will use the modified CER framework to discuss changes in the state of matter.

Objectives

Students will consider how the experimenter character trait is seen in Michael Faraday's ability to ask questions and design simple experiments to find answers.

- In the Play portion of the lesson, students will complete a listening activity about the states of matter of water.

- Students will hear the story *Burn: Michael Faraday's Candle* by Darcy Pattison and discuss how it relates to the word *experimenter* as a character trait.

- In the Explore portion of the lesson, students will make observations about melting an ice cube, melting ice cream (or a chocolate bar), popping popcorn, and toasting bread.

- In the Discuss portion of the lesson, students will use the modified CER framework to discuss the changes in matter they observed.

Learning Outcomes

Students will (1) discuss what being an experimenter means and why being an experimenter is an important trait for scientists and engineers and (2) observe the process of melting an ice cube, melting ice cream (or a chocolate bar), popping popcorn, and toasting bread using the modified CER framework.

Connections to the *NGSS*

The following sections make one set of connections between the instruction outlined in this lesson and the *NGSS*. Other valid connections are likely; however, not all possibilities are listed.

Performance Expectation	Connections to Activity
2-PS1-4: Construct an argument with evidence that some changes caused by heating or cooling can be reversed and some cannot.	• Students will make observations about melting an ice cube, melting ice cream (or a chocolate bar), popping popcorn, and toasting bread and will record their findings as to whether the heating and/or cooling process is reversible.

Science and Engineering Practice	Connections to Activity
Engaging in Argument From Evidence	• Students will make predictions as to which changes are reversible and which ones are not using the CER modified framework.

Disciplinary Core Idea	Connections to Activity
PS1.A: Structure and Properties of Matter Different properties are suited to different purposes. • A great variety of objects can be built up from a small set of pieces. • Different kinds of matter exist and many of them can be either solid or liquid, depending on temperature. Matter can be described and classified by its observable properties.	• Students will make observations about melting an ice cube, melting ice cream (or a chocolate bar), popping popcorn, and toasting bread and will describe the matter of each in relation to temperature change.

Crosscutting Concept	Connections to Activity
Cause and Effect	• Students observe cause and effect in the following changes in matter: melting an ice cube, melting ice cream (or a chocolate bar), popping popcorn, and toasting bread.

Michael Faraday

Overview

In this lesson, students learn how one person used the knowledge he acquired by experimenting to lecture about science and made the lives of children better by sharing his experiments with many people. By reading the featured book, students will learn that men and women from all backgrounds choose careers as scientists. The trait of being an experimenter refers to Michael Faraday's desire to learn about matter.

Materials

You will need a copy of the featured book *Burn: Michael Faraday's Candle* by Darcy Pattison (2016). For the Play portion of the lesson, you will need the Teapot Listening

Activity worksheet (see p. 236); white drawing paper; and colored pencils, crayons, or markers. For the Explore portion of the lesson, you will need the Changes Activity worksheet (see pp. 237–240); an ice cube on a plate or tray; ice cream (or a chocolate bar) on a plate (or in a bowl); popping popcorn kernels in a bowl; a popcorn machine; a toaster; and bread for toasting on a plate.

Safety Notes

(1) Immediately wipe up spilled water—it creates a slip-and-fall hazard. (2) Never eat any food used in an activity.

Setting the Context
Play

Pass out white or plain drawing paper to students. Tell them that this is a *listening* activity. You will read to them from a story and ask them to draw something on their paper. Ask students what might be challenging about this. *(Teacher Note: Some students might say that it might be hard to use only their ears instead of their eyes for this activity.)* Follow the directions on the Teapot Listening Activity worksheet (p. 236).

Guided Reading

Students will be learning about Michael Faraday, a man with a gift for lecturing about science and sharing his experiments with large groups of children. In this way, he shared his passion and knowledge about science with many others. Introduce the book by asking students, *Can you find the person on the front cover? What does it look like is happening on the front cover?* Read the story aloud. Encourage students to notice and think about the challenges Michael Faraday might have faced. This book is unique in that it is actually an adaptation of one of his famous lectures explaining why a candle burns. *(Teacher Note: Explain to students that you won't be able to use a burning candle in the classroom but that there will be an opportunity to observe the changing states of matter.)*

The following questions may be used to guide children's attention to detail as you read. (Page numbers reference unnumbered book pages, beginning with the title page as page 1.)

1. **Pages 1–12:** Michael Faraday described a burning candle with such detail. He said that the melted part of the candle near the wick was "a cup of fuel." What did the cup of fuel do to the flame? *The cup of fuel was burned candle wax that was formed by the rising air outside the candle.*

2. **Pages 13–18:** Michael described capillary action in his lecture. In the case of a burning candle, what does capillary action mean? *Capillary action happens*

Figure 8.7

Sample Experiment Setup

(A)  (B)

when two things won't dissolve into each other but instead bind together. This describes properties of matter.

3. **Pages 19–26:** Why do you think people attended Michael Faraday's lectures? *They attended his lectures to learn about science.*

Making Sense
Explore

In this lesson, students will be exploring four changes in matter to try to determine if a change is reversible or not. You will need to pass out the Changes Activity worksheet for each student or group of students. This experiment will take several days. Select one change observation a day—it does not matter which one you start with. Prompt students to make a prediction of what they think will happen once the change occurs—will it be reversible or irreversible? Have students complete the prediction section on the Changes Activity worksheet for the experiment you decide to do for that particular day. *(Teacher Note: This activity prompts students to develop a claim based on evidence. For this activity, it should be very easy for them to distinguish the type of change, but it may become more challenging when they have to provide evidence for their claim.)* Encourage students to summarize their observations and evidence. Figure 8.7 shows what the experiment (ice, chocolate bar, and ice cream) might look like when it is set up in your classroom.

When students seem to have developed their claim, ask them *How do you know?* This is their *evidence.* Begin by asking students to state their ideas (predictions) about the changes and how they can tell they are sorted into the correct category (reversible and irreversible). As they share their evidence or observations, encourage students to give you as many pieces of evidence as possible. *(Teacher Note: Students are now focused on the evidence—the data that support their claim.)* Tell students that you have one last question for them: What makes you think so? This is the *reasoning* phase of the lesson, where students are called to justify or connect evidence to their claim. Finally, encourage students to write about or illustrate their observations and reasoning in their science notebooks.

Discuss

Use the Changes Activity worksheet to begin science talk about the changes. Talk through each of the examples and ask students if they agree as a group about whether each change is reversible or irreversible.

Evaluate

Summative evaluation of this lesson will include assessment of students' understanding of (1) the character trait of being an experimenter and (2) their observations of melting an ice cube, melting ice cream (or a chocolate bar), popping popcorn, and toasting bread using the modified CER framework.

CHARACTER TRAIT

Why is being an experimenter an important character trait for scientists to have? Ask students to work in groups to tell each other about a time when they were experimenters. Discuss students' answers as a class.

CONTENT

Encourage students to find ways to share their observations. Have students share two or three observations about change reversals and irreversibles. Ask students to record their claims, evidence, and reasoning about the changes in their science notebooks. Use the rubric shown in Table 8.3 to evaluate their CER frameworks.

Table 8.3 ——————————————————————————————————————

Assessing the CER Rubric

Criteria	Not Yet	Beginning	Developing	Secure
Claim	Student does not provide a claim.	Student provides an inaccurate claim.	Student provides a claim, but it is either inaccurate or incomplete.	Student provides a complete and accurate claim.
Evidence	Student does not provide evidence.	Student provides inaccurate evidence.	Student provides evidence, but it does not support the claim.	Student provides appropriate evidence suitable to support the claim.
Reasoning	Student does not provide reasoning.	Student provides inaccurate reasoning.	Student provides reasoning, but it is not connected to evidence.	Student offers reasoning that connects evidence to the claim.

References

Buzzeo, T. 2015. *A Passion for elephants: The real life adventure of field scientist Cynthia Moss.* New York: Dial Books.

Lionni, L. 2017. *Little blue and little yellow.* Decorah, IA: Dragonfly Books.

Lyon, G. E. 2003. *Mother to tigers.* New York: Atheneum Books for Young Readers.

Pattison, D. 2016. *Burn: Michael Faraday's candle.* Little Rock, AR: Mims House.

Schwartz, C. V., C. Passmore, and B. J. Reiser. 2017. *Helping students make sense of the world using next generation science and engineering practices.* Arlington, VA: NSTA Press.

Resources

Ma Daemicke, S. 2018. *Cao Chong weighs an elephant.* Mount Pleasant, SC: Arbordale Publishing.

Roy, K. 2018. *How to be an elephant: Growing up in the African wild.* New York: David Macaulay Studio.

TEAPOT LISTENING ACTIVITY

Have students prepared to do this activity with a blank piece of drawing paper (9 × 12 in., if possible) and some art materials such as crayons, colored pencils, or markers. Here is what you should say to your students and what you should do as they work. Be sure to pause after each instruction so students have time to draw. Some extended pauses are indicated in brackets.

This is a listening activity. You will be given a series of directions, and you should listen to the directions to the best of your ability. Each picture will be each person's own creative masterpiece; therefore, it is not important for yours to look like your neighbor's.

You have a blank paper in front of you on your desk. Begin by drawing a teapot at the center. The sprout of the teapot should be to the left.

[Wait ... and walk around the room.]

Decorate your teapot and pretend it is boiling. Draw some steam coming out of the teapot.

At the top of your paper, draw an ice cube.

[Wait ... and walk around the room.]

In the east and west locations, of your paper draw a cup of water.

[Wait ... and walk around the room.]

Now draw arrows (in pencil) in between each of the pictures.

Use your red crayon to trace over the arrow to show that heat is added to water to produce a change.
Now use your blue crayon to trace over the arrow to show that heat is taken away to produce a change.
We have all experienced changes with water. Water is matter, and matter can take different forms: solid, liquid, or gas.
Label the solid, liquid, and gas to the best of your ability on each picture.

[Wait ... and walk around the room.]

CHANGES ACTIVITY WORKSHEET

Prediction (circle one)

I think the change will be   reversible   irreversible

This is what we did:

_____

_____

_____

_____

This is what we saw:

_____

_____

_____

_____

Ice Cube

Name: _____

CHANGES ACTIVITY WORKSHEET

Prediction (circle one)

I think the change will be   **reversible**   **irreversible**

This is what we did:

_____
_____
_____
_____

This is what we saw:

_____
_____
_____
_____

Ice Cream

CHANGES ACTIVITY WORKSHEET

Prediction (circle one)

I think the change will be   reversible   irreversible

This is what we did:

_____

_____

_____

_____

This is what we saw:

_____

_____

_____

_____

Popcorn Kernel

Name: _____

CHANGES ACTIVITY WORKSHEET

Prediction (circle one)

I think the change will be   reversible   irreversible

This is what we did:

_____

_____

_____

This is what we saw:

_____

_____

_____

Bread/Toast

9

Obtaining, Evaluating, and Communicating Information

The practice of obtaining, evaluating, and communicating information is germane to both science and engineering. This chapter will focus on three scientists—Leonardo da Vinci, Katherine Sessions, and Elizabeth Blackwell—who all obtained, evaluated, and communicated information in the work they did to better society. The amazing flying creations that were invented years before their time (da Vinci), the appreciation of different kinds of trees in our environment (Sessions), and challenging gender stereotypes in science careers (Blackwell) improved the lives of many people. It is easy to see why the words *inventive, generous,* and *determined* best define the character traits of these three individuals. We believe that helping your students to identify each of these traits will allow you to humanize the work and procedures of science and engineering while you teach science lessons to your students.

The *Next Generation of Science Standards* (*NGSS*; NGSS Lead States 2013) expect students to be critical consumers of information. This requires not only the ability to read and understand reports in the media but also the ability to be critical of that information. It is important for students to be able to understand science and engineering methodologies so they can recognize flaws in experimental design when they research issues on the internet and in the press as adults. Therefore, it is

important for elementary students to gather data and understand what makes an investigation valid; in the classroom, this is called a *fair test*. The concept of knowing what does and does not make a fair test will carry over to future science understanding and, ultimately, science communication. One of the best ways to facilitate and reinforce the importance of data collection, evaluation, and communication is to do science and become scientists and engineers in K–2 classrooms.

In the K–2 classroom, this begins with communicating information or designing solutions with others both verbally and in written form. Children should be encouraged to use their prior knowledge and prior observations to communicate new information. Students should be encouraged to find information in grade-appropriate texts and/or media to determine patterns in the natural world. Likewise, they should also seek information that will help them answer their scientific questions.

Donna's Personal Story

The practice of obtaining, evaluating, and communicating information is one that is becoming extremely important in our information age. Today even students in the youngest grades have iPads in their classrooms (and some students have them at home). As a result, information is available to students in a way that we have never experienced before in education. One does not need to be a scientist to discriminate information from the media—we need this skill to be productive members of society. Children need to be taught how to obtain information from credible sources, how to evaluate it, how to compare these sources with other sources of information, and—most importantly—how to communicate this information to others. In upper elementary grades, global warming, heart disease, and cancer would be appropriate topics to gain experience with this practice. With grades K–2, we have to think of more developmentally appropriate ways to implement this practice, such as with Pokémon cards or fidget spinners (which are discussed in this chapter). It's never too early to teach children how to be resourceful and how to discriminate between sources when acquiring information.

Key Features to Remember When Teaching the Practice of Obtaining, Evaluating, and Communicating Information

- Obtain information from a variety of sources (e.g., websites, books, speeches, magazines).

- Evaluate the information to determine whether it is scientifically credible (and/or useful to the project or the question you are trying to answer).

- Communicate information—this includes students sharing ideas, updates, and findings about their project in a classroom setting.

See Schwartz, Passmore, and Reiser (2017) for more information.

SCIENTISTS AND ENGINEERS ARE
INVENTIVE

Inventive (adj.): having the ability to create or design new things or to think originally

Lesson: Fantastic Fidget Spinners
Description

In this lesson, students will plan and conduct an investigation to provide evidence of the effects of balanced and unbalanced forces on the motion of an object.

Objectives

Students will consider how the character trait of being inventive helped Leonardo da Vinci design inventions that would foreshadow those of modern times.

- In the Play portion of the lesson, students will play with fidget spinners and talk about motion.

- Students will hear the story *Neo Leo: The Ageless Ideas of Leonardo da Vinci* by Gene Barretta and discuss how it relates to the word *inventive*.

- In the Explore portion of the lesson, students will design a fidget spinner and test it.

- In the Discuss portion of the lesson, students will draw conclusions about their fidget spinners.

Learning Outcomes

Students will (1) discuss what being inventive means and why being inventive is an important trait for scientists and engineers and (2) compare their fidget spinners and demonstrate their understanding of how the shape and weight relate to the number of continuous rotations in one minute.

Connections to the *NGSS*

The following sections make one set of connections between the instruction outlined in this lesson and the *NGSS*. Other valid connections are likely; however, not all possibilities are listed.

Performance Expectation	Connections to Activity
K-2-ETS1-2: Develop a simple sketch, drawing, or physical model to illustrate how the shape of an object helps it function as needed to solve a given problem.	• Students will develop a fidget spinner that will revolve.
Science and Engineering Practice	**Connections to Activity**
Obtaining, Evaluating, and Communicating Information	• Students observe fidget spinners in class and discuss the scientific principles behind how they work; then, students develop their own fidget spinners from the materials provided.
Disciplinary Core Idea	**Connections to Activity**
ETS1.B: Developing Possible Solutions Designs can be conveyed through sketches, drawings, or physical models. These representations are useful in communicating ideas for a problem's solutions to other people.	• Students observe the pattern of motion of the fidget spinner they created by (a fair test) timing the spinner for one minute and counting the number of rotations.
Crosscutting Concept	**Connections to Activity**
Cause and Effect	• Students observe and discuss cause and effect as it relates to the shape and function of their fidget spinner.

Overview

In this lesson, students learn how one inventive person—Leonardo da Vinci—was an artist, inventor, engineer, and scientist. Leonardo was an extraordinary person who thought of innovations well ahead of his time. By reading the featured book, students will learn that men and women from all backgrounds choose careers as scientists. The character trait of being inventive refers to Leonardo's unique thinking and creative attempts to innovate new ideas.

Leonardo da Vinci

Materials

You will need a copy of the featured book *Neo Leo: The Ageless Ideas of Leonardo da Vinci* by Gene Barretta (2016). In the Play portion of the lesson, students will need fidget spinners (have students who have them bring in theirs from home). In the Explore portion of the lesson, students will need a variety of materials to create their fidget spinners, such as cardboard, newspaper, construction paper, buttons, nuts and bolts, washers, card stock, straws, coffee stirrers, tape (Scotch tape, duct tape, or painter's tape), scissors, and safety goggles. In the Discuss portion of the lesson, students will need the Fantastic Fidget Spinners worksheet (see p. 250) to record their measurements and data trials.

Safety Notes

(1) Remind all students that personal protective equipment should be worn during the setup, hands-on, and takedown segments of the activity. (2) Watch for sharp edges on scissors, nuts, bolts, coffee stirrers, and so forth—these can cut or puncture skin.

Setting the Context
Guided Reading

Students will be learning about Leonardo da Vinci, a scientist who was inventive and paved the way for many modern inventions, by reading *Neo Leo: The Ageless Ideas of Leonardo da Vinci*. Students will connect da Vinci's efforts with modern-day inventions. Introduce the book by asking, *What seems to be happening on the front cover?* Read the story aloud. Encourage students to notice and think about the challenges Leonardo da Vinci may have faced as a visionary with hundreds of ideas before his time. *(Teacher Note: This book is not in the typical style of a read-aloud, and you may prefer to read one or two pages a day to your class instead of reading the entire book all at once. Take some time to preview this book to decide how to best meet the needs of your students.)*

The following questions may be used to guide children's attention to detail as you read. (Page numbers reference unnumbered book pages, beginning with the title page as page 1.)

1. **Pages 1–4:** Most of Leonardo's inventions were not built during his lifetime. The book says this was because the designs were too expensive, too sophisticated, or too controversial. Where did Leonardo's inventions live for many years? *His inventions lived as sketches in his notebooks. Each page in this book shows sketches of his ideas, even though it would take many years before these were built or created.*

2. **Pages 5–8 and 17–18:** These pages show three different flying machines Leonardo drew. Why do you think he was so interested in making people fly? *He watched birds and wanted to make people fly like birds flew. (Teacher Note: Students' answers may vary for this question.)*

3. Have the students go through the pages showing Leonardo's inventions and the modern-day versions of his ideas. Which do they think most closely resemble the ideas Leonardo had? Which least resemble the ideas Leonardo had? Why? *(Teacher Note: Answers will vary here, but ask students to make observations and provide evidence for their reasoning.)*

Play

In this lesson, students will be learning about the science of motion as it relates to their fidget spinners. Provide some fidget spinners for children to test and explore. Ask students to record three observations about the fidget spinners in their science notebooks (if you have enough fidget spinners, allow students to work in small groups). Ask the students if they have any idea how fidget spinners work. Once students have had an opportunity to play and explore with the fidget spinners, ask them to turn to pages 27 and 28 of the book *Neo Leo*. Ask students to start to imagine inventions—for this lesson, flying machines. Scientists and engineers often draw their ideas first before creating them. Ask students to capture their images in a sketch.

Making Sense
Explore

Set out all the materials for this lesson. If you have a large class, it might be best to have students work in groups or pairs. These directions will apply to both individuals and groups. This activity will take several days. *(Teacher Note: Our class used the bottom portion of drink holders from fast food restaurants [see Figure 9.1] because they were the perfect shape for a fidget spinner.)*

THE *HOW* OF THE EXPLORE

Have students come up with three observations or things they know about fidget spinners (this can be based on their prior experience from the Play portion of the lesson or based on previous experience). Once they have created their lists, have them jot down some ideas about the fidget spinners they are going to create. This can be how the fidget spinner they want to invent will be like other fidget spinners (Figure 9.2) or different from other fidget spinners (some students might say their fidget spinners will be

Figure 9.1

Fast Food Drink Tray (With the Bottom Four Pieces Missing) Used to Create Fidget Spinners

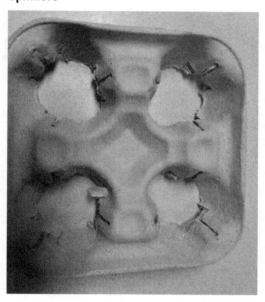

Figure 9.2

Example of a Fidget Spinner

"balanced" or will have "weights"). Then provide students with drawing paper to sketch out their ideas for the fidget spinner. Encourage students to draw and label the fidget spinner they would like to design that will spin the most continuous revolutions in one minute. Have students communicate their ideas to the class with a series of presentations about their designs to meet the challenge. Set aside enough time for students to create physical models of their fidget spinners to build and test. Use the Fantastic Fidget Spinners worksheet (see p. 250) to record data from the trials once the students are finished with their models.

THE *WHY* OF THE EXPLORE

This Explore activity allows students to communicate information or design ideas and/or solutions with others in oral and/or written forms using models, drawing, writing, or numbers. These design ideas should provide details about scientific ideas and practices.

Discuss

Ask students to share the results and observations from their trials. Try to group together observations based on the materials used. For example, all the students who used cardboard—what were their observations? How were the fidget spinners alike? How were they different? How did they compare to fidget spinners made of construction paper or card stock? Gather students' observations in such a way that the entire class can observe (such as on chart paper at the front of the classroom) and guide students to provide evidence to back up their observations. Discuss what a "fair test" is and explain that the trials in this lesson were fair tests.

Evaluate

Summative evaluation of this lesson will include assessment of students' understanding of (1) the character trait of being inventive, (2) how to compare fidget spinners, and (3) how to demonstrate their understanding of how the shape and weight relate to the number of continuous rotations in one minute.

CHARACTER TRAIT

Inventive thinking allows scientists to generate new ideas from ordinary experiences. Therefore, being inventive is an important character trait for scientists. Encourage students to answer the following questions:

1. How was Leonardo da Vinci inventive? *Leonardo created many innovations that were before their time. He did this by reflecting on his ideas and drawing them before creating them.*

2. How important do you think Leonardo's notebook was to him? *His notebook was probably very important to him because it held all his ideas and dreams of the*

future. Leonardo was not only a scientist and inventor; he also used mathematics and art to bring his images to life.

3. Ask students to pair up and tell each other about a time they invented something.

CONTENT

The idea here is that through several trial-and-error experiences, students will be able to communicate the intentions of their designs, the data they collected, and how their fidget spinners compared with those of other students in the class.

Name: _____

FANTASTIC FIDGET SPINNERS

Trial	Number of Spins in a Minute

SCIENTISTS AND ENGINEERS ARE
GENEROUS

Learning About **Katherine Sessions**

Generous (adj.): liberal in giving

Lesson: Trees Are All Around
Description

In this lesson, students will engage in a scientific experiment and observe how light affects a plant leaf.

Objectives

Students will consider how the characteristic of being generous helped Kate Sessions change a city forever.

- In the Play portion of the lesson, students will go outside, find a leaf, and answer five questions about it.

- Students will hear the story *The Tree Lady: The True Story of How One Tree-Loving Woman Changed a City Forever* by H. Joseph Hopkins and discuss the word *generous* as a character trait.

- In the Explore portion of the lesson, students will design an experiment to test what would happen if a leaf did not receive sunlight.

- In the Discuss portion of the lesson, students will draw conclusions about a leaf that did receive sunlight for two weeks.

Learning Outcomes

Students will (1) discuss what being generous means and why being generous is an important trait for scientists and engineers and (2) obtain, evaluate, and communicate what plants need to survive.

Connections to the *NGSS*

The following sections make one set of connections between the instruction outlined in this lesson and the *NGSS*. Other valid connections are likely; however, not all possibilities are listed.

Performance Expectation	Connections to Activity
K-LS1-1: Use observations to describe patterns of what plants and animals (including humans) need to survive.	• Students design an experiment to see what happens when the leaves of a plant do not get sunlight.

Science and Engineering Practice	Connections to Activity
Obtaining, Evaluating, and Communicating Information	• Students generate ideas about what plants need to survive and then develop an experiment to test whether water or light was given to a plant.

Disciplinary Core Ideas	Connections to Activity
ESS3.C: Human Impacts on Earth Systems Things that people do to live comfortably can affect the world around them. But they can make choices that reduce their impacts on the land, water, air, and other living things. LS1.C: Organization for Matter and Energy Flow in Organisms All animals need food in order to live and grow. They obtain their food from plants or from other animals. Plants need water and light to live and grow.	• Students learn from the story that they can make choices that reduce their impact on the land, water, air, and other living things.

Crosscutting Concept	Connections to Activity
Cause and Effect	• Students design a simple test to see whether plants need sunlight.

Overview

In this lesson, students will be introduced to one scientist who was generous with her love of trees. Katherine Sessions discovered drought-resistant native plants and relocated them to San Diego. Before Kate did this, people did not think that such plants would grow there. She made the area perfect for growing a variety of trees and plants and showed people that these plants could indeed thrive in that environment by planting greenery. By reading the featured book,

Katherine Sessions

students will learn that men and women from all backgrounds choose careers as scientists. The character trait of being generous refers to Kate Sessions's ability to convert her generosity for the environment into a reality for the city. She became known as the Mother of Balboa Park. In this way, she communicated what the people of San Diego did not know: that their environment could sustain lush plants. In doing so, Kate forever changed the city. Kate believed that people would love the trees and plants so much that they would protect nature once they experienced its beauty.

Materials

You will need a copy of the featured book *The Tree Lady: The True Story of How One Tree-Loving Woman Changed a City Forever* by H. Joseph Hopkins (2013). For the Play portion of the lesson, students will need access to tree leaves. It is best to go outside with students, but if that is not possible, you can bring in leaves for them to observe. You will also need the Five Questions worksheet (see p. 258) and rulers. For the Explore portion of the lesson, you will need two identical plants with big, broad leaves; black construction paper; and Scotch tape. Individual students will need their science notebooks.

Setting the Context
Play

Tell students that today they are going to be learning about a scientist who was very generous. Ask them if they know what *generous* means, or if they have ever been generous to others. Allow them to share their ideas. Kate Sessions loved plants and trees so much that she asked for as many different plants as she could get and planted them in a place that had few trees. She was generous with her time and effort to make her city a better place. Ask students to share their ideas about what trees mean to them. Instruct students to go outside together as a class and find one leaf to observe for this portion of the lesson. *(Teacher Note: If you do not have an area outside your classroom to collect leaves from, then bring leaves in and allow students to pick through them to identify one they want to study. If students are gathering leaves from outside, remind them to pick leaves off the ground rather than off living trees.)* Hand out the Five Questions worksheet (see p. 258) when students return inside with their leaves.

Guided Reading

Katherine Sessions was transformational with her generosity. Students will be learning about a scientist who was especially generous when they read *The Tree Lady: The True Story of How One Tree-Loving Woman Changed a City Forever*. Introduce the book by asking, *Can you find the person on the front cover? What does it look like is happening on the front cover?* Read the story aloud. Encourage students to notice and think about the challenges Katherine Sessions might have faced as a woman who loved science and nature during a time when it was not acceptable for women to become scientists.

The following questions may be used to guide children's attention to detail as you read. (Page numbers reference unnumbered book pages, beginning with the title page as page 1.)

1. **Pages 1–2:** As a child, Kate Sessions was a curious and determined little girl who spent a lot of time exploring the woods and gathering leaves from oaks and elms. What did Kate do that girls were not supposed to do? *Kate loved*

playing outside and getting her hands dirty. In the 1860s, this was not considered appropriate for little girls because they were supposed to be little ladies.

2. **Pages 3–4:** Kate worked hard in school. Why were most girls discouraged from studying science? *Most girls were discouraged from studying science because it was deemed inappropriate for girls at the time. Girls were to grow up and be wives and mothers, not scientists. Kate was different because she did not let others discourage her from studying science.*

3. **Pages 6–10:** Kate graduated from college and took a job in a new town. What did Kate notice as soon as she arrived? *Kate was surprised to find that her new town was a desert and did not have any trees. (Teacher Note: There is a huge difference in the landscape of Northern California compared with that of Southern California. Northern California is known for its large redwoods—back then, Southern California was considered the desert [until Kate helped plant many trees]. Students may think that moving from one part of the state to another would not be much different in terms of habitat and climate, but that's not always true. Ask students if they think a person moving from Alaska to Florida would notice a difference in habitat and climate. Show students on a map where California is located and discuss why such a long state might have dramatic changes in the environment. Use longitude and latitude to help fuel your discussion with students.)*

4. Kate was a teacher for two years but found that she missed studying science. Soon Kate became a "tree hunter." What does this mean? *Kate started "hunting for trees"—she wrote a letter to gardeners all over the world and asked them to send her some seeds. People did not think that the climate would support such seeds, but Kate proved them wrong. Soon trees began to sprout up everywhere.*

5. **Pages 26–30:** In 1892, Kate made a deal with city leaders to use the land in City Park for a plant nursery. Why was Kate called the Mother of Balboa Park? *She promised city leaders that she would plant 100 trees in the park every year and give the city 300 more trees to plant in other places. City Park would be renamed Balboa Park (it is still Balboa Park today), and it certainly does have a beautiful assortment of greenery. Kate was called the "Mother of Balboa Park" because she initiated this project and tended to the landscape in the park.*

Making Sense
Explore

Students will be designing a class experiment to better understand the needs of plants. Begin this portion of the lesson by asking students what plants need to survive. Students from the youngest ages will have no problem telling you: food, sunlight, and water. Once students have supplied these answers, write them on the board. Remind the class that they are trying to develop an investigation about plants, which means that they will ask a question and conduct a "fair test" to come up with an answer (at this point, you can show students the two identical plants you have purchased for the test). It may be easiest to begin with water because most students have prior experience with plants that have not been watered and can share what will happen to plants that do not receive enough water. Allow students to share and discuss their observations.

THE *HOW* OF THE EXPLORE

As a class, you might be able to determine that you could ask the question *What would happen if we had two plants and watered one but did not water the other?* However, you would not learn much since you already know the answer. You should direct the class to think of a new question they could ask about the plants. Direct the students to the topics of sunlight and food—the students already know that plants need these to live. The students can then begin to discuss the connection between sunlight and food. You can ask, *What do plants eat?* At some point, a student should mention that water helps plants make food. Once this idea has been verbalized, ask students if they think they can test this.

To begin the experiment for this lesson, get two plants that are identical and cover just one leaf with black construction paper on one of the plants and compare it with a leaf on the other plant that is completely uncovered (see Figures 9.3. and 9.4). Encourage students to record the question in their science journals and begin to think through what they need to do to test what will happen to the plant. Before covering the leaf with black construction paper, have students record their observations in their science journals under *Before*. Leave the two plants on the windowsill and water both plants with exactly the same amount of water at the same time each day. Then wait about two weeks and observe the plants again.

Figure 9.3

Two Identical Plants

Figure 9.4

Leaf Covered With Construction Paper So No Sunlight Can Touch It

THE *WHY* OF THE EXPLORE

Students may know from their life experience that plants need sunlight, but to actually see a leaf become discolored from lack of sunlight is another thing entirely. It gives students a visual representation of how plants make food through photosynthesis. Thinking through how plants need sunlight, food, and water in this activity means using students' ideas first and developing the question to be investigated second.

Discuss

Ask students to predict what they think the leaf will look like when it is revealed. Have the leaf covered for at least two weeks. Once students have shared their predictions, as a class begin to remove the black construction paper from the leaf and observe changes in the leaf. Ask students to record their observations in their science journals under *After. (Teacher Note: You should notice discoloration in the leaf, meaning that it has become less green. Depending on what kind of plant you started with, the veins and broad leaves will show the discoloration. This is because for the last two weeks when the leaf was covered with black construction paper, light was not able to shine on the leaf and produce food for the plant—a process called photosynthesis. So, depending on the initial question for this experiment, the class should have answered the question Do plants need light to grow?)*

Evaluate

Summative evaluation of this lesson will include assessment of students' (1) understanding of Katherine Sessions's generosity and (2) demonstrated ability to plan and carry out investigations to answer questions based on fair tests, which provide data to support explanations or design solutions.

CHARACTER TRAIT

Encourage students to answer the following question:

1. Why is being generous an important character trait for scientists? *Being generous is important in terms of communicating your passions and ideas to people in society. Katherine Sessions was generous and known for her ability to convince others to include plants and trees in the Southern California landscape. (Teacher Note: Helping students think about Katherine Sessions's generosity will encourage them to think about how scientists improve the lives of many.)*

2. Describe a time when you were generous.

CONTENT

Evaluate students' journals based on their ability to communicate about their investigation. Were the students able to carry out an investigation? Did they ask a question? Form a prediction? Conduct a fair test as a means of answering the question?

Name: _____

FIVE QUESTIONS

1. Where did you find your leaf?

2. How long is your leaf? How wide is it?

3. What color is your leaf?

4. Describe any distinguishing marks or holes on your leaf.

5. Describe how your leaf feels.

SCIENTISTS AND ENGINEERS ARE
DETERMINED

Learning About **Elizabeth Blackwell**

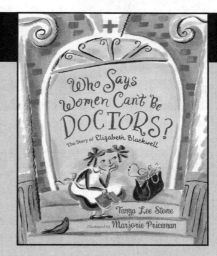

Determined (adj.): having a strong feeling that you are going to do something and that you will not allow anyone or anything to stop you

Lesson: One Big Question
Description

In this lesson, students learn about the first female doctor in the United States and explore scientist careers.

Objectives

Students will consider how being determined helped Elizabeth Blackwell succeed despite gender stereotypes in science careers.

- In the Play portion of the lesson, students will draw a picture of a doctor.

- Students will hear the story *Who Says Women Can't Be Doctors? The Story of Elizabeth Blackwell* by Tanya Lee Stone and discuss how it relates to the word *determined*.

- In the Explore portion of the lesson, students will sort scientist cards.

- In the Discuss portion of the lesson, students will discuss the tools that scientists use and discuss what scientists look like.

Learning Outcomes

Students will (1) discuss what being determined means and why being determined is an important trait for scientists and engineers and (2) ask questions and define problems as they sort the scientist cards.

Connections to the *NGSS*

The following sections make one set of connections between the instruction outlined in this lesson and the *NGSS*. Other valid connections are likely; however, not all possibilities are listed.

Performance Expectation	Connections to Activity
K-2-ETS1-1: Ask questions, make observations, and gather information about a situation people want to change to define a simple problem that can be solved through the development of a new or improved object or tool.	• Students will ask questions and make observations about attributes of scientists.
Science and Engineering Practice	**Connections to Activity**
Obtaining, Evaluating, and Communicating Information	• Students will obtain, evaluate, and communicate information from the scientist sort cards.
Disciplinary Core Idea	**Connections to Activity**
Note: There is no disciplinary core idea for this lesson related to content (earth, life, physical science); this lesson is about the human endeavor of science.	• Students will learn about who can become a doctor by drawing pictures of doctors.
Crosscutting Concept	**Connections to Activity**
Patterns	• Students will observe patterns in processes and tools during the scientist sort game.

Overview

In this lesson, students learn how one woman was responsible for paving the way for women to go to medical school (currently 50% of all medical students are women). Elizabeth would go on to open a hospital and a medical college, proving that women are just as capable as men at becoming doctors. This inspiring true story demonstrates that one question can start a revolution: Who says women can't be doctors? And with a lot of hard work and determination, many women today do become doctors. By reading the featured book, students will learn that men and women from all backgrounds choose careers as scientists. The scientist character trait of being determined refers to Elizabeth Blackwell's journey to become a physician during a time when it was not culturally accepted for women to do so.

Elizabeth Blackwell

Materials

You will need a copy of the featured book *Who Says Women Can't Be Doctors? The Story of Elizabeth Blackwell* by Tanya Lee Stone (2013). Each student will need one piece of white drawing paper; artist materials such as crayons, colored pencils, or markers; and the scientist sort cards (cut out and laminate each of these cards).

Setting the Context
Play

Ask students to draw a picture of a doctor. Distribute a large piece of paper so they can draw a doctor with crayons, colored pencils, or markers. Think about sharing the drawings before you read *Who Says Women Can't Be Doctors? The Story of*

Elizabeth Blackwell. Keep the illustrations close by as you prepare to read. Summarize information from the students' illustrations (e.g., "I noticed all of your doctors had lab coats on," "I noticed all of your doctors were men," "I counted five stethoscopes"). Discuss these observations with the entire class.

Guided Reading

Students will be learning about Elizabeth Blackwell, the first female doctor in the United States. Introduce the book by holding up the cover and asking, *What do you think this story is about?* Read the story aloud. The following questions may be used to guide children's attention to detail as you read. (Page numbers reference unnumbered book pages, beginning with the title page as page 1.)

1. **Pages 1–4:** The notion of female doctors may not be new to your students. This story tells of a woman who dared to be different in the 1830s and became the first female doctor in the United States. Ask students if they have ever met a female doctor and, if so, where. Encourage them to share their experiences. *(Teacher Note: Students' responses will vary. The idea of a female doctor may not be new to students today, but it is important that they realize from a historical perspective that women were not always allowed to become doctors.)*

2. **Pages 5–10:** The book describes how Elizabeth did not always want to be a doctor. What kind of a girl was young Elizabeth? *Elizabeth is described as a young girl who "wanted to toughen herself up" by sleeping on the floor. She was not a "typical" little girl—she was always looking for a way to be tougher. She was curious and brave at a time when girls were not supposed to have these traits. (Teacher Note: Elizabeth Blackwell was born in England in 1821, and her father insisted on making sure that his daughters were as well educated as his sons. When Elizabeth was 11, her father moved the family to the United States.)*

3. **Pages 9–10:** How did Elizabeth come to want to be a doctor? *When Elizabeth was 24 years old, she visited her friend Mary Donaldson, who was ill at the time. Mary shared with Elizabeth that she would much rather be examined by a female doctor and planted the idea in Elizabeth's head to become a doctor. (Teacher Note: The most important part here is that Mary believed in Elizabeth and told her she could do it.)*

4. **Pages 13–18:** The idea of becoming a doctor gnawed at Elizabeth. How did people react to this idea? *Some people laughed at her; others thought she was joking. (Teacher Note: Elizabeth worked as a teacher to earn money while applying to medical schools. Twenty-eight schools rejected her application until finally she was accepted at the 29th!)*

5. **Pages 20–28:** People in town and at school laughed at Elizabeth when she arrived. They thought it was a joke for a woman to attend medical school.

How did Elizabeth prove she was just as smart as a man? *She completed medical school and became the first female doctor in the United States. She graduated with the highest grades in her class. Once she graduated, no one would hire her, so she rented an office and started her own practice. When patients did not come to her, she went out on the streets and found many poor women and children on the streets in need of care. Over the years, Elizabeth and her sister Emily healed hundreds of people.*

Setting the Stage
Explore

Invite teams of two to three students to use the science sort cards on pages 265–267 (see also Figure 9.5). Have students read each card and decide if it has something to do with being a scientist. Instruct students to sort the cards into three piles: "yes," "no," and "maybe." As students look for matches in tools scientists use and things scientists do, they should work as a team. Once students have completed the science sort, they should begin to work on the If I Were a Scientist worksheet (p. 268).

Making Sense
Discuss

Discuss the correct answers of the scientist sort with students. Select a place to display the If I Were a Scientist worksheet in the classroom. Ask students to come forward and share their ideas about being a scientist with the class. Look for differences and similarities in the students' presentations and explicitly guide the class discussion to the realization that both boys and girls can be scientists today.

Evaluate

Summative evaluation of this lesson will include assessment of students' understanding of (1) the character trait of being determined and (2) the scientist sort and the If I Were a Scientist worksheet.

Figure 9.5

Student Completing the Scientist Sort

CHARACTER TRAIT

Encourage students to answer the following question:

1. Why is being determined an important disposition for scientists and engineers to have? *(Teacher Note: Answers will vary, but some kind of an acknowledgment about going through struggles to become a scientist should be the focus of the discussion. In this story, it was gender; it could be economic struggles, struggles in society, etc.)*

2. Describe a time when you were determined.

CONTENT

Challenge students to think about scientists and where they work. As a class, list all the places where scientists might work. The idea here is for students to recognize that scientists can look different, work in a variety of places, and do a variety of activities. They should be able to begin to verbalize attributes about scientists that do not reflect the stereotype of a white man in a laboratory with crazy hair blowing up chemicals (see Figure 9.6). You might want to evaluate students' matches from their scientist sort with the students working in small groups. Encourage students to repeat the scientist sort and arrive at new configurations if possible.

Figure 9.6

Stereotypical Scientist

References

Barretta, G. 2016. *Neo Leo: The ageless ideas of Leonardo da Vinci.* New York: Square Fish.

Hopkins, H. J. 2013. *The tree lady: The true story of how one tree-loving woman changed a city forever.* Beach Lane Books.

NGSS Lead States. 2013. *Next Generation Science Standards: For states, by states.* Washington, DC: National Academies Press. *www.nextgenscience.org/next-generation-science-standards.*

Schwartz, C. V., C. Passmore, and B. J. Reiser. 2017. *Helping students make sense of the world using next generation science and engineering practices.* Arlington, VA: NSTA Press.

Stone, T. L. 2013. *Who says women can't be doctors? The story of Elizabeth Blackwell.* New York: Henry Holt.

SCIENTIST CARD SORT

Cut out and laminate each of these cards. Read each card and decide if it has something to do with being a scientist. Instruct students to sort them in three piles: yes, no, maybe.

Using a ruler to measure something	**Making predictions**
Using a magnifying glass	**Throwing a baseball**
Making dinner for guests	**Planting trees**

Driving a dump trunk

Looking in microscope

Observing trees

Testing water

Observing dolphins

Using graph paper

Observing mosquitoes

Asking questions

Recycling old materials

Thinking about how
to help others

Painting a picture

Teaching a class

Name: _____

IF I WERE A SCIENTIST

Color yourself in this outline and fill in the blanks to thr right.

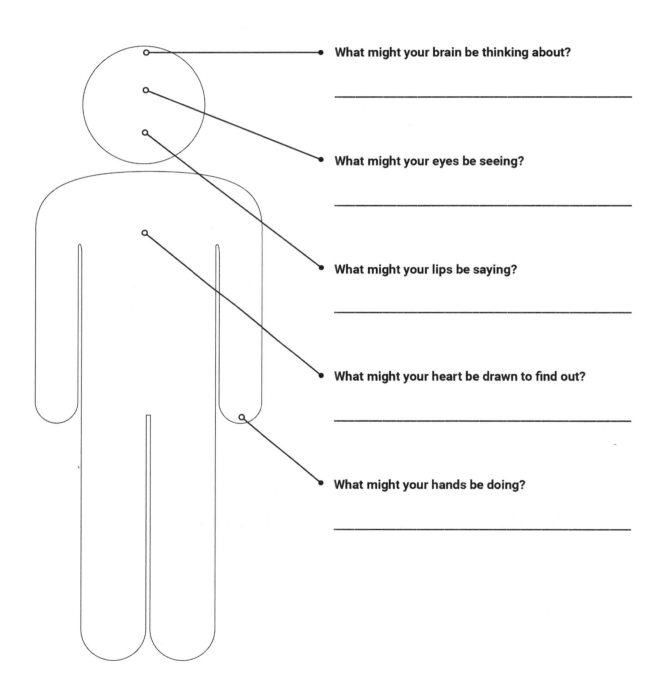

What might your brain be thinking about?

_____

What might your eyes be seeing?

_____

What might your lips be saying?

_____

What might your heart be drawn to find out?

_____

What might your hands be doing?

_____

10

Thinking Beyond *Eureka, Again!*
Teaching How Scientists and Engineers Work

As we researched biographies of scientists to include in this book, it became clear that there are some fiction books that don't quite achieve the goal of introducing the life and work of successful scientists and engineers but do model the thinking skills of scientists and engineers. These books are tremendously beneficial because they will help you to encourage your students' science and engineering practices by helping them to ask questions, solve problems, and design solutions. This chapter will focus on three sections. In the first section, we will discuss using books without a focus on science content that highlight the practices of scientists and engineers: *Ada Twist, Scientist; Not a Box;* and *Noa the Little Scientist*. In the second section, we present guidelines for introducing biography-themed trade books in your class. In the last section, we provide an outline of how to develop and plan your own lessons that combine the character traits of scientists with the core disciplines based on one of the eight practices of the *Next Generation Science Standards* (*NGSS*; NGSS Lead States 2013).

Three Books That Highlight the Practices of Scientists and Engineers

Ada, the main character in *Ada Twist, Scientist*, asks questions as she grows up throughout the story. This story encourages children to understand scientists' sense of wonder and countless questions. An accompanying scientific investigation lesson provides a starting point for linking scientific investigations and processes to the work of scientists and engineers.

In *Not a Box*, a bunny insists that his inventions are not boxes and instead imagines that they are, among other things, a burning building and a rocket ship. In this way, the bunny's imagination has a life of its own. This book is important because oftentimes all the work of science and engineering can be traced back to one idea. The book encourages children to welcome unique ideas and nurture them (a creative thinking skill we do not always directly teach).

Noa the Little Scientist is a chapter book about a little girl who wants to be a scientist. This book is important to share with young children because it is a real-life story about a girl who wants to embark on a science career in a nonstereotypical way. Like Noa, students will conduct a simple experiment as a result of this lesson. If you have done some explicit instruction about scientists in your classroom, then this chapter can build on some of your prior experiences as we introduce some scientist role models: a fictitious young African American girl (*Ada Twist, Scientist*), a bunny (*Not a Box*), and

Figure 10.1 ———————————————

The Laboratory Coat Was the First Thing to Be Drawn

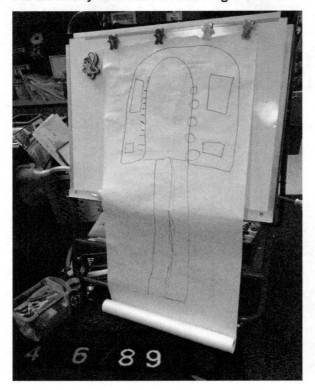

Figure 10.2 ———————————————

The Body Was Drawn After the Laboratory Coat

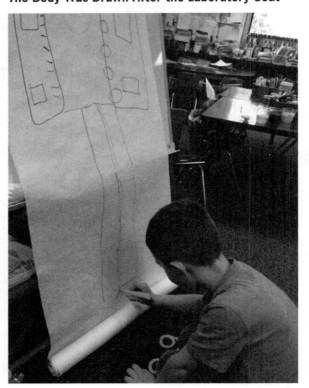

a real-life young African American girl (*Noa the Little Scientist*).

Donna's Personal Story

I have spent the last 15 years asking children to draw a picture of a scientist. I have learned a lot about what children, from the youngest ages, can and cannot tell us. I learned early on in my research that asking children this in second grade was a bit of a risk because they cannot always accurately express what they want to say in illustrations. For this reason, I focused my research only on grades 3 and up—that is, until recently. Anytime I visited K–2 classrooms, the students could always tell me about scientists, and their stories were always quite entertaining and interesting. While waiting for the kindergarten bus

one day, my eldest son proclaimed that he was going to be a "mad scientist" for Halloween, and my heart just sank. Yet in that instant I realized that it was developmentally appropriate to think about scientists in such ways and that I had better expose my son to concepts of scientists other than that of the "mad scientist" he had seen on TV (despite my best efforts to monitor everything he watched). This interaction with my own son reinforced for me what I had known—that children almost always learn this inappropriate stereotype if we do nothing to unpack it and expose them to scientists who are not mad but successful and real.

I soon started volunteering in his class and offered to teach about scientists. This proved to be educational, not only for the kindergarten

Figure 10.3

My Son Added Detail During His Turn

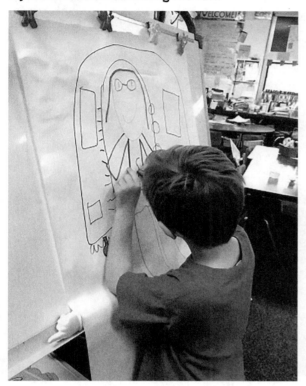

Figure 10.4

The Final Touches When a Child, Unprompted, Drew a Beaker and Chemicals

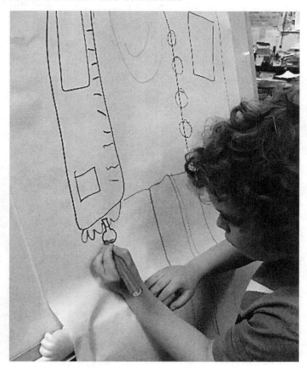

students but for myself as well. The students required a lot of dialogue—what I call "science talk" in this book—to unpack their ideas and discover new ones. They also required visual prompts of scientists working in places other than laboratories and with something else other than beakers and chemicals. But I still struggled as a researcher and as a teacher. How could I explicitly teach toward the stereotype to broaden their thinking? Then one day I came to visit my son's class during "science time" and together the class created a picture of a scientist. All I had brought was a brown bag with all the students' names in it and a large piece of chart paper. The teacher provided markers. I had no plan, but I was so curious as to how to tease their ideas out in the open, especially because one of those children

sitting "criss-cross applesauce" belonged to me. I began to call out the names from my brown paper bag one by one and invite children up independently to add to our class drawing. I sat watching, amazed, as the first child drew a body with a laboratory coat, even before the face (see Figures 10.1 and 10.2)—confirmation that this stereotype had found its way to my son's first-grade class by Christmas break. Each child added details and provided the attributes of a scientist with markers (see Figure 10.3), but what I learned from this activity was priceless.

I learned that I could unpack students' ideas one by one and that we could challenge them as a class. The body emerged by the time the third and fourth volunteers came up, and the fifth child added the face. I anxiously waited to see if the students were in fact drawing a man or a woman. When it became clear that the drawing was indeed a man, it was not surprising, but the fact that none of the other classmates challenged this was. This prompted me to ask if only boys could be scientists, to which the group shouted "No!" Each child added another detail, including glasses and facial hair. But the beautiful part was that we got a chance to honor and recognize each person's addition while recognizing that scientists could, in fact, be different. And as the final child approached the poster and made sure that the beakers and chemicals were in the scientist's hands (see Figures 10.4 [p. 271] and 10.5), we all had a good laugh—the students knew that scientists do more than work with beakers and chemicals. If only picking apart stereotypes piece by piece were so easy out in the world. I was grateful for this experience as a mom and as a researcher. And, as always, I left that first-grade classroom a better educator.

Figure 10.5

The Final Picture

MAKE OBSERVATIONS OVER TIME

Lesson: Ada Twist, Scientist
Description

In this lesson, students will recognize that scientists and engineers make observations over time as they design an experiment to see what would happen to marshmallow confections such as the commercial brand Peeps in different liquids.

Objectives

Students will explore experimental design.

- In the Play portion of the lesson, students will make choices about the kinds of liquids to test.

- Students will hear the story *Ada Twist, Scientist* by Andrea Beaty and discuss the experimental design process Ada used throughout the story to investigate her questions.

- In the Explore portion of the lesson, students will test their ideas about the marshmallow treats in different liquids.

- In the Discuss portion of the lesson, students will observe, record, and discuss what happens to the marshmallow treats after several weeks.

Learning Outcomes

Students will be able to design and test their own investigations using the marshmallow treats and different liquids over time.

Connections to the *NGSS*

The following sections make one set of connections between the instruction outlined in this lesson and the *NGSS*. Other valid connections are likely; however, not all possibilities are listed.

Performance Expectation	Connections to Activity
2-PS1-1: Plan and conduct an investigation to describe and classify different kinds of materials by their observable properties.	• Students will plan an investigation to see how different liquids affect the marshmallow treats.

Science and Engineering Practice	Connections to Activity
Asking Questions and Defining Problems	• Students try to figure out what will happen to the marshmallow treats in different liquids and use their observations to find out more information about the natural and designed world.

Disciplinary Core Idea	Connections to Activity
PS1.A: Structure and Properties of Matter • Different properties are suited to different purposes. • A great variety of objects can be built up from a small set of pieces. • Different kinds of matter exist and many of them can be either solid or liquid, depending on temperature. Matter can be described and classified by its observable properties.	• Students will learn that matter (the marshmallow treats) can be described based on its observable properties.

Crosscutting Concept	Connections to Activity
Cause and Effect	• Students will learn that the liquids selected cause the marshmallow treats to change.

Overview

Ada Twist, Scientist is a story about a fictional young scientist. Ada Marie Twist was named for two of the many women whose curiosity and passion led them to make great discoveries. Marie Curie discovered the elements polonium and radium, and her work led to the invention of x-rays. Ada Lovelace was a mathematician and the very first computer programmer. The female character in the story, Ada Twist, finds herself captivated by simple questions and curiosities. The question that sends her off investigating is *What is the source of that terrible stinking?* Eventually, with classmates nearby, she will try to answer her question. This story models the nature of scientists' work in that many investigations and trials sometimes need to be completed before the work is done.

Materials

You will need a copy of the featured book *Ada Twist, Scientist* by Andrea Beaty (2016) and the following materials: marshmallow confections such as the commercial brand Peeps *(Teacher Note: These are now available almost year-round due to the many holidays celebrated in the United States. If you cannot find Peeps, you can use marshmallows or gummy bears)*; four clear cups; and three different types of liquids to place the marshmallow treats in. *(Teacher Note: It doesn't really matter what liquids are selected—it matters that the students choose the liquids.)* Some possibilities are water, milk, soda, and so on. You will also need the Scientists Ask Questions worksheet (see p. 280), and students will need safety goggles.

Safety Notes

(1) Remind all students that personal protective equipment should be worn during the setup, hands-on, and takedown segments of the activity. (2) Immediately wipe up any liquid spilled on the floor—it creates a slip-and-fall hazard. (3) Never eat food or liquids that are used in a class activity.

Setting the Context
Play

Students will be learning how to conduct an experiment like *Ada Twist, Scientist.* Leave several different types of liquids (in closed bottles) and the marshmallow treats in your science center. Ask students to predict what might happen when a marshmallow treat is placed in the liquid for a day or two—or even a week. Would the marshmallow treat look the same, or would it look different? Talk with students about how they would plan and conduct this experiment in sequential steps. For example, *To test the liquids to see how they would affect the marshmallow treats, what would need to happen first? Second?* And so on.

Guided Reading

Introduce the book *Ada Twist, Scientist* by asking, *Can you find the person on the front cover? What does it look like is happening on the front cover?* Read the story aloud. Encourage students to notice and think about the challenges the main character Ada faced as a scientist. The following questions may be used to guide children's attention to detail as you read. (Page numbers reference unnumbered book pages, beginning with the title page as page 1.)

1. **Pages 1–10:** When Ada was a toddler, she did not speak. Her parents became concerned. Once she got older, she could not stop asking questions. Why do you think it is important for scientists and engineers to ask questions? *It is important for scientists to ask questions so they understand how things work and just accept what they think they know about something. Most discoveries come from simple questions that people have not asked.* (*Teacher Note: It is important to point out that Ada asked simple questions such as* When? Where? *and* How?)

2. **Pages 10–11:** Ada's teacher said that she had all the great traits of a scientist. What do you think she meant by this? *Most likely her teacher meant to point out to the other students that Ada's willingness to question ideas and things and her curiosity are great traits for a scientist to have. Page 11 goes on to tell of the "testing" of ideas Ada was involved in. The text also suggests that Ada loved mysteries and puzzles. This is another great trait of a scientist: perseverance—the willingness not to give up easily on difficult problems. Ada impressed her teacher with her spirit of curiosity, perseverance, and passion.*

3. **Pages 20–28:** Ada's parents were supportive of her endeavors to ask questions about the world we live in. What do you think it means when the story says her parents helped her sort fiction from fact? (*Teacher Note: Provide some examples of stories you read together as a class, both fact and fiction. Ask students to identify the difference between the two and ask why someone would need to sort fact from fiction.*)

Doing the Activity
Explore

In the story, Ada investigates questions she has about the world. This story teaches us that investigations require planning, testing, observing results, and designing new investigations to answer questions. This story focuses on and models the process of asking questions. This lesson is built on a developmentally appropriate question and teaches students how to find answers to a question by making observations and collecting data. Sometimes in science, the students develop questions; other times the teacher develops a question for students to investigate. This lesson is a combination of both. The teacher poses the initial question: *What would happen if we place the marshmallow treats in different types of liquids?* The students design the experiment by defining the liquids to be tested and developing guidelines about the time intervals for observation.

To begin the lesson, gather four clear cups and place one marshmallow treat in each. The first cup will serve as the control (see Figure 10.6). A control in an experiment serves as the reference point for the experimental items. Decide with the class the three types of liquids they want to test and observe the reaction with the marshmallow treat over a period of one week (see Figure 10.7). Our class selected cola (the commercial brand Coke), milk, and citrus soda (the commercial brand Mountain Dew). Have students predict on their worksheets what might happen to each marshmallow treat (see p. 281; larger versions of the day observations are available at *www.nsta.org/EurekaAgain*). Fill the cups halfway with each liquid, and each day observe the changes in the cups.

Figure 10.6

Setting Up the Control for the Experiment: One Marshmallow Treat in an Empty Cup

Figure 10.7

The One Control Cup and the Three Experimental Cups After One Week

Figure 10.8 ———————————————————————————————

Experiment After Two Weeks: (A) Marshmallow Treat in Citrus Soda and (B) Marshmallow Treat in Milk

(A)

(B)
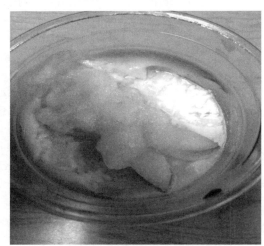

Making Sense
Explain

As a class, share your observations about each cup. What do the students notice? Explain that a scientist analyzes data. Ask students how a scientist would rank the liquids in order of how they actually worked from best (1) to worst (3). Come up with a way to judge the breakdown of the marshmallow treats that is agreeable to all students. Explain that scientists record observations. Walk around the room and look at the observations students have made. Make sure they have labeled as many words as they can on their worksheets for this activity. Finally, explain that scientists make conclusions. Conclusions are usually statements about what was learned. To form a conclusion, go back to the original question that was asked. In this lesson, the original question was *What would happen if we place the marshmallow treats in different types of liquids?* Therefore, a suitable answer might begin *We learned that when we place the marshmallow treats in three different types of liquids ….* Students should complete this phrase and then write a sentence about each liquid. Encourage students to formulate new questions from their experiment. For example, our class wondered what would happen if we left the marshmallow treats in the liquid for an additional week. Figures 10.8 and 10.9 show the results.

Evaluate

Encourage students to summarize their observations and questions prompted by this investigation. Which character trait describes Ada Twist and why?

Summative evaluation of this lesson might focus on students' predictions and observations according to the Scientists Ask Questions worksheet (p. 280).

1. **Prediction:** Did students make a prediction about what the marshmallow treats might look like in the three different kinds of liquids? *(Teacher Note: Accuracy is not important here. Although predictions often rely on some observational data, these may come from prior experiences. The point here is to encourage children to think a bit about what they already know before engaging in the experiment phase.)*

2. **Observation:** Did students record their observations on their worksheets? Are the observations accurate? Do they include correct labeling?

3. **Conclusion:** Did students summarize what they learned and tie up their predictions and observations? Look for indication of student learning and understanding of the scientific method (i.e., recognition of data to evidence new understanding).

Figure 10.9

Marshmallow Treat in Cola After Two Weeks

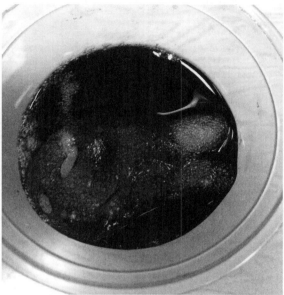

LIQUIDS

Our class brainstormed the following list of liquids:

Select three liquids (as a class) to test and record below.

SCIENTISTS ASK QUESTIONS

Our question is

Name: _____

MARSHMALLOW TREATS OBSERVATIONS

DAY 1

Three describing words

1._____

2._____

3._____

DAY 5

Three describing words

1._____

2._____

3._____

DAY 10

Three describing words

1._____

2._____

3._____

DAY 14

Three describing words

1._____

2._____

3._____

SCIENTISTS AND ENGINEERS

USE "OUT OF THE BOX" THINKING

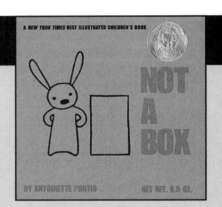

A *NEW YORK TIMES* BEST ILLUSTRATED CHILDREN'S BOOK

NOT A BOX

BY ANTOINETTE PORTIS   NET WT. 8.5 OZ.

Lesson: Not a Box
Description

In this lesson, students brainstorm ideas of what to turn boxes into.

Objectives

Students will recognize how ideas become inventions.

- In the Play portion of the lesson, students will hear the story *Not a Box* by Antoinette Portis and discuss what kinds of things they imagine the boxes brought into the classroom to be.

- In the Explore portion of the lesson, students will design new inventions made from boxes.

- In the Discuss portion of the lesson, students will observe, record, and discuss the problem the invention tried to address.

Learning Outcomes

Students will be able to brainstorm an idea as a group and create something from a box.

Connections to the *NGSS*

The following sections make one set of connections between the instruction outlined in this lesson and the *NGSS.* Other valid connections are likely; however, not all possibilities are listed.

Performance Expectation	Connections to Activity
Note: There is no performance expectation connected to this lesson. However, there is a Nature of Science connection: Scientific investigations use a variety of methods.	• Students will learn that science investigations begin with a question and that scientists use different methods to study the world.

Science and Engineering Practice	Connections to Activity
Developing and Using Models	• Students will develop a model from a cardboard box.

Disciplinary Core Idea	Connections to Activity
ETS1.A: Defining and Delimiting Engineering Problems • A situation that people want to change or create can be approached as a problem to be solved through engineering. Such problems may have many acceptable solutions. • Asking questions, making observations, and gathering information are helpful in thinking about problems. • Before beginning to design a solution, it is important to clearly understand the problem.	• Students will create inventions from either a problem or an idea and make an invention using a cardboard box.

Crosscutting Concept	Connections to Activity
Structure and Function	• Students will learn that the structure (shape of the box) relates to what things it might be imagined to be (i.e., its function).

Overview

Not a Box by Antoinette Portis is the story of a bunny that imagines many things that can be made from a box. The bunny's imagination takes over each page, and the illustrations reflect what the child is imagining superimposed over a regular cardboard box. The story relates to the work of scientists and engineers because their work requires new ideas. This is an encouraging story about managing new ideas and giving them time to grow.

Materials

You will need a copy of the featured book *Not a Box* by Antoinette Portis (2006). Student groups will need boxes, markers, and ideas.

Setting the Context
Engage
Ask students if they have ever played with boxes. What kinds of things did they imagine the boxes were? *(Teacher Note: Encourage students to think about the possible things boxes could be. Typically if they have ever had the opportunity to be around a really big box, they most likely got inside. If students have not had these experiences, then brainstorm what kinds of things could be made for play out of a large box such as a refrigerator box. In this lesson, children should focus on using their imagination and creativity. There is no wrong answer for what their box can become.)*

Guided Reading
The following questions may be used to guide children's attention to detail as you read. (Page numbers reference unnumbered book pages, beginning with the title page as page 1.) Although this book is very easy to comprehend, some questions may be worth asking.

1. **Pages 1–26:** As the story begins, the bunny appears to be standing next to an empty box. The text asks, "Why are you sitting a box?" On the next page, the bunny is in an imaginary race car and says, "It's not a box." This theme is replayed on the remaining pages. Why do you think the bunny was insistent that "it's not a box"? *The bunny was insistent probably because it was not a box to him. He imagined the box as a race car, a burning building, and a rocket ship. (Teacher Note: Ask students,* Have you ever played with a box like this? What kinds of things did you create or imagine?*)*

2. **Pages 1–26:** The bunny in the story had a lot of different ideas of what he could do with a box. Why is a box a good toy to play with? *You can be creative with a plain box and imagine whatever you want when you play. You have unlimited possibilities, and this is what makes a box a good toy.*

Doing the Activity
Explore
The first step in this phase is to decide if you want students to work in groups or in pairs. Once you have made that determination, the next step is to have the students decide if they want to create a new invention to solve a problem or create a replica of something they already know (see Figure 10.10). Figure out a timeline for this project—it may range from a few days to a couple weeks, depending on how frequently students have to engage in the design process.

Arrange students into groups and encourage them to answer this question: *What are the steps to creating something new?* It will be easier for most children if you limit the number of steps to three or five. If students are struggling at this point, create a class list on the chalkboard of some of the words (generated as a class) to describe the invention process. *(Teacher Note: Prompt students to think about whether a scientist or engineer creates an invention perfectly the very first time. How do they know when it is perfect? What evidence do they have? This will help guide students to realize that revision is a natural part of the process. There is no perfect model or correct answer here—whatever the students want to create from their box should be what they make.)* Once

Figure 10.10

Rocket Ship Made Out of Cardboard Boxes

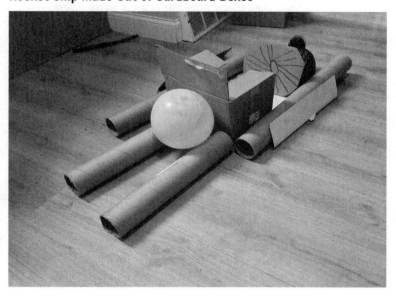

all children have some sort of box—or each group of two students has a box—begin by asking, *What would you like to make?*

Making Sense
Explain

As students finish, begin to group them in groups of four or five with other children who have finished. Instruct them to begin sharing their new designs with the entire class. *(Teacher Note: You may want to do a gallery walk with the students in your class or share your newly reused and repurposed boxes with another class. These boxes would make a great addition to family night or open house events for parents. They make an important statement that creativity, imagination, and play still have a place in early childhood education.)*

Evaluate

Invite the children to think about the scientist character traits they have learned about so far. (These are listed in Appendix A on p. 299.) Which scientist character traits describe the bunny in this story and why?

Students should be able to provide evidence as to what they created with their boxes and why. Depending on their age group, students might include illustrations and explanations in their science notebooks. You can provide formative feedback to your students throughout the lesson by encouraging them to be mindful of their own thinking skills—and not to be discouraged during the test and retest sequences. At a specified time, prompt students to gather feedback from their peers on the design and function of their inventions. *(Teacher Note: Think about pairing students together so they can assess each other's re-created boxes. The simple rubric shown in Table 10.1 will help students provide feedback to one another.)*

Table 10.1

Rubric for Not a Box Activity

Question	Yes	No	Maybe/Unsure
Did we use our imagination?	☺	☹	😐
Did we create a "new thing" from the box?	☺	☹	😐
Can we explain what we did?	☺	☹	😐
Can we explain why we did it?	☺	☹	😐

Note: A larger version of this table is available at *www.nsta.org/EurekaAgain.*

DO EXPERIMENTS TO ANSWER THEIR QUESTIONS

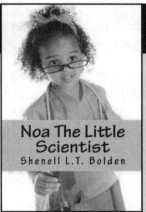

Noa The Little Scientist
Shenell L.T. Bolden

Lesson: Noa the Little Scientist
Description

In this lesson, students perform a simple experiment that is developmentally appropriate for their age group to gain experience with how science experiments are conducted.

Objectives

Students will become familiar with a simple science experiment like the girl in the story.

- In the Play portion of the lesson, students will ask questions they would like to investigate and think about how they could do the experiment to observe, record, and test out their ideas.

- Students will hear the story *Noa the Little Scientist* by Shenell L. T. Bolden and discuss the experimental design process Noa uses in the story.

- In the Explore portion of the lesson, students will observe, record, and test out their ideas about the melting rate of different-colored popsicles.

- In the Discuss portion of the lesson, students will discuss their observations and the data they have collected about the melting popsicles.

Learning Outcomes

Students will work cooperatively in a group to perform a simple science experiment.

Connections to the *NGSS*

The following sections make one set of connections between the instruction outlined in this lesson and the *NGSS*. Other valid connections are likely; however, not all possibilities are listed.

Performance Expectation	Connections to Activity
2-PS1-4: Construct an argument with evidence that some changes caused by heating or cooling can be reversed and some cannot.	• Present the question of how temperature causes things to change and allow students to argue about the causes of changes.

Science and Engineering Practice	Connections to Activity
Planning and Carrying Out Investigations	• Students will develop a model from a cardboard box.

Disciplinary Core Idea	Connections to Activity
ETS1.A: Defining and Delimiting Engineering Problems • A situation that people want to change or create can be approached as a problem to be solved through engineering. Such problems may have many acceptable solutions. • Asking questions, making observations, and gathering information are helpful in thinking about problems. • Before beginning to design a solution, it is important to clearly understand the problem.	• Students will ask questions about different-colored popsicles in the sun.

Crosscutting Concept	Connections to Activity
Cause and Effect	• Students see the cause and effect between popsicles and heat from the Sun.

Overview

Noa is a little girl in first grade who wants to be a scientist. She loves school, loves her parents (who are both scientists), and has an overall positive outlook on life. She has big plans to be a scientist and is not afraid to share her plans with anyone. This book is different from almost all the others in *Eureka, Again!* because it is a chapter book with five chapters (34 pages) that are easy to read. This is helpful for students who are just beginning to read. *(Teacher Note: You may want to do this book as a read-aloud, or you may want to get several copies for a reading group because it is perfect for children learning to read. The reading level is unavailable for this book.)* The author, Shenell L. T. Bolden, intentionally wrote this book for the Girls in Science Collection to encourage girls in science and let them know that it is OK to be smart.

Materials

You will need a copy of the featured book *Noa the Little Scientist* by Shenell L. T. Bolden (2014), three small tin disposable loaf pans, the worksheet for this activity (see p. 293), and a variety of popsicles in different colors.

Safety Notes

(1) Remind all students that personal protective equipment should be worn during the setup, hands-on, and takedown segments of the activity. (2) Immediately wipe up any liquid spilled on the floor—it creates a slip-and-fall hazard. (3) Never eat food that is used in a class activity. (4) Wash hands with soap and water upon completing the activity.

Setting the Context
Play

Ask students if they have ever tried to do a science experiment before. What kinds of things have they done at home? What did they learn? Have students generate a list of words that describe what scientists and engineers do when they want to test out an idea. *(Teacher Note: The purpose of the Play portion of the lesson is to discuss how children have "played" being scientists, just like they might "play school" at home. I [Donna] recall when I was about five, I played being a scientist with my sisters' lotions to create a new perfume. I ended up getting this concoction all over my brother's Linda Ronstadt record, and I never "played" being a scientist again because I got into a lot of trouble. You should also share a time when you "played" being a scientist at home.)*

Guided Reading

The following questions may be used to guide children's attention to detail as you read.

1. **Chapter 1:** Noa is a 6-year-old girl in first grade who loves reading, writing, and exploring the world. Her goal in life is to become a scientist and discover something great. As we meet Noa in the first chapter, she is getting ready for school. She almost misses the bus because she has forgotten to feed Watson. Who is Watson? *Watson is her pet hamster. She runs back to her bedroom, where Watson lives in a cage, to feed him some pellets.*

2. **Chapter 2:** Noa's class does a science experiment in which they place lima beans in a cup with a paper towel so they can watch them sprout. Noa enjoys her science experiment, but what is she most excited about? *Noa is excited about her mom and dad coming to visit her class. They are both scientists, and her teacher has invited them into the classroom to talk to the students about what being a scientist is like.*

3. **Chapter 3:** Noa's mom visits the first-grade classroom (Noa's dad is not able to attend because he has a meeting at work). She teaches the children about the importance of keeping their hands clean by washing them. She brings in a Petri dish for the children to observe germs in to try to convince them. Noa leaves school early after her mom's visit. Where does she go? *Noa goes to her mom's laboratory. (Teacher Note: This is a wonderful opportunity to talk about children's experiences of going to work with their parents. Many children will be able to relate to the feeling of visiting their parents' work and feeling excited and important.)*

4. **Chapter 4:** At her mother's laboratory, Noa takes part in a special experiment. What is the special experiment the scientist at her mother's workplace had Noa doing? *The scientist had her growing crystals, which Noa would later bring into class to show the other students. (Teacher Note: These sorts of experiences—doing science experiments while NOT in school—actually help children see themselves as scientists. Encourage students to talk and share any experiences they have had like Noa's.)*

5. **Chapter 5:** Noa shows the class her crystal experiment and shares with them some simple scientific methods (like how she checks it every day). Then the class checks their lima bean experiment. What can't Noa wait to be when she grows up? *A scientist, of course! (Teacher Note: This book is so unique because we do not often read stories about young African American girls who cannot wait to grow up and become scientists. Noa's story sends a positive message to both boys and girls that you don't have to be a "geek" to be a scientist, which is the typical stereotype.)*

Doing the Activity
Explore

Invite students to do a simple science experiment just for fun. This basic experiment is included, but feel free to explore others on your own. Ask students how science experiments usually begin. Some students will say that they may start from an observation or a question (either answer is OK; there is no one scientific method but rather several scientific methods). Ask students if they think the color of a popsicle affects how fast it melts. Gather three or four colors of popsicles and ask students to predict which one will melt the quickest in the sun (see Figure 10.11). *(Teacher Note: It is very important to use the word* prediction *rather than* hypothesis *here because it is developmentally appropriate for this age group. Hypotheses are different because they include an if–then statement. Young children should be taught to predict first so they can gain experience with making predictions before using predictions to examine cause-and-effect patterns.)* Ask students to design the experiment. This involves going outside and testing which popsicle will melt the fastest. They will need to design a fair test in terms of the placement of the popsicles and the time they set each popsicle out in the sun so that there are no additional variables (differences) besides color. As students watch the popsicles melting, have them sketch on their worksheets or in their science journals what hap pened during the beginning, middle, and end of the experiment.

Making Sense
Explain

Invite students to think about how Noa's story influenced their thinking during this exercise. Encourage students to summarize their observations and questions prompted by this experiment. Students are simply working together toward answering the question of which color melted the fastest, and they should draw and/or write down what they have found. Prompt students for additional experiments you

Figure 10.11

An Example of What the Experiment Looks Like

could do in class or at home. *(Teacher Note: Essentially anything that they can test and that is safe with parental permission and supervision would be appropriate.)*

Evaluate

Evaluate the students' worksheets or journals based on their complete ideas about the experimental process. Were they able to answer the original question of which color melted the fastest? Do students' beginning, middle, and end pictures reflect accurate data? Were they able to formalize a new question to investigate?

Invite the children to think about the scientist character traits they have learned about so far. (These are listed in Appendix A, p. 299.) Which scientist character traits describe Noa and why?

References

Beaty, A. 2016. *Ada Twist, scientist*. New York: Harry N. Abrams.

Bolden , S. L. T. 2014. *Noa the little scientist*. Golden Butterfly Publishing. Charleston, SC: CreateSpace.

Corey, S. 2016. *The secret subway*. Toronto, ON: Schwartz & Wade.

Locker, T. 2004. *Rachel Carson: Preserving a sense of wonder*. Golden, CO: Fulcrum Publishing.

McDonnell, P. 2011. *Me … Jane*. New York: Little, Brown Books for Young Readers.

NGSS Lead States. 2013. *Next Generation Science Standards: For states, by states*. Washington, DC: National Academies Press. *www.nextgenscience.org/next-generation-science-standards*.

Portis, A. 2006. *Not a box*. New York: HarperCollins.

Name: _____

NOA WORKSHEET

QUESTION:

Draw your experiment.

CONCLUSION: We learned that _____

Guidelines for Selecting Biography-Themed Trade Books in Your Class

One way teachers can evaluate science trade books for use in their classroom is by using the Science Trade Book Evaluation Rubric devised by Atkinson, Matusevich, and Huber (2009) to assess the science- and literature-related appropriateness of trade books. This rubric includes two main sections: science content and literacy criteria. With respect to literacy criteria, the rubric looks at plot development, imagination, and continuity if the story is fictional or whether the book contains sufficient information that is clearly organized in appropriate text structures if the story is nonfiction. The rubric further looks at writing style; the suitability of the book's illustrations and graphics for the text it relates to; and the presentation of positive ethical and cultural values, including gender and racial representation. With respect to science content criteria, the rubric's key elements address the following: whether the science content is substantial, accurate, and current; whether the content has a "human face" (is personalized); and whether the content is intellectually and developmentally appropriate for the target audience. However, one aspect of science trade books not clearly addressed in the Science Trade Book Evaluation Rubric is the representation of scientists, particularly within the context of "science as a human endeavor."

We have yet to find a rubric for selecting trade books that is specifically designed to evaluate the accurate representation of scientists. Some places to begin looking for quality books include the National Science Teachers Association and Children's Book Council's annual Oustanding Science Trade Books for Students K–12 list. The Caldecott, Newbery, and Orbis Pictus Award lists are also useful. This section of *Eureka, Again!* is designed to provide some guidance for intentionally selecting trade books about scientists that do not reinforce a negative stereotype of scientists to the children in your classroom.

Protocol for Selecting Science Trade Books

We developed a protocol elementary teachers can use when selecting excellent science trade books with a focus on science as a human endeavor for their classroom science instruction. The protocol has six major considerations in no specific order.

1. The trade book must focus on science or on a scientist, regardless of the gender or ethnicity of the person(s) included within its pages. The storytelling aspect of the book is more likely to reflect science as a human endeavor than are presentations of sets of facts. For example, in *Preserving a Sense of Wonder*, Thomas Locker focused on one scientist—Rachel Carson—and how hearing stories of robin deaths linked to pesticides led her to write a story in which the songbirds of the world had disappeared. She followed that up with *Silent Spring*, in which she explained how every strand within the web of life is

connected to the other strands and how the collapse of one endangers all the others.

2. The trade book must contain accurate information. There are two things you should consider: (1) the accuracy of the scientific information (Rice and Snipes 1997) and (2) the attributes of the process(es) of science as delineated by the *NGSS*.

3. The trade book must include a nonstereotypical representation of a scientist. The trade book should include images of both men and women while remaining historically accurate. Patrick McDonnell's portrayal of Jane Goodall in *Me … Jane* is both historically accurate and nonstereotypical. A young woman, outside, not wearing a laboratory coat is the opposite of the stereotypical perception that scientists are white, middle-aged men in laboratory coats.

4. The story presented in the trade book should illustrate the roles of people engaging in the scientific enterprise. A good example is Shana Corey's *The Secret Subway,* in which the author describes how an engineer became interested in and persisted in creating a means for underground travel.

5. The illustrations in the trade book should be aesthetically pleasing in a way that encourages children to want to enjoy the book over and over again. All of the books in *Eureka, Again!* are excellent examples of books with high-quality illustrations. These trade books stand out because they are so different from the typical information texts currently found in the science sections of the bookstore. Informational texts are read for information, and we encourage students to read trade books for enjoyment.

6. The trade book must be age appropriate, and the practice of science must include students' practice and learning. The content of the trade book must be both age and developmentally appropriate for its intended audience so that readers can cognitively connect with what is being presented.

Gather the science trade books you use for teaching. Then do the following:

- Assess their science content for accuracy and developmental appropriateness so the books clearly suit your students' reading ability ranges, interests, and abilities. Students should be able to grasp the scientific concepts that are being presented.

- Assess the books' literacy qualities, including the narrative, style of writing, and cultural appropriateness.

- Determine how well the books show the personal side of science for the main characters (i.e., determine how well the books describe science as being a human endeavor).

- Consider the quality of the illustrations that help tell the story. For the age and developmental level of your students, consider the brightness of the colors and whether the photographs or other types of illustrations are understandable and appropriate.

Helping teachers make good choices about what trade books they introduce to their students may affect students' understanding of where scientists work and what they do.

Planning Lessons on Your Own

The simple steps outlined in the 27 lessons in this book are summarized as follows:

1. Determine an appropriate trade book.

2. Read the book and determine which character trait the scientist or engineer depicts most clearly.

3. Find a way to connect the story with the disciplinary core ideas.

4. Design your objective(s) and assessment.

5. Develop guided reading questions.

6. Test out the lesson!

References

Atkinson, T. S., M. N. Matusevich, and L. Huber. 2009. Making science trade book choices for elementary classrooms. *Reading Teacher* 62 (6): 484–497.

Rice, D. C., and C. Snipes. 1997. Children's tradebooks: Do they affect the development of science concepts? Paper presented at the annual meeting of the National Association for Research in Science Teaching, St. Louis, MO.

Appendix A

Overview of Featured Books

Chapter	Scientist or Engineer	Book Title	Author(s)	ISBN	Character Trait or Disposition	Lexile Measure	Publisher	Year
2	Jane Goodall	Me ... Jane	Patrick McDonnell	978-0316045469	Observant	740	Little, Brown Books for Young Readers	2011
2	Albert Einstein	On a Beam of Light: A Story of Albert Einstein	Jennifer Berne	978-0811872355	Imaginative	680	Chronicle Books	2013
2	Kathy Sullivan	To the Stars: The First American Woman to Walk in Space	Carmella Van Vleet and Kathy Sullivan	978-1580896443	Explorer	680	Charlesbridge	2016
3	Alfred Ely Beach	The Secret Subway	Shana Corey	978-0375870712	Thinker	810	Schwartz & Wade	2016
3	Citizens of Samsø	Energy Island: How One Community Harnessed the Wind and Changed Their World	Allan Drummond	978-0374321840	United	920	Square Fish	2015
3	Maria Merian	Summer Birds: The Butterflies of Maria Merian	Margarita Engle	978-0545662697	Artistic	600	Henry Holt	2010
4	Amelia Earhart	I Am Amelia Earhart	Brad Meltzer	978-0803740822	Brave	580	Dial Books	2014
4	Isaac Newton	Newton and Me	Lynne Mayer	978-1607188667	Playful	600	Arbordale	2010
4	Temple Grandin	The Girl Who Thought in Pictures: The Story of Dr. Temple Grandin	Julia Finley Mosca	978-1943147304	Examiner	680	Innovation Press	2017
5	George Washington Carver	A Picture Book of George Washington Carver	David A. Adler	978-0671664909	Diligent	640	Holiday House	2000

Overview of Featured Books (*continued*)

Chapter	Scientist or Engineer	Book Title	Author(s)	ISBN	Character Trait or Disposition	Lexile Measure	Publisher	Year
5	Mary Anning	*The Fossil Girl: Mary Anning's Dinosaur Discovery*	Catherine Brighton	978-0711213241	Curious	580L	Frances Lincoln	1999
5	Rachel Carson	*Rachel Carson: Preserving a Sense of Wonder*	Thomas Locker and Joseph Bruchac	978-1555916954	Persuasive	Not available	Fulcrum	2009
6	Eugenie Clark	*Shark Lady: The True Story of How Eugenie Clark Became the Ocean's Most Fearless Scientist*	Jess Keating	978-1492642046	Fearless	730	Sourcebooks Jabberwocky	2017
6	Margaret Hamilton	*Margaret and the Moon: How Margaret Hamilton Saved the First Lunar Landing*	Dean Robbins	978-0399551857	Problem Solver	630	Knopf Books for Young Readers	2017
6	Marie Curie	*Little People, Big Dreams: Marie Curie*	Isabel Sánchez Vegara	978-1847809629	Resilient	Not available	Frances Lincoln	2017
7	Thomas Edison	*Timeless Thomas: How Thomas Edison Changed Our Lives*	Gene Barretta	978-1250114785	Inspiring	900	Henry Holt	2012
7	Isatou Ceesay	*One Plastic Bag: Isatou Ceesay and the Recycling Women of The Gambia*	Miranda Paul	978-1467716086	Catalyst	480	Millbrook	2015
7	John Muir	*John Muir: America's Naturalist*	Thomas Locker	978-1555917050	Dedicated	Not available	Fulcrum	2010

Overview of Featured Books (*continued*)

Chapter	Scientist or Engineer	Book Title	Author(s)	ISBN	Character Trait or Disposition	Lexile Measure	Publisher	Year
8	Cynthia Moss	*A Passion for Elephants: The Real Life Adventure of Field Scientist Cynthia Moss*	Toni Buzzeo	978-0399187254	Passionate	1030	Dial Books	2015
8	Helen Martini	*Mother to Tigers*	George Ella Lyon	978-0689842214	Caring	610	Atheneum Books for Young Readers	2003
8	Michael Faraday	*Burn: Michael Faraday's Candle*	Darcy Pattison	978-1629440453	Experimenter	Not available	Mims House	2016
9	Leonardo da Vinci	*Neo Leo: The Ageless Ideas of Leonardo da Vinci*	Gene Barretta	978-1250079602	Inventive	930	Square Fish	2016
9	Katherine Sessions	*The Tree Lady: The True Story of How One Tree-Loving Woman Changed a City Forever*	H. Joseph Hopkins	978-1144241420	Generous	760	Beach Lane Books	2013
9	Elizabeth Blackwell	*Who Says Women Can't Be Doctors? The Story of Elizabeth Blackwell*	Tanya Lee Stone	978-0805090482	Determined	560	Henry Holt	2013
10	—	*Ada Twist, Scientist*	Andrea Beaty	978-1419721373	—	550	Harry N. Abrams	2016
10	—	*Not a Box*	Antoinette Portis	978-0061123221	—	240	HarperCollins	2006
10	—	*Noa the Little Scientist*	Shenell L. T. Bolden	978-1419721373	—		CreateSpace	2014

Appendix B

Timeline of Featured Scientists and Engineers

2018 ●

Isatou Ceesay (1971–)

Rachel Carson (1907–1964)

Helen Martini (1912–1994)

Eugenie Clark (1922–2015)

Jane Goodall (1934–)

Margaret Hamilton (1936–)

Cynthia Moss (1940–)

Katherine Sessions (1942–)

Temple Grandin (1947–)

Kathy Sullivan (1951–)

Amelia Earhart (1897–disappeared 1937)

Elizabeth Blackwell (1821–1910)

Alfred Ely Beach (1826–1896)

John Muir (1838–1914)

Thomas Edison (1847–1931)

George Washington Carver (c. 1860–1943)

Marie Curie (1867–1934)

Albert Einstein (1879–1955)

Mary Anning (1799–1847)

Michael Faraday (1791–1867)

Maria Merian (1647–1717)

Isaac Newton (1643–1727)

Leonardo da Vinci (1452–1519)

1400 ●

Appendix C

Lesson Connections to the *NGSS*, Grades K–2

Disciplinary Core Ideas†	2—Goodall	2—Einstein	2—Sullivan	3—Beach	3—Citizens	3—Merian	4—Earhart	4—Newton	4—Grandin	5—Carver	5—Anning	5—Carson	6—Clark	6—Hamilton	6—Curie	7—Edison	7—Ceesay	7—Muir	8—Moss	8—Martini	8—Faraday	9—da Vinci	9—Sessions	9—Blackwell*	10—Ada Twist	10—Not a Box	10—Noa
ETS1.A: Defining and Delimiting Engineering Problems													●													●	●
ETS1.B: Developing Possible Solutions				●																		●					
ETS1.C: Optimizing the Design Solution					●																						
ESS1.A: The Universe and Its Stars														●													
ESS1.B: Earth and the Solar System																											
ESS1.C: The History of Planet Earth											●																
ESS2.B: Plate Tectonics and Large-Scale Systems																											
ESS2.C: The Role of Water in Earth's Surface Processes																											

*This lesson does not correspond with a disciplinary core idea.

†PS = physical science; LS = life science; ESS = Earth and space science; ETS = engineering design

Lesson Connections to the *NGSS*, Grades K–2 (*continued*)

Disciplinary Core Ideas[†]	2—Goodall	2—Einstein	2—Sullivan	3—Beach	3—Citizens	3—Merian	4—Earhart	4—Newton	4—Grandin	5—Carver	5—Anning	5—Carson	6—Clark	6—Hamilton	6—Curie	7—Edison	7—Ceesay	7—Muir	8—Moss	8—Martini	8—Faraday	9—da Vinci	9—Sessions	9—Blackwell*	10—Ada Twist	10—Not a Box	10—Noa
ESS2.D: Weather																											
ESS2.E: Biogeology																											
ESS3.A: Natural Resources																											
ESS3.C: Human Impacts on Earth Systems																	●	●					●				
PS1.A: Structure and Properties of Matter															●						●				●		
PS1.B: Chemical Reactions																											
PS2.A: Forces and Motion							●	●																			
PS2.B: Types of Interactions																											
PS3.B: Conservation of Energy and Energy Transfer			●																								
PS3.C: Relationship Between Energy and Forces																											
PS4.A: Wave Properties																●											

*This lesson does not correspond with a disciplinary core idea.

[†]PS = physical science; LS = life science; ESS = Earth and space science; ETS = engineering design

Disciplinary Core Ideas[†]	2—Goodall	2—Einstein	2—Sullivan	3—Beach	3—Citizens	3—Merian	4—Earhart	4—Newton	4—Grandin	5—Carver	5—Anning	5—Carson	6—Clark	6—Hamilton	6—Curie	7—Edison	7—Ceesay	7—Muir	8—Moss	8—Martini	8—Faraday	9—da Vinci	9—Sessions	9—Blackwell*	10—Ada Twist	10—Not a Box	10—Noa
PS4.B: Electromagnetic Radiation		•																									
PS4.C: Information Technologies and Instrumentation																											
LS1.A: Structure and Function																											
LS1.B: Growth and Development of Organisms																			•								
LS1.C: Organization for Matter and Energy Flow in Organisms	•																			•			•				
LS1.D: Information Processing																											
LS2.A: Interdependent Relationships in Ecosystems						•				•																	
LS3.B: Variation of Traits																											
LS4.D: Biodiversity and Humans									•			•					•										

*This lesson does not correspond with a disciplinary core idea.

†PS = physical science; LS = life science; ESS = Earth and space science; ETS = engineering design

Lesson Connections to the *NGSS*, Grades K–2 (*continued*)

Science and Engineering Practices[†]	10—Noa	10—Not a Box	10—Ada Twist	9—Blackwell	9—Sessions	9—da Vinci	8—Faraday	8—Martini	8—Moss	7—Muir	7—Ceesay	7—Edison	6—Curie	6—Hamilton	6—Clark	5—Carson	5—Anning	5—Carver	4—Grandin	4—Newton	4—Earhart	3—Merian	3—Citizens	3—Beach	2—Sullivan	2—Einstein	2—Goodall
Asking Questions and Defining Problems			•																						•	•	•
Developing and Using Models		•																				•	•	•			
Planning and Carrying Out Investigations	•																		•	•	•						
Analyzing and Interpreting Data																•	•	•									
Using Mathematics and Computational Thinking													•	•	•												
Constructing Explanations and Designing Solutions										•	•	•															
Engaging in Argument From Evidence							•	•	•																		
Obtaining, Evaluating, and Communicating Information				•	•	•																					

*This lesson does not correspond with a disciplinary core idea.

[†]PS = physical science; LS = life science; ESS = Earth and space science; ETS = engineering design

Lesson Connections to the *NGSS*, Grades K–2 (*continued*)

Crosscutting Concepts[†]	2—Goodall	2—Einstein	2—Sullivan	3—Beach	3—Citizens	3—Merian	4—Earhart	4—Newton	4—Grandin	5—Carver	5—Anning	5—Carson	6—Clark	6—Hamilton	6—Curie	7—Edison	7—Ceesay	7—Muir	8—Moss	8—Martini	8—Faraday	9—da Vinci	9—Sessions	9—Blackwell	10—Ada Twist	10—Not A Box	10—Noa
Structure and Function	•			•	•		•		•				•				•									•	
Cause and Effect		•	•			•		•		•						•					•	•	•		•		•
Stability and Change											•																
Patterns												•		•				•	•					•			
Energy and Matter															•												
Systems and System Models																				•							

*This lesson does not correspond with a disciplinary core idea.

[†]PS = physical science; LS = life science; ESS = Earth and space science; ETS = engineering design

Appendix D

Glossary of Character Traits

artistic (adj.): having or showing the skill of an artist

brave (adj.): bold or courageous

caring (adj.): feeling or showing concern for other people or animals

catalyst (n.): a person or event that quickly causes change or action

curious (adj.): having a desire to learn or know more about something or someone

dedicated (adj.): devoted to a task or purpose; having single-minded loyalty or integrity

determined (adj.): having a strong feeling that you are going to do something and that you will not allow anyone or anything to stop you

diligent (adj.): putting forth constant effort to accomplish something; attentive and persistent in doing anything

examiner (n.): one who looks at something closely and carefully to learn more about it

experimenter (n.): a person who tries out new ideas, methods, or activities

explorer (n.): one who travels in search of geographical or scientific information

fearless (adj.): not afraid; very brave

generous (adj.): liberal in giving

imaginative (adj.): having or showing an ability to think of new and interesting ideas

inspiring (adj.): to have the effect of encouraging others

inventive (adj.): having the ability to create or design new things or to think originally

observant (adj.): good at noticing things

passionate (adj.): having or showing strong feelings

persuasive (adj.): having the power or ability to convince others

playful (adj.): showing that you are having fun and not being serious

problem solver (n.): one who solves difficulties

resilient (adj.): able to become strong, healthy, or successful again after something bad happens

thinker (n.): one who has an idea or opinion

united (adj.): involving people or groups working together to achieve something

Image Credits

CHAPTER 2

p. 14: Jane Goodall. Public domain, Wikimedia Commons, *https://en.wikipedia.org/wiki/Jane_Goodall#/media/File:Jane_Goodall_2015.jpg*

p. 28: Albert Einstein. Public domain, Wikimedia Commons, *https://commons.wikimedia.org/wiki/File:Albert_Einstein_Head.jpg*

p. 39: Kathy Sullivan. Public domain, Wikimedia Commons, *https://commons.wikimedia.org/wiki/File:Kathryn_D._Sullivan_NOAA_Leadership.jpg*

CHAPTER 3

p. 49: Alfred Ely Beach. Public domain, Wikimedia Commons, *https://commons.wikimedia.org/wiki/File:Alfred_Ely_Beach.jpg*

p. 57: The People of the Island of Samsø. Shutterstock, *www.shutterstock.com/image-photo/solar-panels-local-brewery-samsoe-island-456316315*

p. 66: Maria Merian. Public domain, Wikimedia Commons, *https://commons.wikimedia.org/wiki/File:Merian_Portrait.jpg*

CHAPTER 4

p. 79: Amelia Earhart. Public domain, Wikimedia Commons, *https://commons.wikimedia.org/wiki/File:Amelia_Earhart_standing_under_nose_of_her_Lockheed_Model_10-E_Electra,_small.jpg*

p. 91: Isaac Newton. Shutterstock, *www.shutterstock.com/image-photo/isaac-newton-16431727-engraved-by-escriven-81842473?src=86WD0WtOe-7F2YoGcXK6Yg-1-2*

p. 101: Temple Grandin. Steve Jurveston, Wikimedia Commons, CC BY 2.0, *https://commons.wikimedia.org/wiki/File:Temple_Grandin_at_TED.jpg*

CHAPTER 5

p. 114: George Washington Carver. Shutterstock, *www.shutterstock.com/image-illustration/george-washington-carver-18641943-african-american-238329505?src=ow4hYvFdVbCEZe7ijYWZBQ-1-0*

p. 125: Mary Anning. Public domain, Wikimedia Commons, *https://commons.wikimedia.org/wiki/File:Mary_Anning_painting.jpg*

p. 133: Rachel Carson. Public domain, Wikimedia Commons, *https://commons.wikimedia.org/wiki/File:Rachel-Carson.jpg*

CHAPTER 6

p. 145: Eugenie Clark. U.S. Department of Labor, Public domain, *https://commons.wikimedia.org/wiki/File:Eugenie_Clark.jpg.*

p. 154: Margaret Hamilton. Daphne Weld Nichols, Wikimedia Commons, CC BY-SA 3.0, *https://commons.wikimedia.org/wiki/File:Margaret_Hamilton_1995.jpg*

p. 166: Marie Curie. Shutterstock, *www.shutterstock.com/image-photo/marie-curie-18671934-polishfrench-physicist-who-242816158?src=FvXlJxgP6Lt6oOrBxNrp3g-1-0*

CHAPTER 7

p. 177: Thomas Edison. Public domain, Wikimedia Commons, *https://commons.wikimedia.org/wiki/File:Thomas_Edison2.jpg*

p. 187: Isatou Ceesay. Luke Duggleby, Redux Pictures, *www.reduxpictures.com/portfolio/editorial/luke-duggleby*

p. 197: John Muir. Public domain, Wikimedia Commons, *https://commons.wikimedia.org/wiki/File:John_Muir_by_Carleton_Watkins,_c1875.jpg*

CHAPTER 8

p. 213: Cynthia Moss. Professional photo provided by Elephant Voices, *www.elephantvoices.org/about-elephantvoices/history.html*. Used with permission.

p. 223: Helen Martini. Madeline Thompson, "Helen Martini and Her Bronx Zoo Family," *http://blog.wcs.org/photo/2015/06/04/tbt-helen-martini-and-her-bronx-zoo-family-panther-cub-baby*. Used with permission.

p. 231: Michael Faraday. Shutterstock, *www.shutterstock.com/download/confirm/252133891?src=Au2zZlKCmdEswtokXB9yXg-1-1&size=huge_jpg*

CHAPTER 9

p. 245: Leonardo da Vinci. Shutterstock, *www.shutterstock.com/image-illustration/leonardo-da-vinci-14521519-italian-renaissance-242291527?src=WYj9WB75ibXFFdNXNTVv4Q-1-0*

p. 253: Katherine Sessions. Public domain, Wikimedia Commons, *https://commons.wikimedia.org/wiki/File:Kate_Sessions.jpg*

p. 261: Elizabeth Blackwell. Public domain, Wikimedia Commons, *https://commons.wikimedia.org/wiki/File:EBlackwell1905.jpg*

Index

Page numbers printed in **bold** type indicate tables, figures, or illustrations.